USA

modern architectures in history

This international series examines the forms and consequences of modern architecture. Modernist visions and revisions are explored in their national context against a backdrop of aesthetic currents, economic developments, political trends and social movements. Written by experts in the architectures of the respective countries, the series provides a fresh, critical reassessment of Modernism's positive and negative effects, as well as the place of architectural design in twentieth-century history and culture.

Series editor: Vivian Constantinopoulos

Already published:

Britain
Alan Powers

Finland
Roger Connah

Forthcoming:

Brazil
Richard Williams

France
Jean-Louis Cohen

Germany
Iain Boyd Whyte

Greece
Alexander Tzonis and Alkistis Rodi

India
Peter Scriver

Italy
Diane Ghirardo

Japan
Botond Bognar

Netherlands
Nancy Stieber

Spain
David Cohn

Switzerland
Stanislaus von Moos

Turkey
Sibel Bozdogan

USA

modern architectures in history

Gwendolyn Wright

REAKTION BOOKS

For Tom, with joy

Published by Reaktion Books Ltd
33 Great Sutton Street
London EC1V 0DX, UK

www.reaktionbooks.co.uk

First published 2008
Copyright © Gwendolyn Wright 2008

The publishers gratefully acknowledge support for the publication of this book by the
Graham Foundation for Advanced Studies in the Fine Arts.

Printed and bound in Slovenia
by MKT Print d.d.

British Library Cataloguing in Publication Data
Wright, Gwendolyn
      USA. – (Modern architectures in history)
      1. Modern movement (Architecture) – United States
      2. Architecture – United States – 20th century
      I. Title
      720.9'73'0904

      ISBN-13: 978–1–86189–344–4
      ISBN-10: 1–86189–344–2

Contents

Frank Lloyd Wright 1867-1959 Fallingwater Mill Run PA

Architecture USA 20c

Mies van der Rohe 1886-1969 Illinois Inst Tech Chicago

Architecture USA 20c

Walter Gropius 1883-1969 Gropius House Lincoln MA

Architecture USA 20c

Eero Saarinen 1910-1961 Dulles Airport Washington DC

Architecture USA 20c

Introduction

American modern architecture is as lively and mutable as quicksilver. Artists in every medium have delighted in the surprising play of forms and types. Architects claim freedom and democracy as birthrights for every citizen, sometimes presuming these are assurances rather than aspirations. Popular culture has eagerly appropriated icons of modern architecture and design without generating much respect for architects.

Praise has mixed freely with invective. The European avant-garde lauded Midwestern factories and grain elevators as the magnificent evidence of a new age. Americans were considered liberated from the past, or ignorant of its lessons and beholden to commerce. New York remains unfinished, impossible to pinion, simultaneously 'a new Babel and a City Divine'.[1] Countless observers have deplored the vulgar consumerism of Los Angeles, Las Vegas and Miami – then enjoyed their pleasures. Modern office buildings and housing came under widespread attack in the late 1960s, condemned as cold and callous or gaudy and 'plastic'. The most contemptuous critics may be those who denounce all aspects of American modern architecture as a debased bastardization of 'true Modernism', revering the European Modern Movement as the sole incarnation of progressive values.

Can there be any coherence among these wildly divergent opinions and the works they seek to describe? No single definition can encompass the phantasmagoria of American modern architecture, but that doesn't mean that everything qualifies. The designation is stitched together by ambitions, processes and effects more than any formal rules. Modernism confronts contemporary life rather than seeking to escape; it tries to redirect, improve or at least enliven present-day realities. The goals extend beyond noble intentions about artistic innovation and social progress, for we can no longer exclude the modernity of spectacles, self-promotion and profit incentives, even if they should not be embraced wholeheartedly. The actors include world-renowned figures but also relatively unknown clients and designers. Some are not architects at all, since professionals account for only about 10 per cent of what

'Architecture USA' stamps, 1982 issue, showing Frank Lloyd Wright's Fallingwater (1937), Walter Gropius House (1937), Mies van der Rohe's Crown Hall at the Illinois Institute of Technology, Chicago (1956), and Eero Saarinen's Dulles International Airport (1962).

gets built in America. I am suggesting an inclusive, dynamic and contested perspective, not a harmonious consensus.

A century of canonical histories has defined modern architecture in terms of universal beliefs and forms, a worthy aspiration yet one dismissive of the multifarious conditions in which all people operate, including architects. We have recently become more aware of ecological issues and the fact that 'modern man'– the presumed beneficiary of well-intended reforms – marginalized people who did not fit one model of needs and desires. National and local cultures still seem problematic, however, given legitimate apprehensions about xenophobic fervour and provincialism. Yet nations remain salient factors even in today's global world. The materiality of building responds to formal regulations and informal conventions. National imaginaries sustain shared notions about the public sphere and private life, influencing even those who want to challenge such norms. These configurations are never cohesive. No formulas or essences, in other words, but definite patterns.

The Modern Architectures in History series considers such patterns inside and across the boundaries of many nations. Each instance reveals distinctive imageries and meanings that often reverberate elsewhere once we know to look for them. The United States shared many qualities with European Modernism: a commitment to social reform, confidence in the sciences, a passion for new technologies and a pervasive fascination with 'the new'. It appropriated from Africa, Asia and Latin America as well in a flow of ideas, capital and people that was always multi-directional. By the late nineteenth century, most of the world saw America as the epitome of modernity, with architectural advances assuming a key role in this mental construction: towering skyscrapers, rationalized factories, vibrant settings for popular culture, verdant parkways and mass-produced, moderate-cost dwellings.[2]

Like all cultures, America's is paradoxical. Traditions coexist with innovations; utopian visions of the future with nostalgic fantasies about the past – including earlier stages of Modernism. Americans follow trends, yet they remain deeply suspicious of orthodoxies, mindful of contingencies and unintended consequences. This inclination aligns with pragmatist tendencies, both the late nineteenth-century philosophers William James and John Dewey, who asked what ideas actually do in the world, and the less systematic predilections of countless others, including architects and designers, eager to tinker with (and sometimes to transform) established practices. Such an approach tends inevitably towards 'patchwork', but it is not inherently anti-theoretical. As James put it, 'Pragmatism unstiffens all our theories, limbers them up and sets each one at work.'[3]

Joseph Stella, *Battle of Lights, Coney Island, Mardi Gras,* 1913–14, painting, oil on canvas.

In that spirit, this book unstiffens some familiar premises in order to expand canonical histories, reframe customary narratives, unravel tangled ambiguities. Such an unwieldy subject requires a clear structure. Each chapter is organized around three realms of modern life: work spaces, domestic spaces and public spaces – including infrastructure linkages and urban/suburban design. Typologies provide an alternative to more usual classifications based on individuals or stylistic trends. They encourage a broader spectrum, juxtaposing exceptional buildings with 'minor' or generic examples that history so often erases. Readers can admire the impressive achievements of American modern architecture, singular and collective, without denying destructive tendencies, lacklustre replications and unequal access to modern improvements. Cultural history reaches beyond the hermetic limits of a supposedly autonomous 'architecture culture'.[4] Just as reformulations in other disciplines have affected design, so they provide fresh insights in my conceptualization. For example, Bruno Latour's Actor-Network-Theory traces the multiple, mostly unanticipated associations of humans and 'things' as agents in the world. An historian of science, Latour was thinking of microbes or information – but why not buildings?[5]

Too many architects and historians still insist that European émigrés and their loyal American disciples brought Modernism to the United States, as if in a suitcase, with the 1932 exhibition *Modern Architecture* at New York's Museum of Modern Art (MOMA). The chronology of this book overturns that myth. American modern architecture has a much earlier lineage beginning in the late nineteenth-century aftermath of the Civil War, a struggle about unity and equality that engendered a full-fledged modern nation with a transcontinental infrastructure, a national economy, extensive industrialization, pervasive media and a thriving consumer culture – all of which directly affected architecture.

A brief discussion about language helps clarify some of the conundrums.[6] *Modernism* is a broad cultural phenomenon with striking shifts in forms and intentions between (and within) different intellectual or artistic domains. While these inevitably change over time, the word also refers to specific radical artistic movements of the early twentieth century – and to right now. *Modernization* is the mission of various specialists, including architects, who viewed economic rationalization, standardized norms and expanded markets as an inexorable historical trajectory. The experience of *modernity* has elicited conflicting human responses, exhilarating liberation but also materialism, alienation, a sense of loss or foreboding. This makes it untenable to speak of a single *modern consciousness* rather than passionate, contradictory and contentious variations. The *modernist project* envisions social amelioration through radical change. Early certainties have disappeared, giving way to more personal experiments and aesthetic games. A resigned nihilism now seems to prevail; as the art historian T. J. Clark recently lamented, 'The modernist past is a ruin . . . our antiquity.'[7] Fortunately, aspirations for progress continue, responding to contemporary conditions, utilizing the latest technologies while drawing upon what has come before. The modernist project still moves forward, seeking a more sustainable, equitable and, yes, a more beautiful world.

If the history of American modern architecture is diverse and contradictory, there are some clear consistencies. This book emphasizes five interconnected themes, each resonant in today's world. First, Americans like to mix genres and sources. Terms like *creole* or *mestizaje* apply to architecture as well as to language and physiognomy. Regional inflections have long infused American Modernism. Architects have drawn on local vernaculars to reinvigorate the inevitable stiffness of official or 'universal' languages (as with literature at least since the fifteenth century).[8] *Hybridity*, once a term of disdain, has become a positive value, whereas purity relies on exclusion. These qualities, so conspicuous in an American context, remind us that creativity is always multivalent in its origins as well as its consequences.

Second is the indisputable role of commercial culture, its effects often crudely imitative, sometimes daringly inventive. Popular culture has contaminated but also re-energized high art, infusing it with unexpected outside influences. The search for new markets frequently adopted modern motifs, if only for their upbeat imagery. The private sector has been dominant – especially wealthy clients, corporations and major cultural institutions, which come under state auspices in most countries. As a result, American architects have rarely enjoyed the authority of their colleagues in other places. Not just clients, but businessmen and bankers, merchant builders and marketing experts, politicians of every stripe, an ambitious middle class of consumers, labour unions and immigrants all have their say. These voices often collide with those of architects or draw them into insidious webs of power.

Third, industrial production in the United States has accentuated growth and diversity rather than uniformity, anticipating today's 'mass customization'. This is especially true in the realm of housing, a fundamental concern in every instauration of Modernism. Designers have experimented with production systems and modern materials ranging from steel to synthetics and recycled timber. Like most Americans, architects have typically embraced the latest technologies with enthusiasm, presuming them to be inherently positive, their reach all-pervasive. The result has stimulated rising standards for human

TIME
The Weekly Newsmagazine

Volume XXXI

FRANK LLOYD WRIGHT
His city would be everywhere and nowhere.
(See Art)

Number 3

TIME
THE WEEKLY NEWSMAGAZINE

ARCHITECT
EERO SAARINEN

$6.00 A YEAR

VOL. LXVIII NO. 1

TIME
THE WEEKLY NEWSMAGAZINE

ARCHITECT RICHARD NEUTRA
What will the neighbors think?

TIME

R. BUCKMINSTER FULLER

VOL. 83 NO. 2

comfort, efficiency and individual self-expression – together with relentless consumerism and inequalities.

The media have been a fourth influence, including both popular and highly specialized professional publications or events. New currents in the mainstream profession, the academic discipline and the self-declared avant-garde have all been heavily mediated. Designers eagerly seized on each new format: lithographs, photographs, mapping, cinema and digital imagery. Advertising connected architecture with business, industry, fashion and popular culture. Some individuals have made their mark as celebrities – most notably Frank Lloyd Wright, who figures in every chapter of this book until his death in 1959, and Philip Johnson, as arbiter and architect since 1932. The media also enhanced the allure of verbal language with labels, analogies and buzzwords.

Fifth and most auspicious is a long-standing environmental sensibility. Thoughtful site planning has enhanced many individual structures and large-scale building groups. Many architects have accentuated natural landscapes and tried to mitigate ecological or climactic problems. American Modernism has rightly been characterized as 'Geo-Architecture', given how often it highlights surroundings, especially dramatic sites, and fuses structure with infrastructure. Unfortunately, the belief in the regenerative power of nature also tolerated a rapacious

Some of the architects featured on the cover of *Time* from 1938, 1949, 1952, 1963, 1964 and 1979.

Hoover Dam (now Boulder Dam), Colorado (1928–38): 'American "Geo-Architecture"', from the *Magazine of Art* (January 1944).

GEO-ARCHITECTURE: AN AMERICAN CONTRIBUTION TO THE ART OF THE FUTURE

disregard for land and ecological balance, as if these were eternal resources.

Every history inevitably engages present-day circumstances. This book raises questions about architecture in the twenty-first century even as it analyses the past. Contemporary debates about ecologies, technologies, patronage, symbolism and form build upon a lineage even as they go beyond it. If today's architecture seems inchoate, this is nothing new and even potentially positive, since the tendency towards rigid dichotomies is equally ingrained, each faction using the threat of the other to legitimate its own narrowly self-righteous position. Neo-traditionalists deform history by evoking imaginary pasts and facile accusations that modern architecture is inherently inhuman. Neo-avant-gardists likewise distort reality, disdaining history and public opinion outside their own bubble, rekindling suspicions of modern architecture as narcissistic indulgence. But why should anyone have to choose between illusions of a return or a rupture? The 'excluded middle' – what William James simply called the 'in-between' – is a fascinating and capacious realm to explore.[9]

A broader historical perspective will always challenge established assumptions, but it will not undermine individual talents or distinctive architectural concerns to place them in a larger context. My selection emphasizes breadth and diversity, balancing major buildings, some incontestable masterworks, with lesser-known trends and examples. I have not hesitated to point out overlaps with the world of builders and popular culture which determines the vast majority of what is built, and with architects who were significant in their time but since forgotten. Rather than simply describing stars I highlight constellations that can be read in multiple ways and seen from different perspectives.

History is an ongoing and fluid process, not a sacred narrative. It can illuminate alternative positions, so necessary within the homogenizing forces of today's global economy. This book is an effort to suggest myriad influences, dominant tendencies and counter-currents, a maelstrom of possibilities that sustains a vigorous culture. It would be foolish to deny that American modern architecture has been a tool of power, and equally foolish to see that domination as totalizing, as if change were impossible. The options are never equal, yet the outcome is not predetermined. I hope that readers will actively engage the broad currents and anomalies of the past, and then draw upon this legacy to imagine new possibilities in the present.

chapter one

Modern Consolidation, 1865–1893

The aftermath of the Civil War has rightly been called a Second American Revolution.[1] The United States was suddenly a modern nation, interconnected by layers of infrastructure, driven by corporate business systems, flooded by the enticements of consumer culture. The industrial advances in the North that had allowed the Union to survive a long and violent conflict now transformed the country, although resistance to Reconstruction and racial equality would curtail growth in the South for almost a century. A cotton merchant and amateur statistician expressed astonishment when he compared 1886 with 1856. 'The great railway constructor, the manufacturer, and the merchant of to-day engage in affairs as an ordinary matter of business' that, he observed, 'would have been deemed impossible . . . before the war'.[2]

Architecture helped represent and propel this radical transformation, especially in cities, where populations surged fourfold during the 30 years after the war. Business districts boasted the first skyscrapers. Public buildings promoted a vast array of cultural pleasures, often frankly hedonistic, many of them oriented to the unprecedented numbers of foreign immigrants. Real-estate speculators built comfortable apartments and oppressive tenements, while residential suburbs enjoyed a surge of growth within or just outside city limits, touting bucolic pleasures and the latest conveniences. Chicago's John Root articulated the challenge for architects: 'The frankest possible acceptance of every requirement of modern life in all its conditions,' he wrote, 'without regret for the past or idle longing for a future and more fortunate day'.[3] Americans lived in the present, a realm of ever-changing and contested realities.

New technological connections intensified the pace of progress. Local events could take on national significance almost immediately. Crowds all over the country shared in the 1869 'golden spike' ceremony that marked the culmination of a transcontinental railroad. Ideas, images and materials as well as people could now move quickly across the country, encouraging a more unified culture, although regional distinctions and metropolitan heterogeneity continued to grow apace. The drive for

Brooklyn Bridge opening celebration, New York City, 1883, lithograph.

systemic coordination would affect time itself in 1883 when the railroads imposed the four standard time zones we know today, supplanting more than fifty local variants. The telephone would further dissolve spatial barriers following the first call in 1876 (the centennial year of national independence), eventually connecting all would-be modern buildings.

Linkages could be simultaneously symbolic and practical. Steel suspension cables allowed the Eads Bridge (1874) to traverse the Mississippi River at St Louis. Young Louis Sullivan 'followed every detail', finding the ideal modern 'man in his power to create beneficently'.[4] A decade later, New Yorkers celebrated the opening of the Brooklyn Bridge, a fusion of steel cables and neo-Gothic piers that unified two cities into boroughs of what had now become the nation's premier city. Celebrants touted the bridge as a beacon for immigration, a tourist attraction, an engineering marvel. They audaciously asked: 'Will New York Be the Final World Metropolis?' The critic Montgomery Schuyler called this 'gossamer architecture' the leading monument of the age precisely because it was not a palace or a place of worship, but 'an exquisite refinement of utility in which the lines of forces constitute the structure'.[5] Electricity transformed spaces, too, with urban crowds drawn by the dazzling lights of some streets and urban entertainment venues, fuelled by Edison's central power stations. Electrified public streetcars transported a new social category, the middle class, beyond the city limits.

Inexpensive media saturated America with images of these and other spectacles. Pictures and texts about architecture attracted the general public and all manner of competing producers. *American Builder and Journal of Art* (founded in 1868) was joined by *Carpentry and Building* (1870), *American Architect and Building News* (1876), Chicago's iconoclastic *Inland Architect* (1883), *Architectural Record* (1890), *National Builder* (1885) and scores of others. Family magazines like *Scribner's* and *Scientific American* also analysed the latest trends. Pattern books by architects and builders offered multiple house designs, urging readers to alter and combine the suggestions as they saw fit. This coverage was part of a larger phenomenon: the advent of postcards, comic strips, amateur photography and omnipresent advertising. If the national appetite for commercial illustrations elicited fears among the elite that popularization would subvert the standards of fine art, the population as a whole delighted in the visual stimulation that surrounded them everywhere.

The architectural profession acquired its modern structure during these years of cultural maelstrom. The Massachusetts Institute of Technology offered the nation's first professional classes in 1865, and ten other schools followed in the next two decades, dispersing professional training beyond the East Coast. The scene remained cosmopolitan since

German, British and Irish architects continued to wield considerable authority across the country, and ambitious Americans still studied in Europe, most often at the Ecole des Beaux-Arts in Paris. Anyone could call himself an architect, so a resuscitated American Institute of Architects (AIA) joined other professional organizations to ostracize competitors and command respect. Licensing exams in the 1890s conferred state-approved credentials and gave registered architects exclusive rights over major public buildings. Most professional offices remained quite small (as they do today), although multiple commissions in a few firms required large staffs since corporate clients demanded speed, driven in part by steep financing costs. As Daniel Burnham told Louis Sullivan in 1874, 'my idea is to work up a big business, to handle big things, deal with big businessmen, and to build up a big organization.'[6]

Rationalized Business Structures

Rapid expansion and economies of scale fostered concentration of all sorts, beginning with the railroads, then mergers and the emergence of

large corporations – modernity's most powerful clients and economic arbiters. Businesses large and small, including architecture, calculated managerial practices and profit margins with far greater precision, in part through 'process spaces' to facilitate more resourceful operations.[7] Large-scale producers moved their clerical and administrative employees into downtown 'headquarters', away from the gritty world of factories. Up-and-coming companies invested in commercial architecture that trumpeted prosperity, recognizing that this could give them a distinctive edge in a fiercely competitive laissez-faire economy. Insurance companies and newspapers set the pace, followed by otherwise conservative banks, since their growth thrived on fears and excitement about change. In the words of the pre-eminent business historian Alfred Chandler,

Gilman & Kendall and George B. Post, Equitable Life Insurance Headquarters, New York, 1867–70.

'Modern business enterprise' became viable 'only when the visible hand of management proved to be more efficient than the invisible hand of market forces'.[8]

New York increasingly stood out, 'part Paradise, part Pandemonium', in the words of an 1868 best-seller; 'Order and harmony seem[ed] to come out of the confusion.'[9] In the 1870s, the tumultuous world of speculative booms and busts brought thousands of tourists to Wall Street, the 'engine room of corporate capitalism', whose 'Robber Baron' magnates were both admired and despised.[10] These circumstances generated the first skyscrapers – still a quintessential expression of modernity. A search for 'firsts' tends to obscure dynamic processes of appropriation and adaptation, essential to any innovation. Nonetheless, many contemporary historians give the prize to New York's Equitable Life Insurance Building (1867–70), the flagship of a company less than a decade old whose assets set a world record in 1868.

The Equitable Building was certainly not a 'proto-skyscraper', as some later historians contended, implying a teleological course towards an inevitable outcome.[11] The evolution of its design instead fused modern concerns for cost-effectiveness with high-risk stakes and publicity. Although one firm, Gilman & Kendall, won a competition for the new building in 1867, Henry Hyde, founder and vice-president of the company, immediately asked runner-up George B. Post to revise their scheme, making it 'rational' – by which he meant that it should abide by the cost guidelines while providing both higher rents and more rentable space. Post complied in ingenious ways. Most importantly, following Hyde's lead, he incorporated two steam-powered elevators so all floors would be equally valuable. (Elisha Otis had installed the first safety elevator for passengers a few blocks away in 1857, but it was expensive and clumsy.)

Only eight storeys high, the Equitable reached 43 metres, more than twice as tall as comparable structures, for Hyde understood both the allure of double-height ceilings and the emergent competition to create the tallest structure. The building enjoyed immediate success when it opened in 1870, drawing thousands of people to ride in the elevators and enjoy what one newspaper called 'the most exciting, wonderful, and instructive view to be had on our continent'.[12] Equitable continued to expand,

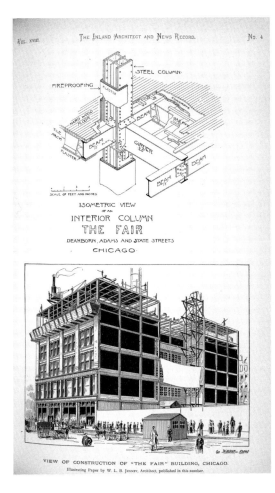

STEEL COLUMN.

FIREPROOFING

PLASTER

HARD WOOD FLOOR

TILE ARCH

BEAM

BEAM

GIRDER

BEAM

DEAM

PLASTER

SCALE OF FEET AND INCHES

ISOMETRIC VIEW
OF AN
INTERIOR COLUMN
THE FAIR
DEARBORN, ADAMS AND STATE STREETS
CHICAGO

VIEW OF CONSTRUCTION OF "THE FAIR" BUILDING, CHICAGO.
Illustrating Paper by W. L. B. Jenney, Architect, published in this number.

William LeBaron Jenney, Fair Department Store, Chicago, construction drawing with column-and-beam detail, 1890–91, from the *Inland Architect and Building News*.

although the nearby towers of media giants like Western Union (designed by Post) and Newspaper Row, congregated east of City Hall Park, soon usurped its once-remarkable prominence. Promotions for each new set of skyscrapers would continue to tout a fusion of rational constraints and exceptional splendour in costs, height and visibility.

William LeBaron Jenney of Chicago has been called the father of the skyscraper. Paternity claims rest on evidence of iron-skeleton construction – a hidden genetic code for Modernism – and a desire for legitimate parentage. Thin structural members support their own weight and that of the floors; the outer wall hangs on this frame, a curtain of natural light, weatherproofing and ornament. Jenney's Home Insurance Building (1884–5) did use such a system, but only on two façades, as an expert committee ascertained in 1931 during the first stage of the building's demolition.[13] The skeleton frame evolved through multiple experiments on diverse structures, including Jenney's Fair Building, a department store of 1890–91. Figures like Jenney reveal changing cultural biases. First seen as archetypal American 'inventors', they fit later historians' critique of obliging practitioners who merely fulfilled the will of powerful capitalists. 'The [Chicago] frame was convincing as fact rather than as idea,' Colin Rowe would contend, 'whereas [in Europe] it was more often an essential idea before it was an altogether reasonable fact.'[14]

Astute late nineteenth-century critics like Montgomery Schuyler understood that 'Architectural forms are not invented,' but evolve in response to multifaceted, unpredictable shifts in business, technology and culture.[15] Successor generations of modernists instead promulgated myths of a preternatural creative force, with Chicago akin to Renaissance Florence. Siegfried Giedion's book *Space, Time and Architecture* (initially published in 1941 and known as 'Giedion's Bible' for decades among architects) acclaimed what soon came to be known as the Chicago School – its

Modernism incarnate in the 'constituent element' of steel-frame construction – and dismissed New York's towers as signs of frivolous 'troubadour spirit'.[16] This limited vantage highlighted a few remarkable examples as prescient exceptions to the American norm. They supposedly embodied the Zeitgeist of their age because they anticipated later preferences. These judgements denied legitimacy to most other structures, erasing them from consideration. Architectural debate is still burdened by the narrow oppositions that resulted from this purview: lonely exceptions versus evolving norms, modern versus eclectic, progressive versus backward, pure spirit versus contaminated amalgams.

Skyscrapers appeared in downtown areas – officially designated 'central business districts' – where economic concentration and social prestige combined with high property values. *Downtown* is a distinctly American word and concept that originated in the 1880s, in clear contrast to the dispersed and variegated commercial districts of Europe. (The term *downtown* only appeared in dictionaries in the early 1900s after several decades of widespread colloquial use.) Spatial concentration intensified as more companies demanded proximity to legal, financial and other services, causing the price of real estate to increase dramatically, which then encouraged owners to expand vertically. Venturesome investors anticipated future concentrations since the locations and boundaries of each city's downtown were highly volatile, especially in early years.

Chicago gained prominence when its commercial leaders rebuilt quickly after the devastating fire of 1871, despite an ensuing economic depression. The new downtown was known as the Loop, taking its name from the surrounding cable-car tracks, re-inscribed by elevated trains in the late 1890s. To this day, all major transit lines still lead to this area, even though its prominence has declined markedly since the 1920s. The Loop was concentrated, occupying a 1.3-square-kilometre area, hemmed in by water and railroad yards. Crowds and congestion were seen as assets, evidence of a vigorous economy. Tourist guidebooks promoted itineraries of Chicago's new skyscrapers, touting it as the world's most characteristically modern metropolis, the 'City of Speed'.

Two Boston developers, Peter and Shephard Brooks, helped define Chicago's modernity. By the turn of the century they had financed 9.3 square kilometres of new office space, together with Owen Aldis, their local manager. Combined with the other buildings that Aldis managed, this accounted for nearly one fifth of the Loop. Peter Brooks explained his specifications for the Monadnock Building (1884–91) to his architect, John Root: a marginal site required masonry construction to reassure clients, while economy and maintenance meant 'no projecting surfaces or indentations . . . everything flush, or flat and smooth with the walls'.

Burnham & Root, Monadnock Building, Chicago, 1884–91, with Holabird & Roche addition of 1893 at left.

Root's alchemy turned these constraints into creative architecture. Sheer walls of deep brown brick rise sixteen storeys. The building's effect depended solely 'on its massiveness and the correct relation of its lines', marvelled one local newspaper, and Schuyler described it as an essence, 'the thing itself'.[17] Unfortunately, elegant minimalism is notoriously expensive, and cost overruns were one reason that Aldis hired another firm, Holabird & Roche, for an addition two years later.

Technological innovations provided essential underpinnings for the modern skyscraper. Some went far below ground. Power-operated derricks made deeper foundations possible; pneumatic caissons allowed buildings to rise to more than twenty storeys high in 1890 – at which

time Chicago and other cities began imposing height limits. Elevators
were prominent, but hidden systems of sewage, heating, ventilation and
plumbing were equally important, while advances in non-combustible
materials and sprinkler systems eased fears about fires. Whereas large
office buildings of the 1850s had housed some 300 employees, new skyscrapers might have 4,000 with several times that number of business
visitors per day. By 1890 the sequence of experimental construction procedures had coalesced into a pattern, still much the same today,
including general contractors with comprehensive schedules. Designed
to be replicated, the 'Chicago system' took root in Kansas City,
Cleveland, Atlanta and Los Angeles.

Major changes in communications and record-keeping spurred a
sometimes desperate demand for skilled employees. Small offices accord-
ingly gave way to larger spaces and movable partitions. Business, only
recently an entirely male domain, now rapidly feminized, in part because
of pay disparities that continue today. New equipment like typewriters,
telephones and vertical filing cabinets helped generate a female clerical
force whose members became interchangeable elements arrayed in rows
in large central areas under the scrutiny of male managers.[18]

If office efficiency and rentability determined interior design, both
required access to natural light. Burnham and Root's headquarters for
the Chicago, Burlington and Quincy Railroad (1883) introduced spacious
light courts within large perimeter blocks. Chicago's Reliance Building
transformed the office façade, converting most of its surface to plate
glass. The fourteen-storey building was erected in two stages. John Root
designed the ground floor (1890–91) with capacious windows set in dark

D. H. Burnham & Co.,
Reliance Building,
Chicago; base by John
Root, 1890–91; upper
floors by Charles
Atwood, 1894–5.

masonry; Charles Atwood, who replaced Root after his death, conceived
the upper floors (1894–5) quite differently, using glazed terracotta around
ample 'Chicago windows' consisting of tripartite bays with smaller operable sashes to each side. Commentators of the era disliked the bright
white cladding as the embodiment of the 'money-getting spirit of the
age'. Eighty years later, the Marxist architectural historian Manfredo
Tafuri concurred, calling it a pure sign of laissez-faire capitalism. More
formalist critics saw the cladding as a mirage; they read the exterior as a
transparent, virtually immaterial glass curtain wall, drawing in part on
Root's early translations of Gottfried Semper, who had alluded to walls as
textiles, and therefore 'an architectural anticipation of the future'.[19]

More than ever, Americans now worried that their aggressive business culture might have negative repercussions, not just on architecture
but on the larger social order. Louis Sullivan was not alone in asking:
'How shall we impart to this sterile pile, this crude, harsh, brutal

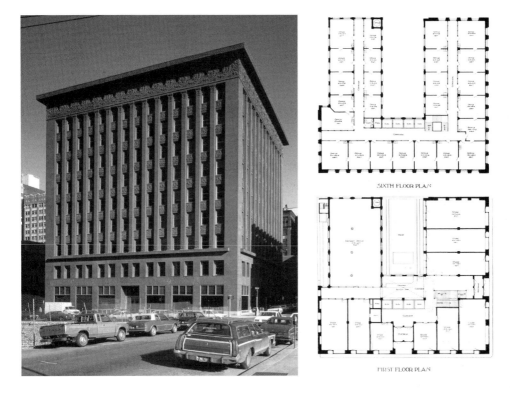

SIXTH FLOOR PLAN

FIRST FLOOR PLAN

Adler & Sullivan,
Wainwright Building,
St Louis, Missouri,
1890–91.

Wainwright Building,
plan of sixth (typical)
and first floor.

George Wyman,
Bradbury Building,
Los Angeles, 1890,
light court.

agglomeration, this stark staring exclamation of eternal strife, the graciousness of those higher forms of sensibility and culture?'[20] Ornament seemed an antidote, articulating higher cultural values over bottom-line frugality, especially when the public could see it. The incised granite bases of skyscrapers reasserted human scale and even a civic presence on busy downtown streets. Grand entrances invited the public into handsome lobbies and interior courts where light filtered through the filigree around stairs, cantilevered balconies and elevator cages.

Sullivan himself insisted on synthesis, fully integrating rich colours and ornament (derived from studies of nature and geometry) in his eloquent office buildings. Three of Adler & Sullivan's masterpieces are outside Chicago: the Wainwright in St Louis (1890–91), the Guaranty in Buffalo, New York (1894–5) and the Bayard in New York City (1897–8). The Wainwright, fully ten storeys high, was the firm's first steel-frame structure. Sullivan claimed to have created the initial 'logical and poetic expression' for skyscrapers in a 'volcanic' moment of inspiration. Celebrating verticality, making 'every inch a proud and soaring thing', he transliterated the classical concept of a tripartite column of base, shaft

H. H. Richardson, Marshall Field Warehouse, Chicago, 1886.

Harry Wild Jones, Lindsay Brothers Warehouse, Minneapolis, Minnesota, 1895, upper-level addition 1909; photographed in 1990 following renovation as River Walk lofts.

and capital into monumental scale: a tall, handsome base with public lobby, 'an indefinite number of stories' for office rentals, and mechanical equipment at the top, concealed behind a frieze whose vibrant pattern was visible from the street.[21] The lush ornament counterbalanced the elemental structure, providing a 'life force', which, Sullivan believed, could neutralize the oppressive forces of capitalism. Famously declaring that 'form ever follows function', he considered lyricism a fundamental human need, especially in a crowded, often alienating metropolis. His was a 'liberal, expansive, sumptuous' Modernism, bringing joy to 'the daily life of our architecture'.[22]

Industrial architecture also favoured functional beauty, although, given constant changes in use, adaptability was far more important than visibility. Urban manufacturing surged in the 1870s and '80s as small-scale capitalists built hundreds of structures typically known as lofts, renting out each floor for storage or small-scale industry, notably garment sweatshops. Larger companies soon hired well-known architects to provide more specialized functions and aesthetic impact, notably in urban wholesaling, which dwarfed retail in economic and architectural terms throughout the 1890s. Marshall Field's wholesale store in Chicago (1886), designed by Henry Hobson Richardson, became an icon. The headquarters for a prestigious business, its exterior majesty and internal organization provided a stable point of reference not just for architects but also for merchants and shopkeepers throughout the region. Architects in other cities often emulated this example for relatively inexpensive warehouses, sturdy enough to support heavy loads, their

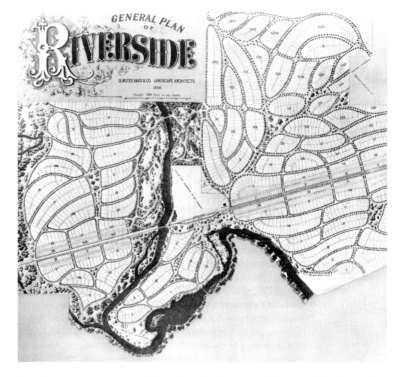

handsome restraint considered 'a wholesome architectural influence' at the time.[23] A century later, many of these handsome buildings were converted into high-status residential lofts.

Housing the Emergent 'Middle Class'

The landscape architect Frederick Law Olmsted expressed pleasure in another geographical shift of the post-Civil War era, one that separated 'compact and higher buildings' in business districts from 'broader, lower, and more open building in residence quarters' beyond the city limits. *Industrial Chicago* (1891) likewise praised the 1880s for the new commercial style downtown *and* the 'modern cottages' going up outside the city.[24] Olmsted and Vaux's 1868–9 design for Riverside, just outside Chicago, created the first large-scale comprehensive design for a residential suburb.[25] Unlike patrician suburbs of the 1850s such as Llewellyn Park, Riverside used skilful site planning to integrate natural beauty with modern technology – notably the inclusion of public transit with a railroad station – together with adjacent shops and apartments. Almost half of the 650 hectares comprised dedicated public land, ensuring a lush bucolic

Edmund Quincy, Jr, and Ware & Van Brunt, Model Houses for the Quincy German Homestead Association, Dedham, Massachusetts, 1871.

setting. William LeBaron Jenney became chief architect and engineer after 1870, designing a number of eclectic houses and a hotel. Like Olmsted, he was an environmental strategist, gearing each building to near and distant views. Frank Lloyd Wright's Tomek House (1907) and Coonley House (1908) in Riverside would reinterpret this tradition in a daring new idiom.

The Riverside typology was an eloquent ideal that few could afford to match. Less expensive streetcar suburbs attracted a middle-income market – indeed they helped create the middle class. Antebellum society had presumed unchanging categories (the 'vicious' poor, 'hard-working' mechanics or farmers, the elite 'best men'), giving little thought to a vague entity sometimes called the 'middling classes'. The American designation 'middle class' emerged in the 1870s, marking a heightened awareness of status among the fast-growing ranks of service employees, clerks and professionals. If class depended on job and salary, the right house converted these into a visible commodity. Although most people still rented, home ownership rose as banks and builders offered better mortgage terms. A more informal market emerged for ambitious working-class families with ethnic-based building-and-loan societies underwriting workers' cottages in Polish, German and other enclaves close to urban industrial zones.[26]

Suburbia embodied and exaggerated the idea of separate gender spheres, supposedly protecting women and children from the brutal male world of commerce and industry. Yet here, too, we find alternative currents. Intent on modernizing this female realm, in 1869 Catharine Beecher published *The American Woman's Home*, co-authored with her sister, Harriet Beecher Stowe. A former art teacher, Beecher adapted several dwelling types 'with the latest and most authentic results of science applicable to domestic life'. She focused almost obsessively on her suburban model. It featured two full bathrooms, built-in furnishings, movable partitions and a 'workroom' that concentrated plumbing, heating and storage in a compact service core.[27] In defining the home as a virtually autonomous setting, the shrine of health and efficiency,

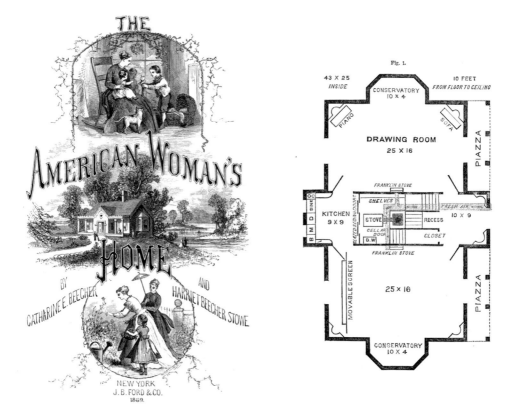

Catharine Beecher,
frontispiece and
floor plan of a model
suburban house,
from *The American
Woman's Home* with
Harriet Beecher
Stowe, 1869.

Beecher endorsed what would later be called 'family values'. Her ideal home was strictly separated from the work of business, although not from work as such, at least not for women. Giedion and others have portrayed Beecher's ideas as premonitions of 1920s Modernism. In fact, her remarkable scheme highlights an intriguing aspect of Victorian culture, Modernism's *bête noire*. The widespread appeal of Victorian homes, then and now, is in part their ability to symbolize deep human longings for familial and personal well-being while deftly incorporating the latest provisions for convenience, comfort and health. Builders' advertisements routinely promised 'A.M.I. – All Modern Improvements' – or higher standards for everyday life.

Even today, modern residential architecture in the United States draws on four themes that emerged in the late nineteenth century. The first is new media. The latest house designs were favourite topics in popular and professional journals and early mass-market shelter magazines, which focused exclusively on the topic. Second, modern technologies raised standards for public infrastructure and household comfort. Site planning is third. The Civil War made Americans keenly aware of the 'environment' as a potent cultural phenomenon and a prime determinant of public health. Well-to-do suburbs set aside some open space and adopted a regular pattern of curving street layouts that seemed organic. Most dwellings connected to the outdoors with one or more porches and long verandas that in turn led to lawns or gardens. Finally and most pronouncedly, American dwellings linked individualization with standardization. Mass-market commerce still relies on surface images of individuality, illusions of autonomy fused with predictable uniformity.

The post-Civil War era marks the birth of that entrenched American belief that your home expresses who you are. Whereas antebellum domestic architecture had stressed collective standards (variations were based on climate and class), American houses now accentuated self-expression. Street façades and interiors mixed materials in distinctive, eye-catching patterns, while irregular massing supposedly signalled the distinctive interests of those inside. In reality, of course, home-builders relied on mass-market pattern books and popular magazines for ideas. Clarence Cook, a well-known New York art critic, declared zealously in *The House Beautiful* that 'there never was a time when so many books and magazines written for the purpose of bringing the subject of architecture – its history, its theory, its practice – down to the level of popular understanding as in this time of ours.'[28]

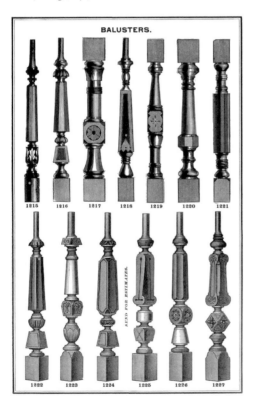

Factory-produced stair balusters from *Universal Moulding Book* (Chicago, 1871).

Equally important, stock fixtures and factory-made ornament allowed builders to conjure up the effect of uniqueness at a reasonable price. As American mass production reached unprecedented output, it churned out the appearance of personalized diversity for dwellings, a precursor to contemporary building practices. Only a quarter of most suburban households in 1890 owned their own homes (and half of these were owned by mortgage-financing institutions), making appearance all the more important an indication of status and stability.

'Queen Anne' was the most common label for these variegated, supposedly individualized houses, although builders and

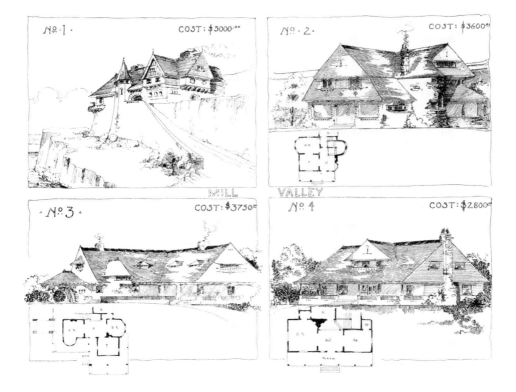

Joseph Cather Newsom, designs from his pattern-book, *Modern Homes of California* (1893).

architects borrowed widely from French, Japanese and other English vernaculars and from their own New England Colonial houses. The amalgams could be serendipitous or garbled ('hallucination and morbid delirium tremors', fretted *Scientific American*).[29] However, architecture rarely fits into precise categories like pastiche or pure, traditional or modern. The seductive ease of stylistic labels brings a semblance of order to the messy vitality of art, science and politics, but it tends to dismiss all sorts of creative work that do not fit into narrow classifications.

Besides, labels are often applied long after the fact. Art historian Vincent Scully invented the term Shingle Style in the late 1940s to describe the rambling, informal houses of the 1880s especially popular in wealthy New England suburbs and resorts. Illustrations underscored bold, asymmetrical compositions, a continuous flow of 'natural' shingles (usually factory-produced) on the façades and a relatively open flow of spaces inside – each one a stage for special everyday 'events'. This trend spread all the way to California and is often replicated today. A French architect in 1886 extolled 'an audacity which is astounding', predicting

Frank Lloyd Wright, Wright house, Oak Park, Illinois, 1889.

The Oak Park Wright house, living-room inglenook.

that these imaginative yet restrained American houses could 'lay the groundwork of a more modern style'.[30] Yet Scully was not content to describe a phenomenon. Taking the rhetoric of the time far too literally, he claimed an inherent and conscious meaning: the incarnation of an American 'democratic' spirit.[31] Past or present, architects and builders rarely adhere to stylistic rules, much less mythic cultural imperatives.

Frank Lloyd Wright adapted these ideas for his own home and studio in the Chicago suburb of Oak Park in 1889, when he was just 22 years old. The principal façade features an exaggerated triangular gable atop two

bay windows, the whole covered with shingles. This paradigmatic signifier of shelter emphasized simplicity, even restraint; it also extended
beyond the private sphere. Following the tenets of Chicago progressives,
especially women reformers, Wright integrated work and family life
under one roof. (He also shared a Chicago office with like-minded colleagues for business meetings and collaborative discussions.) The bold
geometries continued inside, notably his refinement of a conventional
fireplace alcove as a series of interlocked rectangles around an arch. His
treatment of space would become increasingly assured and complex over
the next decade.

Modern systems of production and distribution underlay most
Victorian residential architecture. Domestic production of plate glass
after 1875 led to stock windows to fit stock window-sash. Portable prefabricated houses were shipped from contractors, many of them in Chicago,
to American homesteads and overseas. Schoolhouses, churches, courthouses, stores and taverns were also available. Most suburban and urban
houses were constructed in small groups from three or four to twenty at
a time, each one quite similar in structure and floor plan, but made to
seem distinctive with still commonplace devices like reversing the placement of a porch or gable. The 1880s also saw a new breed of builder who
dramatically increased the number of dwellings and consolidated a
panoply of services. These 'sub-dividers' produced advertising; designed
and built dwellings; laid out street plans; financed transit systems; and

Advertisement for
S. E. Gross's
'Enterprises' in the
Chicago suburbs,
1889.

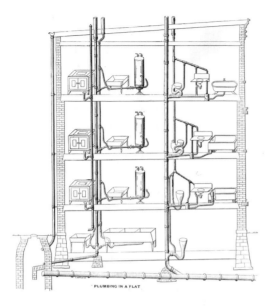

PLUMBING IN A FLAT

Section of plumbing
in a typical Chicago
apartment house,
c. 1890.

installed landscaping and infrastructure, even when the standards were meagre. San Francisco's Real Estate Associates built over a thousand row (terrace) houses in one decade. Two architect-brothers, Joseph and Samuel Newsom, produced hundreds of custom-designed dwellings, speculative row-house blocks and eleven pattern books with titles like *Modern Homes of California* (1893). Samuel E. Gross surpassed everyone, laying out more than 40,000 lots in 16 towns and 150 smaller subdivisions in and around Chicago between 1880 and 1892. His ads for houses and neighbourhoods appeared in English and foreign languages, using comic-strip art to assert the enduring developer's promise: happiness and prosperity in 'your own home'.

Meanwhile, apartment buildings were setting off a 'Revolution in Living', declared the *New York Times* in 1878.[32] Large cities soon reported thousands of multi-family residences under construction every year, spurred by the rising cost of land. Working-class areas had distinctive patterns, such as New York's 'walk-ups' and New England's 'triple-deckers', with one family to a floor, though renters and boarders were common. Apartment houses could be 'cheap flats' or more prestigious 'French flats', so locations and façades had to ensure status. Interiors were visibly ornate, sometimes awkwardly so, but certain forms of convenience were an asset. By the 1880s, architects were experimenting with innovative plans and technological advances such as gas lighting, elevators, central vacuum-cleaning systems, telephone switchboard operators, central hot-water heating and that American obsession, fully equipped bathrooms, for every unit. Apartment-hotels upped the ante with centralized services like professional laundries and kitchens to service individual units, as well as dining rooms, cafés and reception areas on the main floor. Progressive buildings added childcare and kitchen-less units. The feminist Charlotte Perkins Gilman called this a boon for women, a model of cooperative living, proof that Americans were willing to innovate, always ready 'to throw aside good for better, and better for best'.[33]

Apartment buildings thrived by transforming the image of multi-unit housing from poverty to luxury. The New York courts helped, ruling in 1878 that collective services distinguished apartment houses from tenements, since no one dared suggest 'communistic' efficiencies for the poor. Philanthropists constructed suburban enclaves and a few 'model tenements' in cities. Both kinds of reforms were relatively conservative, based on small interventions, not grand architectural 'solutions'. The site planning did make a difference, however, since large parcels of land allowed for spacious central courtyards to maximize sunlight, fresh air and common areas for the residents.[34] These efforts merged belief in the market with environmental determinism – the notion that good or bad environments directly affect human behaviour – an especially deep-rooted conviction in American culture. Model housing presumed a twofold effect: better architecture would change the bad habits of both residents and speculative builders.

Public Entertainment

Frederick Law Olmsted, Back Bay Fens Park and parkway to Boston Commons, 1887 site plan.

American cities were segregating commercial and residential environments, yet urban social life retained a dynamic creole mixture. Despite the fierce antagonisms that divided citizens along class, ethnic and racial lines, all were simultaneously voyeurs and actors in the show. American and European scholars studied crowds, hoping to find ways to control

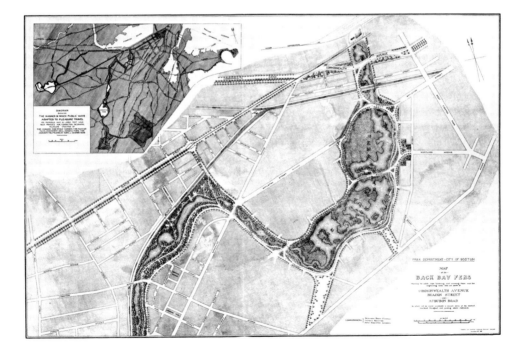

John Kellum, rotunda of the A. T. Stewart Department Store, Astor Place, New York City, 1862–70.

the strikes and the 'mob' violence of urban riots that intensified in the 1880s. Some American reformers built institutions and outdoor spaces to bring people together, seeking to mitigate the tensions and pressures of modern life. The bustling crowds also spurred entertainment moguls to create a kaleidoscopic world of commerce and culture with architecture to match. The rise of spectator sports provided acceptable outlets for emotion. The Cincinnati Red Stockings launched professional baseball in 1869, and the spread of teams in the 1880s provided key sites for male camaraderie. These ballparks are still beloved fixtures in national imaginaries and collective symbols of hometown pride.

Urban parks accommodated a broad mix of people and pursuits, encouraging amateur sports, various leisure activities and some contact with what is now designated 'the Other'. The quintessential example is New York's Central Park, designed by Olmsted and Vaux in 1857 and under construction until 1880. Olmsted's Boston landscapes grew into a network of differentiated yet coordinated public spaces, much admired by European visitors, starting in 1878 with a park in the Back Bay Fens and a proposed parkway to Boston Commons. Olmsted would encompass various efforts throughout the entire metropolitan area to create a regional park system known as the 'Emerald Necklace' (1890). Designers in Chicago, Minneapolis, Kansas City, San Francisco and other cities implemented similar large-scale landscape designs. This integration of nature and infrastructure, planning and 'non-planning', provides the foundation for today's ecological architecture and Landscape Urbanism.

The department store was a transatlantic phenomenon, its origins and trajectory almost as elusive as the consumer fantasies it fueled. A. T. Stewart's Italianate Marble Palace in New York (1846) was a prototype, although the Bon Marché in Paris (1852) was far more inventive in its iron structure and fantastic displays. Stewart then constructed a grand cast-iron store and, just after the Civil War, a larger emporium further uptown. By this time, a congruence of modern conditions was affecting time, space and desires. National transport systems of roads, waterways and railroads moved goods quickly. Business principles like high volume, varied choices and fixed prices, including mark-downs, increased sales. Lively advertising became omnipresent, heightening both fears and fantasies about class mobility. Marshall Field initiated a concentration on Chicago's State Street with his opulent 'palace', and an even grander replacement whose construction began just one day after the 1871 fire. New York also generated a retail district called 'Ladies' Mile'. The Cincinnati merchant John Shillito created the country's largest store under one roof in 1878, using James McLaughlin's design for an iron-skeleton frame to obtain maximum open space for display. Department-store managers claimed their buildings embodied universal progress by democratizing luxury.

The scale, space and grandeur of these emporia sought to transform frugal women into avid shoppers. Consumer culture redefined self-fulfilment in terms of immediate gratification, displacing the earlier national ethic of hard work, thrift and faith. Edward Bellamy's *Looking Backward*, a popular utopian novel first published in 1888, imagined

twenty-first-century Boston as a cooperative society of leisure and pleasure centred on a vast emporium where the buyer 'found under one roof the world's assortment in whatever line he desired'.[35] Most social critics of the past century have condemned consumerism as insidious seduction that trapped the masses, although Walter Benjamin, the brilliant commentator on modern Paris, recognized the allure of commodities intensified by 'the crowd that surges around them and intoxicates them'.[36] Some theorists now argue that consumer culture can be liberating as well as manipulative, allowing people, especially women, to imagine alternative possibilities for their lives. People do take pleasure, albeit fleeting, in the exhilarating aura that pervades shopping environments.

Nineteenth-century department stores provided fantasy settings for women and direct contact with goods unimaginably more luxurious than the simple products they had only recently made themselves. The combination was intentionally irresistible. Tantalizing entries proclaimed an open-access policy, welcoming the 'shawl trade' of immigrant women as well as the upper-tier 'carriage trade'. (The working-class protagonist of Theodore Dreiser's 1900 novel, *Sister Carrie,* loved 'the delight of parading here as an equal'.)[37] Once inside, women discovered a wonderland focused around cathedral-like rotundas that featured spectacular displays and concerts. Open balconies ascended upward, crowned by brilliant stained-glass skylights. The grand emporiums also provided safe and comfortable places for female customers to rest and recuperate in ladies' restrooms, lounges, tearooms and nurseries. Shoplifting may have been inevitable given the enticements for immediate gratification of one's desires, but surveillance could not break the illusion that miraculous transformations were within anyone's reach. So the grand stairways and balconies proved doubly useful, drawing customers further into a seemingly magical realm while allowing for discreet monitoring. For good or bad, this modern building type provided intense, if ephemeral, spectacles, fusing private desires and public space, an amalgam that is now difficult to dissolve.

Window systems were crucial in department stores, as in other kinds of modern architecture. Upper-level offices and shopping floors required maximum light to supplement the central skylights. Street-level 'show windows' were a more complex transitional realm geared to a new pastime dubbed 'window shopping'. Early displays that exhibited products for sale were soon eclipsed by dream-like settings that encouraged a suspension of disbelief. Architects experimented with new types of plate glass to eliminate reflections, making the barrier virtually invisible yet solid, while a new breed of design specialist, the window-dresser, conjured up magical micro-environments. The most famous of these was Chicago's L. Frank Baum, author of *The Wizard of Oz* (1900).

Adler & Sullivan, Schlesinger and Meyer Department Store (today Carson Pirie & Scott), Chicago, 1891–4, 1903–4.

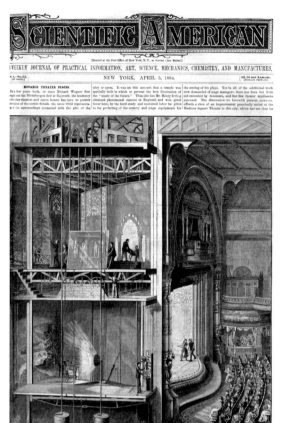

Scientific American

[Entered at the Post Office of New York, N.Y., as Second Class Matter.]

WEEKLY JOURNAL OF PRACTICAL INFORMATION, ART, SCIENCE, MECHANICS, CHEMISTRY, AND MANUFACTURES.

NEW YORK, APRIL 5, 1884.

THE MOVABLE STAGE AT THE MADISON SQUARE THEATER, NEW YORK.

Francis Kimball and Thomas Wisedell, Madison Square Theater, New York City, 1879–80, backstage technology and electric footlights.

Perhaps the most alluring American department store of the era was Sullivan's Schlesinger and Meyer (1891–4, 1903–4) in Chicago (now Carson, Pirie, Scott). The show windows set innovative, non-glare glass in prismatic boxes, while the ornamentation at street level is the most exuberant of Sullivan's entire career, culminating in a lush, sumptuously curved corner entry. Giedion's photographs in *Space, Time and Architecture* ignored this streetscape to show only the spare Chicago windows above, so that generations of young architects stood outside, asking where to find this modern masterpiece.

Popular entertainment exemplified the technical prowess and pyrotechnic allure of late nineteenth-century American modernity. Small-town 'opera houses' proliferated with lively fare that might combine Shakespeare and Verdi with burlesque. Urban pleasure gardens, vaudeville theatres and dance halls presented lively offerings for diverse audiences. Women of all classes and backgrounds enjoyed greater freedom at night in cosmopolitan cities. Every neighbourhood had bars and brothels, but also scores of more respectable settings. Many facilities were geared to immigrants, who typically separated the propriety of 'family audiences' from prostitutes and saloons (sometimes relegated to another floor or wing rather than eliminated). 'Dime museums' exhibited curiosities, while grand art and natural-history museums displayed masterworks. New York's innovative new theatres spurred the first legends of Broadway with visual spectacles that relied on technologies – electric footlights, complex backstage components for quick changes of scenery, mechanical systems for retractable roofs and light shows – all typically left exposed for ease of work.

Impresarios soon thought of uniting this variety of activities and audiences in huge palladiums. P. T. Barnum had already converted the

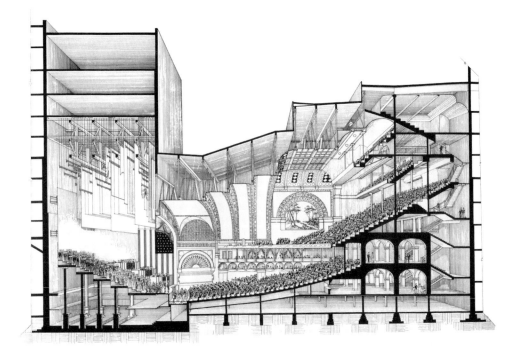

Adler & Sullivan,
Chicago Auditorium,
1886–90, section
through theatre.

abandoned railroad depot at New York's Madison Square into a Great Hippodrome for horse-shows, concerts, religious revival meetings and his own circus when he proposed a grand mixed-use coliseum called Madison Square Garden for the site in 1879. Almost a decade later, an investment syndicate appropriated the term and chose McKim, Mead & White to create a 'Palace of Amusements' with a hippodrome, concert halls, dance halls, theatres, restaurants, baths, a sports amphitheatre, an exhibition hall and outdoor pleasure gardens. The main structure opened in 1890, the roof garden two years later. In the March 1894 issue of *Century Magazine* Mariana van Rensselaer proclaimed that 'nothing else would be so sorely missed by all New Yorkers.'[38] That possibility seemed preposterous at the time, but high upkeep costs led to the Garden's demolition in 1925. Only the name survives today, an empty signifier attached to a mammoth but sterile sports arena near Barnum's original site.

Fortunately, Chicago's Auditorium Building still stands, though it too has been threatened. The difficulty of demolishing so massive a building saved its life more than once. Distressed by the anarchist bombing at Haymarket Square in 1886, the clients, Ferdinand Peck and the Chicago Opera, insisted that the structure be immune to dynamite. Peck wanted a 'public edifice' to unite the city with varied amenities, drawing multiple audiences ranging from national political conventions to subsidized concerts for workers. Begun in 1887 and, like Madison Square Garden, completed in 1890, it was the largest structure in the city's history and the most costly in the country's. Peck chose Dankmar Adler and his young partner, Louis Sullivan, based on their theatre designs. Given such a daunting commission and a site that filled half a city block, Peck encouraged them to emulate Richardson's Marshall Field wholesale store for the exterior. To contrast with the rusticated stone façade, Sullivan created a pulsating sequence of richly chromatic settings for the interiors, culminating in a glorious theatre. Adler's skill in acoustics merged with Sullivan's artistic bravura in the ceiling of elliptical arches embellished with delicate ornament, hundreds of incandescent lights and openings for the ventilation system. Folding ceiling panels and vertical screens could transform the space from a concert hall of 2,500 seats into a convention hall with a capacity of 7,000. Since Peck wanted to make money, he added offices and a hotel to underwrite the civic and cultural spaces. A public observation deck on the roof of the eleven-storey office tower allowed magnificent views of the city. When a building workers' strike stopped construction throughout the city, the Mayor insisted that the Auditorium, a private development, had 'a quasi-public nature', so work continued.[39]

Another extravaganza, the World's Columbian Exposition of 1893, left a more controversial legacy. Some 27 million people, half from abroad, marvelled at the spectacle that brazenly proclaimed American superiority in every realm: technological, social, economic and cultural. Conceived and orchestrated in just over two years under the direction of one man, Daniel Burnham, and more than 465,000 square metres in area, the 'White City' won praise as a cohesive ensemble, a vision of harmony in a world that seemed marred by drudgery and anarchy. Burnham's aesthetic was decidedly Beaux-Arts. The Exposition was modern in its comprehensive planning and its reliance on mass production and new technologies, notably electricity and modern transportation systems like moving sidewalks. The broad vision also appropriated the excitement of commercial and popular culture. Burnham himself chose the theatrical impresario Sol Bloom to oversee the Midway Plaisance, a 1.5-kilometre-long carnival of exoticism, eroticism and escapism right alongside the grandeur of the White City. The Midway featured ethnographic displays, more voyeuristic than educational, and technological wonders like the first Ferris wheel, which provided unprecedented panoramas of Chicago. Department-store and railroad executives dominated the committee that presided over the Exposition, and they wanted a phantasmagoria of enticing variety, not a static, moralistic tableau.

Later critics condemned the Chicago Exposition as deceptive and retrograde, largely because of the opulent Beaux-Arts aesthetic that predominated. Sullivan's blistering attack still resounds: 'The damage wrought by the World's Fair will last for half a century from its date, if not longer.'[40] This exaggerated prophecy was written in the 1920s, when Sullivan was embittered and impoverished. Such vindictive antagonism harmed American architecture, setting up a battle that privileges those who wield the greatest power, such that architects simultaneously dismiss them and try to usurp their supremacy. Montgomery Schuyler recognized the broader implications of the Chicago Exposition. An ardent modernist, he lamented the dominant aesthetic as 'hopelessly prosaic [and] pedantic'. Nonetheless, it was just a 'passing show'. Everyone knew that the white plaster surfaces were 'architectural screens . . . executed on a colossal stage', for this was 'a success of illusion'.[41] Visitors admired the cohesive planning that brought together hundreds of diverse sites, including Sullivan's resplendent Transportation Building. Official photographs or speeches celebrated a grand imperial vision of American culture, but the experience was richer, more incongruous, a mêlée of surprises and juxtapositions.

The spectacular 1893 Exposition died as planned after only six months, though it remains part of the American collective consciousness. Its reassuring thematic cohesion persists in many public settings, from historic districts to shopping malls. The scope of Burnham's control and his corporate values established a significant model for later urban 'revitalization' plans. There are also other more auspicious repercussions in our contemporary world: waterfront reclamation and temporary spaces for illusory images, fleeting events, participatory performances. Can we heed Schuyler's urbane analysis, rejecting simple binaries of good/bad, daring to engage a range of alternatives at the same time? There is something to be learned from the allure of popular success and even historicist fantasies. Surely modern architecture and thought have the strength to engage diverse aesthetic and social worlds? As Schuyler showed so well, tolerance does not mean abandoning critical judgements.

PERSPECTIVE OF QUADRUPLE BLOCK PLAN

QUADRUPLE BLOCK PLAN

A Home in a Prairie Town

By FRANK LLOYD WRIGHT

This is the Fifth Design in the Journal's New Series of Model Suburban Houses Which Can be Built at Moderate Cost

CITY man going to the country puts too much in his house and too little in his ground. He drags after him the fifty-foot lot, soon the twenty-five-foot lot, finally the party wall; and the home-maker who fully appreciates the advantages which he came to the country to secure feels himself impelled to move on.

It seems a waste of energy to plan a house haphazard, to hit or miss an already distorted condition, so this partial solution of a city man's country home on the prairie begins at the beginning and assumes four houses to the block of four hundred feet square as the minimum of ground for the basis of his prairie community.

The block plan to the left, at the top of the page, shows an arrangement of the four houses that secures breadth and prospect to the community as a whole, and absolute privacy both as regards each to the community, and each to each of the four.

The perspective view shows the handling of the group at the centre of the block, with its foil of simple lawn, omitting the foliage of curb parkways to better show the scheme, retaining the same house in the four locations merely to afford an idea of the unity of the various elevations, though based upon a similar plan.

The ground plan, which is intended to explain itself, is arranged to offer the least resistance to a simple mode of living, in keeping with a high ideal of the family life together. It is arranged, too, with a certain well-established order that enables free use without the sense of confusion felt in five out of seven houses which people really use.

The exterior recognizes the influence of the prairie, is firmly and broadly associated with the site, and makes a feature of its quiet level. The low terraces

GROUND FLOOR PLAN

CHAMBER

HALL · HALL

CHAMBER 20·6×12·0

CHAMBER 20·6×12·0

HALL

SECOND FLOOR PLAN

CHAMBER

and broad eaves are designed to accentuate that quiet level and complete the harmonious relationship. The curbs of the terraces and formal inclosures for extremely informal masses of foliage and bloom should be worked in cement with the walks and drives.

Cement on metal lath is suggested for the exterior covering throughout, because it is simple, and, as now understood, durable and cheap.

The cost of this house with interior as specified and cement construction would be seven thousand dollars:

Masonry, Cement and Plaster	$2806.00
Carpentry	3100.00
Plumbing	400.00
Painting and Glass	375.00
Heating — combination (hot water)	318.00
Total	$6970.00

IN A HOUSE of this character the upper reach and gallery of the central living-room is decidedly a luxury. Two bedrooms may take its place, as suggested by the second-floor plan. The gallery feature is, nevertheless, a temptation because of the happy sense of variety and depth it lends to the composition of the interior, and the sunlight it gains from above to relieve the shadow of the porch. The details are better grasped by a study of the drawings. The interior section in perspective shows the gallery as indicated by dotted lines on the floor plan of the living-room.

The second-floor plan disregards this feature and is arranged for a larger family. Where three bedrooms would suffice the gallery would be practicable, and two large and two small bedrooms with the gallery might be had by rearranging servants' rooms and baths.

The interior is plastered throughout with sand finish and trimmed all through with flat bands of Georgia pine, smaller back bands following the base and casings. This Georgia pine should be selected from straight grain for stiles, rails and running members, and from figured grain for panels and wide surfaces.

All the wood should be shellacked once and waxed, and the plaster should be stained with thin, pure color in water and glue.

EDITOR'S NOTE — As a guarantee that the plan of this house is practicable, and that the estimates for cost are conservative, the architect is ready to accept the commission of preparing the working plans and specifications for this house to cost Seven Thousand Dollars, providing that the building site selected is within reasonable distance of a base of supplies where material and labor may be had at the standard market rates.

HALL, LOOKING TOWARD ENTRANCE

THE LIBRARY   LIVING-ROOM AND GALLERY   THE DINING-ROOM

INTERIOR VIEW OF THE FIRST FLOOR OF THIS HOUSE

chapter two

Progressive Architectures, 1894–1918

Herbert Croly considered the 1890s a pivotal decade when 'Americans began to realize that their stock of buildings of all kinds was inadequate, or superannuated'. As editor of *Architectural Record* from 1901 to 1909, Croly called on readers to generate up-to-date building types and assume a new responsibility for directing urban growth. More specifically, they should purge '*meaningless* eccentricities' from houses and impose modern standards for urban design, adapted to changing conditions while still respectful of surrounding contexts, a synthesis he called 'a nationalization of taste'.[1] Croly's small but influential book, *The Promise of American Life* (1909), transferred these ambitions to the national political scene. He contended that the statesman, the philanthropist, the reformer and the architect were modern heroes, leaders whose specialized expertise should command authority. The book helped launch Teddy Roosevelt's Progressive Party in 1912. Two years later, Croly published *Progressive Democracy*, renouncing his earlier demand for expert control. He now emphasized a very different Modernism based on participation, flexibility and 'curiosity' about other modes of thought, other ways of life. Croly thus encapsulates the two somewhat contradictory aspects of the American progressive movement: elite and standardized; popular and diffuse.[2]

The term *progressive* denotes an aspiration for progress as ameliorations, making it virtually synonymous with modern architecture past and present, orthodox and eclectic. The word was also used for a panoply of American reform movements in the 1890s and early twentieth century up through World War One. Croly helped fuse the two trajectories, as did Frank Lloyd Wright, the social reformer Jane Addams, the philosopher and educator John Dewey, the feminist Charlotte Perkins Gilman and many others. American progressivism (the lowercase 'p' distinguishes the diverse and vibrant progressive movement from Roosevelt's formal political party) was a form of social democracy, albeit more closely aligned with incremental improvements than with radical politics. Deeply nationalistic and committed to local action,

Frank Lloyd Wright, 'A Home in a Prairie Town', *Ladies' Home Journal* model house, February 1901.

progressive reformers were also internationalists, exchanging ideas with colleagues across the Atlantic and the Pacific. Theirs was a wide-ranging and pluralistic movement, never unified under one banner. Scholars emphasize multiple realms of action: structural reform of government; regulations to constrain corporations and industries; social ambitions for institutions and public services; moral uplift through nature and religion; housing reform for all classes.[3] Environments provided a shared leitmotif as visible critiques of what was wrong and alternative proposals that were mostly restrained modifications rather than utopian visions, although emotional passions were strong.

Like their European counterparts, *fin-de-siècle* American progressives wanted subjective intensity. Feeling stifled by the 'flatness' of contemporary life, they sought renewal through the 'vital contact' of experience in the world. That experience was often disconcerting. Some responded to what seemed chaos with cries for rigorous controls. Others abandoned established norms and rules, seeking to take account of the incongruous, competing and unconscious modes of thought they encountered. Nietzsche, Bergson and Freud provided key theoretical premises, but so did American thinkers. William James described a belief that resonated in architecture, declaring: 'What really exists is not things made but things in the making.'[4]

Pragmatism emerged in this context, a distinct though not exclusively American philosophy. Conceived as a science, pragmatism sought to deal with conflicting beliefs and ideas that are continuously evolving, contingent upon circumstances, meaningful in terms of actual effects rather than elegant abstractions. James expounded a theory of 'indeterminism … in which no single point of view can ever take in the whole scene'. Spatially and socially, his 'mosaic philosophy' emphasized heterogeneous fringes or patches, potentially linked through an incalculable number of superimposed realities.[5] John Dewey, a professor of education at the University of Chicago and then at Columbia, stressed learning through experience – what is still called progressive education. The arts played a key role, simultaneously instrumental and experiential in an expanded public realm that we today call civil society.[6] The acerbic economist Thorstein Veblen also viewed aesthetics in pragmatist terms. *The Theory of the Leisure Class* (1899) excoriated 'conspicuous consumption' among the wealthy, not just extravagant opulence but the expensive restraint of the arts and crafts as well. Veblen's masterwork, *The Instinct of Workmanship* (1914), affirmed creativity as a fundamental human drive, increasingly more hybrid and rigid under the forces of modern society.

The city became the principal locus and subject for progressive Americans in every realm. The reformer Frederic Howe optimistically

John Marin, cover for
Alfred Stieglitz's
magazine *291* (June
1915).

described the metropolis as an 'experiment station . . . the hope of the future'.[7] New York seemed the quintessential modern metropolis. Representations of the city's architecture destabilized categories such as beauty and ugliness. Numerous visions of contemporary life tenuously coexisted, popular and professional, liberating and oppressive. A self-declared 'Young Generation' of writers and artists synthesized the

Lewis Hine, baseball in a Boston tenement alley, c. 1909, photograph.

emerging currents of realism and plasticity to evoke urban life. Painters like Marsden Hartley wanted to 'release art from its infliction of the big "A"'.[8] So did John Marin, who trained as an architect and who captured the dynamic cadence of skyscrapers that shift and collide like our perceptions of them. Photography also rendered the metropolis through different modalities: the voyeuristic shock of Jacob Riis, the muted indeterminacy of Alfred Stieglitz's circle, the human dignity of Lewis Hine. Adapting Dewey's ideas about the aesthetic dimension of education, Hine sought to convey both what should be respected and what should be changed.[9]

The polyglot mixture of people in large American cities inspired young artists and intellectuals, even as it disturbed their elders. Between 1870 and 1920, some 20 million immigrants arrived in America, principally from southern and eastern Europe. By 1910, one in three Americans was an immigrant or had a foreign-born parent, more than half in large cities. Extreme poverty in overcrowded immigrant 'ghettos' was compounded by inadequate municipal services. Nativists demonized these 'aliens' as a threat to the 'American way of life', but others were fascinated by the 'authentic' (or enticingly exotic) culture of their street life and distinctive social institutions.

The wide-ranging essayist Randolph Bourne seized upon immigration as the basis for a modern national identity. His 'Trans-national America' was cosmopolitan and adventurous. Several articles on architecture expressed the hope that multiculturalism would overturn the 'cultural colonialism' of derivative Beaux-Arts design.[10] While most progressive reformers sought better housing and planned leisure activities for ethnic neighbourhoods, Bourne embraced their energy as a 'New Freedom that really liberates and relaxes the spirit from the intolerable tensions of an over-repressed and mechanicalized world'.[11] Like other sympathizers, he romanticized what he saw, more concerned about creative inspiration than actual conditions. And he remained silent about African-Americans. The Supreme Court's 1896 ruling on Plessy v. Ferguson had established the principle of 'separate but equal' facilities, institutionalizing racial inequalities beneath a modern rhetoric of difference.

Another, sometimes overlapping, group of progressives focused on systematic analysis and objectivity as modern vehicles for change. The engineer, the professional bureaucrat and the technical specialist embodied a rationalized approach that would soon influence every type of work and every building. The social sciences coalesced in the late nineteenth century, taking a dominant role in American research universities, businesses and reform organizations. Many scholars tested theoretical premises in real-life situations, whether factories or urban neighbourhoods, convinced that rigorous analyses would ameliorate the environments they studied; others relied on the subtleties of human observation and interaction. Amateurs and professionals alike compiled arsenals of seemingly unbiased visual material including statistics, maps and documentary photographs, hopeful that evidence would generate both a public demand for reform and the direction it should take. Architects like Daniel Burnham used such data to venture into city planning, both small ensembles and large-scale schemes sponsored by businessmen's clubs. As John Dewey recognized, there were many kinds of modern education ranging from visual to verbal, from the dictums of experts to collaborative exchange.

Progressive-era Americans saw their cities through a kaleidoscope, fractured yet endlessly fascinating. They wanted change and often embraced it, but remained cautious about moving beyond descriptive critiques of what existed. Major architectural innovations occurred despite all the constraints, mainly outside major cities or on their fringes. At least initially, the designers were themselves peripheral to the profession and unknown to one another, although they were involved with local and, later, transnational organizations. Some might even be considered amateurs, with little or no formal education in architecture schools. As such, they had much in common with the remarkable independent inventers who dominated the age, men like Thomas Edison and

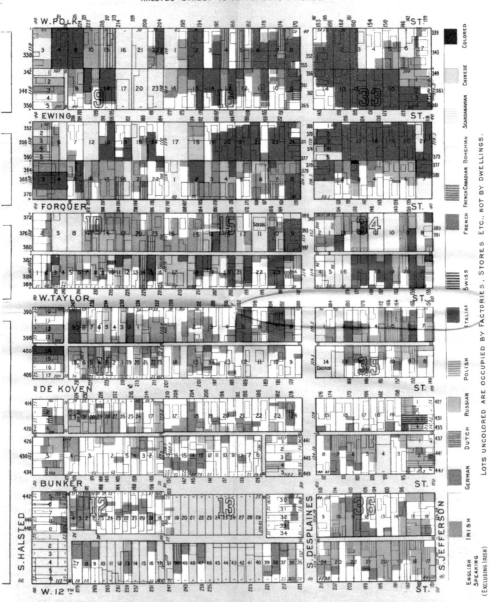

(North)

NATIONALITIES MAP No.I.- POLK STREET TO TWELFTH,
HALSTED STREET TO JEFFERSON, CHICAGO.

Colored

Chinese

Scandinavian

Bohemian

French Canadian

French

Swiss

Italian

Polish

Russian

Dutch

German

Irish

English Speaking
(Excluding Irish)

LOTS UNCOLORED ARE OCCUPIED BY FACTORIES, STORES ETC., NOT BY DWELLINGS.

(South)

Detail of map
showing immigrant
ethnicities in blocks
of West Chicago from
*Hull House Maps and
Papers* (1892).

Nikola Tesla. Clients were equally unconventional, ranging from middle-class families to small businessmen. Popular culture embraced this work, as much as, if not more than, the professional architecture media. This was unquestionably an anomalous Modernism. But it transformed home lives, work lives and public lives, not just of Americans but of people around the world.

Systems and Battlefields of Business

Americans recognized momentous transformations in the nature of work and the making of products at the turn of the last century. Architecture adapted of necessity to competing demands for more precision and flexibility. The efficiency craze was formalized in the 1910s, under the label of 'scientific management' and the name of engineer Frederick Winslow Taylor. A skilled publicist, Taylor focused on workers' efficient, cost-saving movements through space. The simple precepts of his 1911 book, *The Principles of Scientific Management*, inspired an army of disciples who became professional consultants to business and industry, proclaiming Taylor's maxim that there is always 'one best way'.

Initially focused on industrial production, Taylorism would spread to every sort of workplace, from offices to homes. Yet Taylor and his cohorts did not rethink factory architecture. That process began in the 1880s when the use of electricity and advances in concrete construction, which led to façades becoming more transparent and interior spaces larger and less encumbered. In this as in other fields of technological experimentation, early American innovators drew on experience rather than formal education as architects or engineers. Factories provided the first evidence of change as façades became more transparent and interior spaces larger and less encumbered.

Ernest L. Ransome, an English-born family-trained engineer, seems to have invented the concrete-frame factory in California in the 1880s, partly in response to the danger of earthquakes, then quickly patented his technology and designs even as he went beyond them. Ransome's first East Coast commission was the Pacific Borax plant in Bayonne, New Jersey (1898), which attracted considerable attention when it survived a horrific fire in 1903. Hired that very year for an addition to the plant, he systematically used concrete to mould floors and columns. He recognized that exterior walls, no longer load-bearing, could be transformed into extensive window-walls that improved safety, quality control and worker morale. Fully conscious of this breakthrough, Ransome heralded his 'Daylight Factory' as a 'modern type' of structure. His best-known

Largest Reinforced Concrete Factory in the World
Ransome & Smith Co., Concrete Engineers

Ernest L. Ransome,
United States Shoe
Machinery Company
factory, Beverly,
Massachusetts, 1906,
from a Ransome &
Smith Co. ad in
*System: The Magazine
of Business* (1906).

building, likewise from 1903 to 1906, was a larger facility for the United
Shoe Manufacturing Company in Beverly, Massachusetts. Its starring
role in architectural history came through European validation. The
owner of Germany's Fagus Shoe-Last Company visited Beverly in 1910 to
procure financing for his venture and, on his return, presented Walter
Gropius with photographs of Ransome's building (and of Albert Kahn's
Ford plant in Highland Park, Michigan). Both architect and client called
the 1912 Faguswerk 'an American factory'.[12]

New systems changed factory-building, much like the work inside,
with a continuous flow of work and a shift from skilled to relatively
unskilled labor. The timber-and-masonry construction of 'mill-doctors'
disappeared as reinforced concrete became standard. Structural breakthroughs were in fact adaptations – what came to be called applied (as
opposed to theoretical) knowledge. Engineers continuously tested ideas
in the field, often in collaboration with university-based materials-sci-
ence programmes. Ransome's protégé, C.P.A. Turner of Minneapolis,
invented mushroom-column construction around 1909, unaware of
simultaneous European experiments by Robert Maillart and François
Hennebique. Ransome's book, *Reinforced Concrete in Factory Production*
(1912), resembled a kit-of-parts more than a treatise on structure. Yet
this approach relied on a concept, a pragmatic mode of questions,
experimentation and modifications that can be linked, albeit indirectly,
to the work of James and Dewey.

The iconic industrial buildings of the modern era, grain silos and
grain elevators, developed in much the same way. The cylindrical con-

crete form originated near Minneapolis in 1899, initially ridiculed as 'Peavey's Folly'. (Frank Peavey was an international grain dealer, Charles Haglin his architect.) It protected produce remarkably well and quickly became the industry standard. Meanwhile, American dominance of the world grain market connected scattered rural storage silos to batteries of huge transfer- or terminal-elevators in port cities. The Washburn-Crosby (now General Mills) Elevator in Buffalo was the most photographed example. The first structure was built in 1903, the second in concrete, two years later. European modern architects were awed by these unintentional monuments yet principally concerned with their own artful gaze. Erich Mendelsohn wrote of 'childhood forms, clumsy, full of primeval power, dedicated to purely practical ends'.[13] American Precisionist painters such as Charles Demuth and Charles Sheeler recognized the intelligence that underlay this distinctly American building type, but they, too, romanticized the subject, celebrating grain-elevators as an expression of a new 'certainty' in business and the culture at large. The reality of cultural history lies in between these extremes, cognizant of individual designers and evolving processes, both of which proceed in irregular cadences.

The year 1906 saw two key commissions in the automobile industry: Pierce Arrow's one-storey factory in Buffalo and Packard's Building No. 10 in Detroit. Albert Kahn, a self-educated German-American, designed them both, and his brother Julius invented the innovative concrete truss system that permitted the long spans. Space opened up, free of obstacles, maximizing the potential for endless expansion and improvements. Henry Ford was so impressed that he asked Kahn to design a new facility at Highland Park, a suburb north-west of Detroit. The initial complex of eight buildings, commissioned in 1909, was in operation by 1910. The main structure, soon known as the Old Shop, was dubbed the 'Crystal Palace' because of its window-walls. Ford asked Kahn to combine two massive buildings, cover them with glass and consolidate processes inside. A giant craneway at the centre, set on a monorail and connected to the glass roof above, distributed materials. Greater control over light and ventilation increased equipment tolerance and therefore output. The factory itself was now a productive machine.

Bateman & Johnson, Washburn-Crosby (now General Mills) Grain Elevator, Buffalo, New York, 1903–5, from Erich Mendelsohn's *Amerika* (1926).

Albert Kahn with
Ernest Wilby, Ford
Motor Company,
Highland Park,
Michigan, 1909–10,
in a 1913 photograph.

Ford later identified the salient feature of his approach as 'System, system, system'.[14] Recognizing that systems are never static, he commissioned a sequence of new types. The six-storey New Shop accommodated more processes. This interior focused around a glass-roofed, six-storey craneway that ran the entire 257-metre length; railroad tracks below moved everything directly into place for continuous, calibrated production. A single-level plant in 1913 was specifically designed for a continuous assembly line – again, less a unique invention than a culmination of preceding experiments. By that year Ford had similar assembly plants in other cities. Despite their being filled with light and ergonomically advanced, the relentless control over everyone's place and movements led to higher rates of worker turnover.

Ford's concept of mass production altered workspace, labour conditions and consumerism. His plants produced some 6,000 identical

Model T cars in 1908, 182,000 in 1913 and 741,000 in 1917 – at an ever-lower price. The system, soon called Fordism, and its concomitant architecture spread throughout the world. Kahn's factories had to be modern in a new way, anticipating continual expansion, replication and obsolescence. He did not celebrate the iconic modernity of the automobile, nor did he claim to design the production system. His was an unmediated and direct response, a series of envelopes tailored to Ford's ongoing, almost obsessive advances.

Commercial office buildings faced a related set of issues. The great mergers of 1895–1904 created the major corporations of the twentieth century, names like US Steel, AT&T and DuPont. Most of the country's industrial base came into the hands of about 50 giant corporations known as trusts, which eradicated thousands of small companies. A national, and soon international, scale of distribution extended to other businesses, notably mail-order companies and service industries. Americans' attitudes towards big business ranged from awe to outright hatred, which fed 'trust-busting' crusades and critiques of the 'Soulless Corporation'. Even more than factories, these much larger headquarters had to produce not just efficiency, but a new, more manipulative form of advertising based on the 'science' of public relations.

Not surprisingly, the response differentiated interiors from façades. The Chicago-based magazine *System*, founded in 1900, described interior design as a key weapon in the 'battlefields of business'. Large companies needed multiple floors for a network of differentiated tasks. Elaborate charts and statistical tables organized procedures and people, bringing order to the vast empires. Scientific managers took the factory as their

Albert Kahn, Ford New Shop, Highland Park, Michigan, 1914–15, factory interior with six stories of craneway connectors.

Frank Lloyd Wright, Larkin Company Administration Building, Buffalo, New York, 1904–06.

model, assigning hordes of workers to repetitive tasks at specified spots in huge, open 'bullpens' overseen by foremen. Systemization extended to status, including gender relations. Some companies with large numbers of female clerks segregated the sexes, as much to ensure orderly work relations as to show paternalistic concerns for morals. Most relied on rigid specifications for virtually every space and body. Managerial power seemed dependent on evidence of control, made visible in efficient spatial organization and the subordination of office workers as well as those in factories.

The *annus mirabilis* of 1906 witnessed an example and a partial exception to this trend: Frank Lloyd Wright's Larkin Administration Building just outside Buffalo (demolished in 1950 to make way for a truck-storage garage). This was the headquarters for the fast-growing mail-order business of a soap manufactory. Wright aptly called it both a 'commercial engine' and a 'family gathering' for the employees, including 1,800 clerical workers.[15] He geared the design to specific needs: systematic mail handling, a carefully coordinated hierarchy and a wholesome image – essential advertising for a soap company. Efforts to maximize efficiency led to some of the first architect-designed office furnishings. This ode to work converged at the central atrium where the managers sat alongside their secretaries. Twenty-one metres of open space soared above them, flooded with light from a glass skylight. The upper levels opened onto this majestic volume and connected via half-flights of stairs to an adjacent annex, creating a complex spatial interweaving. The top floor and roof level contained a staff restaurant, conservatory and exercise promenade, thus combining services with surveillance.

Larkin Administration Building, photograph of light court, 1906.

If employee morale supposedly depended on the edifying virtues of orderly work, both management and architect insisted on a pleasant environment. Like other advanced workplaces of the era, the Larkin Building was sealed off from the outside – a necessity given its polluted surroundings consisting of the factory and local rail yards – but Wright provided air conditioning. He installed an air-purifying and cooling device manufactured in Chicago, then augmented it by placing the air-exhaust units in massive stair-towers at the corners. Wright bridged two kinds of Modernism here, one concerned with pure structure and rationality, the other with ongoing improvements in human comfort and control. As we shall see, he brought this same dynamic synthesis of innovations and adaptations to his domestic architecture.

Willis Polk, Halladie Building, San Francisco, 1917–18.

Apart from such exceptional buildings, the commercial buildings of early twentieth-century American cities can pose a challenge to anyone with a modernist education. Metal-and-glass façades on smaller buildings often achieved a lyrical beauty with exterior ornament that obscured the ferocity of capitalism and its concomitant innovations. Façades also functioned as advertising, giving a distinctive image (a brand, we might say today) to the company. Cass Gilbert's extravagant Woolworth Building in New York City (1911–13) was famously called the 'Cathedral of Commerce'. Solon Beman's Studebaker Building in Chicago (1885), both a headquarters and showroom, defined that city's Automobile Row for the next two decades. Large corporations like Singer, Woolworth and Metropolitan Life competed to put their name on the tallest building in the world.

Willis Polk's Halladie Building in San Francisco (1918) boasted the first large-scale curtain wall, its broad glass panels hung a metre in front of the structure and bolted to thin concrete slabs. At the time it seemed a 'frontless building', possibly dangerous and visibly cheap, especially since Polk painted the exuberant ornamental ironwork bright blue and gold to honour the owner, the Regents of the University of California.

Small businesses likewise explored advertisement and public relations. Plate glass and colourful terracotta ornament abounded on Main Streets in large and mid-size towns, even along the new 'taxpayer strips' of inexpensive temporary buildings geared to automobile traffic. (The term meant than owners just wanted to break even on taxes, anticipating more lucrative development in the near future.) Substance was more crucial for financial institutions. Purcell & Elmslie and Louis Sullivan built handsome banks in small Midwestern towns. Interiors and exteriors were striking yet purposefully unostentatious. Sullivan declared that his banks fostered democratic values, 'deifying the commonplace', as with his adaptation of an industrial material – rough-cut, multi-hued tinted bricks – so luminous that locals nicknamed them 'jewel boxes'.[16] These architects showed a deep faith in their society, but we should not take them or their clients too literally. Progressive governments in these states passed legislation that required banks to invest in their local communities and extend credit more liberally. The reforms were not related to the transformative power of architecture

The 'New Woman' and the Simplified Home

Progressive ideals about the public interest had a potent effect on the private realm. A chorus of voices – architects, builders, building-trades unions, feminists and other reformers – condemned the 'costly ugliness',

THE HOME OF THE FUTURE: THE NEW ARCHITECTURE OF THE WEST: SMALL HOMES FOR A GREAT COUNTRY: BY IRVING J. GILL: NUMBER FOUR

"An artist is known rather by what he omits."

inefficient construction, insalubrious sanitation and 'undemocratic' extravagance of Victorian dwellings. Middle-class women wanted to extend their concerns citywide, improving standards for health, comfort, economy and beauty in all dwellings, a concept known as municipal housekeeping. An architecture for 'rational beings' would be simpler, standardized, efficient, economical. 'A busy woman,' wrote Mary Gay Humphries in 1896, 'says her idea of the house of the future is one that can be cleaned with a hose.'[17] Progressive architects never picked up on this particular suggestion, but they often talked with women's reform groups and wrote for popular shelter magazines, following John Dewey's belief in ongoing exchange between experts and users of a similar class.

The 'New Woman' was omnipresent, a distinctly American character who first emerged in the 1890s, demanding greater economic, social, political and sexual freedom. Such women eagerly embraced modernity without abandoning all supposedly traditional comforts or roles, although *Harper's Bazaar* did condemn the single-family dwelling as 'a prison and a burden and a tyrant'.[18] The word *feminism* appeared early in the century, encompassing various ambitions and desires rather than one uniform image. Work became a prime issue since almost one in four American women were earning wages by 1900, whether as servants, labourers, 'working girls' or professionals. Many working women had to plan for childcare and other responsibilities – the 'infrapolitics' of everyday life, too often invisible in political or social analysis.[19] Even those with no outside jobs demanded simpler, more efficient homes to gain extra time for social life and reform. Middle-class domesticity was affected by overlapping changes. The number of children declined markedly, and the number of domestic servants fell by half between 1900 and 1920. Almost a third of the nation's female population lived alone or with other women by 1910, 'adrift' to some observers, 'self-sufficient' to others.[20]

A new profession called home economics or domestic science mediated between women, government and the private marketplace. By 1916 almost 200 colleges and universities had specialized departments to educate female students as modern specialists, consumers and citizens. Home economists always defined modern homes in the plural, never as '*the* modern home'. Three fundamental tenets stood out: private and public realms were fundamentally interrelated; household knowledge relied on biological and social sciences, not fashion; and all kinds of dwellings needed change, from suburban houses to urban tenements. Several home economists praised the work of Frank Lloyd Wright and his cohorts.[21] The radical feminist Charlotte Perkins Gilman leaned strongly towards simplification, standardization, smooth surfaces and efficient spatial organization. Her 1903 book, *The Home: Its Work and Influence*, condemned the 'myth' of domestic economy, explaining that 'the more elaborate the home, the more labour is required to keep it fit'.[22] She also encouraged women to think about cooperative approaches to housing, housekeeping and childcare, such as the recent introduction of kindergartens. The striking exception, Christine Frederick, the self-promoting Martha Stewart of her day, promulgated the authoritarian techniques, charts and rhetoric of scientific management. German modernists like Bruno Taut and Alexander Klein would incorporate Frederick's routing diagrams into their housing texts, drawn to her insistence on expert definitions of 'the one best way' – clearly a reference to Taylor's scientific management.[23]

Health became an aesthetic imperative with the recognition that germs caused disease. Housewives now demanded smooth hygienic surfaces to minimize (and reveal) dust or dirt; every home economist condemned Victorian woodwork detailing as 'abiding-places for germs'. The process of elimination extended from a simplified aesthetic to higher standards for plumbing fixtures. The kitchen and bathroom vied with the informal living room as the symbolic core of the modern American home. Adolf Loos praised American bathrooms as 'genuine Modernism' in his 1898 essay 'Plumbers'.[24]

Higher, more expensive standards for household technologies required smaller, more efficient plans. Built-in furnishings helped maximize the small floor area of an average house. Pantries disappeared as commercial enterprises took over domestic tasks like canning food. Equally important, simplified façades rebuked ostentatious competition and proclaimed democratic equality as a foundation for mental health. Marion Talbot, a professor at the University of Chicago, sought to make the home and family 'effective parts of the social fabric' both in the Department of Sociology and in the city outside.[25]

The shelter media encouraged similar ideas. Edward Bok, editor of *Ladies' Home Journal*, launched a crusade to modernize American domestic architecture in the late 1890s. His definition was functional: a living room to replace the fussy parlour, no 'senseless ornament', at least one bathroom and improved ventilation. This milieu provided the first opportunity for Frank Lloyd Wright to show his alchemy, converting a simple programme into architectural gold. Wright published the first of three houses for *Ladies' Home Journal* in February 1901, calling it 'A Home in a Prairie Town'.[26] The design contains virtually every revolutionary theme he would employ for the next two decades. While the building seems embedded in its landscape, the massing suggests the remarkable spaces within. Wright and others since likened the effect to dynamiting the boxy Victorian home. A similar design was built a year later: the Ward Willitts House in Highland Park, Illinois. Unfortunately, the architect could not find a client for the 'Quadruple Block' site plan in the upper corner of the *Journal* article, which showed various arrangements of four uniform houses.

Wright poured most of his energies into small houses and three grand dwellings: the Martin House in Buffalo (1904), the Coonley House and the Robie House in Chicago (1910). This last, designed for the family of a bicycle- and automobile-parts manufacturer, culminated the process of abstraction ('articulation' in Wright's terms) that he had evolved over a decade. The long, narrow, three-storey house sits on a corner lot in the university neighbourhood of Hyde Park, near what had been the Midway in 1893. The horizontal lines of the masonry walls are high, screening views of the outdoor rooms and the interior. The entry is hidden away, almost insignificant in the formal composition. Low-pitched roofs reinforce the geometry and tie the house to the ground, as in Wright's suburban Prairie Houses of this era.

The Robie House interior is startling to this day. The social area of the main floor is a free flow of space around the solid mass of the central fireplace/staircase, which provides a break between the living and dining areas. A separate wing floats quietly to the rear with a guestroom, kitchen and servants' rooms. The only embellishment is the geometric patterns of leaded-glass windows and the structural elements themselves, including vents for the integrated central-heating system Transverse oak strips in the ceiling hold electric lights, accentuating the sense of technical precision while providing a natural balance. This is

Frank Lloyd Wright,
Frederick C. Robie House,
Chicago, 1908–10.

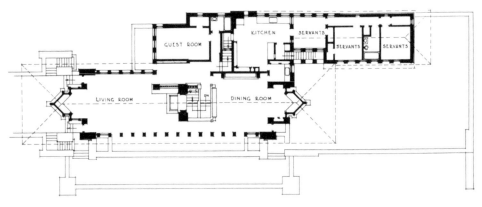

UPPER FLOOR

Robie House, main floor
plan.

Robie House, living room.

undeniably a modern house – abstract, even slightly anonymous. Like Wright's other dwellings, it nonetheless maintains a connection with traditional, almost atavistic ideals of a family shelter, notably in the hearth and the faint allusion to the beamed ceilings of Colonial-era houses.

Only much later, in his 1931 lectures on modern architecture, would Wright establish a nine-point statement of principles, crystallizing ideas that had emerged in his work and in the larger culture. These were: a reduction of elements to achieve unity; horizontal planes to integrate building and site; elimination of basements to raise houses off the ground; spaces defined by screens rather than cellular rooms; windows grouped as banks of 'light screens'; one continuous material for the façade and no applied ornamentation, both to highlight 'the nature of materials'; incorporation of all mechanical features into the architectural scheme; likewise with built-in furnishings; and elimination of decorators in favour of the architect's total-design concept.[27] This list encapsulates the directness that characterized American housing reform of the progressive era, the emphasis on modern processes and effects more than aesthetic representation. Despite metaphors that resembled those of the European Modern Movement – the kitchen was likened to a 'laboratory', a 'surgery', a 'domestic factory' – there was no demand for severity. Wright challenged conventional American ideas about domestic space without trying to disturb the eye or disrupt the harmony of social relations. That would change when he abandoned first his family and Oak Park and then the harmonies of the Prairie House for the more radical clime of the Southwest and California.

Eclectic northern California began to capture the public imagination in the early twentieth century. Bernard Maybeck helped launch what the historian Lewis Mumford would later call the First Bay Area Style, a joyful Modernism that freely mixed local vernaculars with Japanese and European influences, native redwood with industrial materials, compositional order with quirky details. The micro-ecology of this area, distinctive both climatically and culturally, encouraged a cult of well-being through aesthetic restraint and closeness to nature. Charles Keeler's *The Simple House* (1904) affected Maybeck (who built Keeler's house) and colleagues such as Ernest Coxhead, Lillian Bridgman, Willis Polk and Julia Morgan. John Galen Howard was so adamant about process that he only gave client and crew foundation plans; he designed day by day, testing his ideas, integrating interior with exterior, familiarity with innovation. Drawing on Bergson and James, he saw modern houses 'in the making', activated by the memories and possibilities of human lives.[28]

Irving Gill, Lewis
Courts, Sierra Madre,
California, 1910.

Southern California proved equally fertile. The brothers Charles and
Henry Greene fused East and West in their virtuoso designs, notably the
Gamble House in Pasadena (1908), with its crescendos and pianissimos
of woodwork, light and landscape. Irving Gill preferred plain, asymmetrical walls of poured concrete or tilt-up panels, enlivened with cubic
shapes and bold geometric openings. His designs eliminated super-
fluous detail while retaining a palpable sense of grace, the result of
deference to local traditions and a respect for economy. Iridescent interior tints made even small rooms seem 'like living in the heart of a shell'.
Interiors showed Gill's strong feminist sympathies with innovative plans
and smooth surfaces to achieve 'the maximum of comfort . . . with the
minimum of drudgery'.[29] Commissions ranged from the magnificent
Dodge House in Los Angeles, sadly demolished in 1970, to modest
workers' dwellings. Gill's favourite work was Bella Vista Terrace or Lewis
Courts, a group of low-cost dwellings built in 1910. In projects large or
small, grand or spartan, his site plans synthesized public and private
outdoor areas, while the simple 'sanitary' dwellings boasted labour-saving devices as well as simplified forms.

Three popular trends helped disseminate modern ideas and aesthetics
among a broad swath of architects, builders and clients. The first was prefabrication, including pre-cut (or 'Ready-Cut') houses for mail-order
companies. Builders and architects, too, designed limited repertoires of
typologies with distinctive façades to disguise the standardization such as
Frank Lloyd Wright's designs for the American System-Built Houses
Company in Milwaukee from 1915 to 1917. Factory managers and home
economists also provided labour-saving innovations. When Sears,
Roebuck & Company added houses to its well-known catalogue in 1908,

the enthusiastic response generated a special publication, *Sears' Modern Homes*, published from 1909 to 1937. By 1939 Sears claimed that over 100,000 families were living in their homes. This prefabrication relied on a national transportation infrastructure, advertisements in the national media, centralized industrial production and a radically simplified, standardized yet familiar aesthetic.[30]

The second trend came from Gustav Stickley, a furniture designer, whose magazine, *The Craftsman,* published from 1901 to 1916, featured moderate-cost dwellings with simplified elements and local materials. Committed to the socialism and artistic principles of William Morris, Stickley pressed Arts and Crafts ideals about visible evidence of craftsmanship, especially that of carpenters and masons. All the same, he cautiously incorporated industrial techniques to reduce the cost of houses for average Americans. *The Craftsman* published work by architects such as Gill and Sullivan, as well as by builders and ingenious amateurs. Another ardent feminist, Stickley encouraged women professionals while his articles stressed ease of maintenance and fluid connections within the dwelling. The *Craftsman* house ideal spread beyond the magazine and Stickley's short-lived empire.

Third was a type: the bungalow, a comfortable minimal dwelling (usually one or one-and-a-half storeys and under 75 square metres), especially popular from 1900 to the 1920s. Here, too, the media played a role, from the architectural press to scores of popular plan books, magazines and even songs from Tin Pan Alley, as New York's Broadway came to be called. This early global trend made its way from India to Australia, Britain and the US

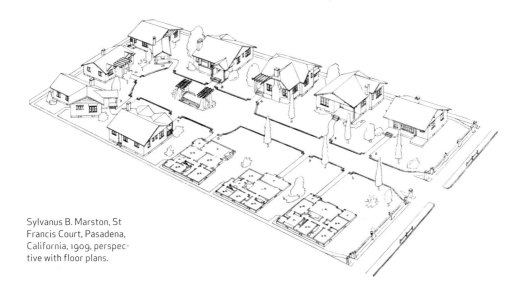

Sylvanus B. Marston, St Francis Court, Pasadena, California, 1909, perspective with floor plans.

Walter Burley Griffin, houses in Trier Center Neighborhood, Winnetka, Illinois, 1913, drawing by Marion Mahoney.

in the 1880s, first as vacation homes on the East Coast, then as moderate-cost mass housing in California. Builders and architects alike were pleased with the potential new market. Distinguishing characteristics included a low-pitched overhanging roof, a front porch with rather hefty supports and abundant built-in furnishings. As both the word and the basic concept swept the country in the 1910s and '20s, regions from Seattle to Chicago to Florida evolved their own distinctive variations.

Site planning posed quite a challenge for small houses, which look dwarfed and out of place along conventional residential streets. Residents sometimes wanted to emphasize shared social activities. The Los Angeles architect Sylvanus Marston was the first to group bungalows

Grosvenor Atterbury, Forest Hills Gardens, Queens, New York, 1909–12, precast concrete panels being lifted into place.

Forest Hills Gardens, concrete-panel houses with neo-Tudor ornament and a recent third storey addition, photographed in 2007.

Fifth Demonstration Group 48 Forest Hills Gardens.
A child's blocks raised to the Nth power, assembled by giant fingers.

off the street around a courtyard. His St Francis Court in Pasadena (1909) combined eleven small houses around a central court to address problems of landscaping, standardization and scale, while he provided collective space. This arrangement spread quickly. Arthur and Alfred Heineman began a series of courts within a year, radically increasing the number of houses per hectare. Bungalow courts with community buildings were especially popular among single women.[31] Ingenious modifications included double bungalows with sliding doors between the living rooms so residents could create a larger joint space when (and if) they wished to. Architects of middle-class subdivisions expanded on the bungalow-court idea with far more spacious grounds. Walter Burley Griffin and Marion Mahoney did several such groupings in the Midwest. They encouraged collective ownership of land, in part out of political conviction, in part to ensure concern for the landscape.

Working-class housing reform likewise integrated individual and collective settings. Frank Lloyd Wright's Francisco Terrace in Oak Park, completed in 1895 for the philanthropist Edward Waller, focused around a courtyard. Grosvenor Atterbury's Forest Hills Gardens (1909–12) relied on a site plan by Frederick Law Olmsted, Jr, to mix apartment buildings, attached houses and single-family dwellings. The Russell Sage Foundation subsidized this model workers' suburb in the New York borough of Queens. Atterbury's efforts to strike a balance between domestic symbolism and economy led to an experimental section using pre-cast concrete panels lifted into place with a crane; he then tacked on neo-Tudor detailing to soften or re-familiarize the rather spare aesthetic. American minimalism thus recast the idea of architectural honesty, acknowledging the truth of ambivalent human desires rather than insisting on pure structural expression. The market triumphed over good intentions, however, when enthusiasm for the high-quality design priced workers out of this middle-class haven.

Mutual Education and Fantastic Recreation

Public buildings of the 'Gay Nineties' and early twentieth century provided another form of advertising, a celebration of collective spirit that used dynamic modern forms and technologies. Local communities sometimes initiated the effort. When St Louis proposed neighbourhood centres in addition to a City Beautiful civic centre, Henry Wright's 1907 prototype included a library, fire/police station, settlement house, model tenement and public market complex. One such example survives in the Czech working-class neighbourhood of Soulard.[32] Nothing, however, matched

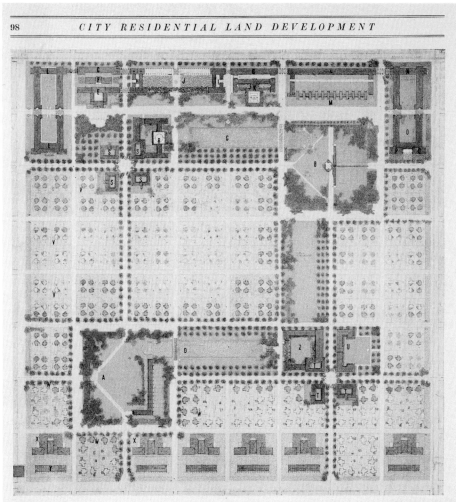

PLAN BY FRANK LLOYD WRIGHT

KEY TO PLAN

A. Park for children and adults. Zoölogical gardens.
B. Park for young people. Bandstand, refectory, etc. Athletic field.
C. Lagoon for aquatic sports.
D. Lagoon for skating and swimming.
E. Theater.
F. Heating, lighting, and garbage reduction plant. Fire department.
G. Stores, 3 and 4 room apartments over.
H. Gymnasium.
I. Natatorium.
J. Produce market.
K. Universal temple of worship, non-sectarian.
L. Apartment building.
M. Workmen's semi-detached dwellings.
N. Four and five room apartments.
O. Stores with arcade.
P. Post Office branch.
Q. Bank branch.
R. Branch library, art galleries, museum, and moving picture building.
S. Two and three room apartments for men.
T. Two and three room apartments for women.
U. Public school.
V. Seven and eight room houses, better class.
W. Two-flat buildings.
X. Two-family houses.
Y. Workmen's house groups.
Z. Domestic science group. Kindergarten.

STATISTICAL DATA

304 Seven and eight room houses.
120 Two-flat buildings, five and six rooms.
18 Four-flat buildings, four and five rooms.
6 Fourteen-family workmen's house groups.
12 Seven-room semi-detached workmen's houses.

6 Apartment buildings, accommodating 320 families in all.
4 Two and three room apartment buildings for women, accommodating 250 to 300.
Total, 1032 families and 1550 individuals (minimum).

Frank Lloyd Wright, model suburb for the outskirts of Chicago designed for the Chicago City Club, 1913.

the potential of Frank Lloyd Wright's brilliant 1913 proposal for a model suburb outside Chicago. Wright used a sequence of parks and playgrounds near the centre to weave together a rich assortment of modern public buildings. His specifications included a school, library, gymnasium, theatre, cinema, art museum and 'a domestic science group'. This indoor/outdoor complex provided a common ground for residents from different social classes and house types, ranging from spacious single-family dwellings to small two-family workers' houses and apartment buildings for single people near the public-transit station. The programme brief had not asked for this mix of incomes and house types, nor for the assortment of activities. They signalled Wright's deep and abiding commitment to social landscapes, a critical though never realized context for his virtuoso private dwellings.

The Chicago City Club had initiated the ideas competition that led to Wright's proposal. (His was a non-competitive entry, since, he explained, he was otherwise bound to win.) Like other civic groups around the country, the City Club sponsored discussions, exhibitions and various projects to enhance the public realm. Public baths, libraries, gymnasia, schools and parks appeared in cities and small towns. Women's clubs were especially active, and, while their facilities were usually quite traditional in appearance, modern buildings sometimes matched the cosmopolitan purpose that defined the early century. These clubs offered an important place for businesswomen to socialize. The programmes usually extended more broadly, including special residences for working women of different classes, notably Chicago's Eleanor Clubs. Julia Morgan built hundreds of clubs and collective residences for the YWCA and Emanuel Sisterhood, as well as women's hotels, hospitals and nursing homes.[33]

Hazel Waterman, Wednesday Club, San Diego, California, 1910–11.

Bernard Maybeck,
First Church of Christ
Scientist, Berkeley,
California, 1909–11.

Churches, too, explored new social and artistic agendas. The progressive movement re-energized American Protestantism, infusing many congregations with a sense of worldly responsibility. Evangelical 'auditorium churches' in large cities provided a precedent for today's mega-churches with their large-scale, dramatic interiors for charismatic ministers together with adjacent social rooms, sports facilities, and lecture halls for outreach programmes among the working classes. Small suburban churches struck a more restrained liberal chord in liturgy and sometimes in architecture. Wright's Unity Temple in Oak Park (1905–8) is concrete, cubic and rather stark, uncannily similar to the Larkin Building. The interior spaces surprise us with their visual and emotional intensity. The spare geometries of the church 'temple' harked back to early Christianity, as did an adjoining auditorium and social hall for 'friendly gathering'. Bernard Maybeck's First Church of Christ Scientist in Berkeley, California (1909–11), is characteristically more exuberant, mixing hand-carved neo-Gothic tracery with industrial materials such as exposed concrete, cement tiles and factory windows. Maybeck was a mystical modernist, a fitting designer for this relatively new religion.

Settlement houses provided another site for intense community life. Social settlements began in London in the 1880s, large cooperative houses in poor urban neighbourhoods where residents, principally college-educated single women, fostered close human contact with nearby residents as a basis for professional services, political representation and expanded social knowledge. By 1910 the United States had 400 settlements. The most famous was Chicago's Hull House, established in

1889 under the leadership of Jane Addams, a social activist who helped achieve the first juvenile court, compulsory education laws and protective labour legislation. Addams defined settlements as 'an attempt to express the meaning of life in terms of life itself, its forms of activity'.[34] Architects Allen and Irving Pond cross-programmed public and private realms in their adaptive reuse of a former mansion for Hull House. By 1912 the complex of twelve buildings encompassed an entire block. The Labor Museum celebrated the heritage of local immigrant groups; Hull House had the nation's first Little Theatre and the Jane Club, a cooperative residence for working women. Kindergartens, clinics, clubs, classrooms and bathing facilities were interspersed with coffee houses, dining rooms and sundry meeting places, which attracted more than a thousand local and international visitors each week.

Chicago's Arts and Crafts Society met at Hull House and shared its commitments. While most such groups idealized handicrafts, this contingent embraced industry, convinced (like the German Werkbund) that the artist's conception of beauty could help overcome oppressive working conditions and poor-quality products. Frank Lloyd Wright delivered his first manifesto there in 1901, 'The Art and Craft of the Machine'. Machines could be tools for artistic and democratic advancement, he contended, but a machine aesthetic was not itself the incarnation of progress. Only a modern architecture of 'mutual education' could direct technological energies to free artists from tedious work, improve the lives of ordinary people and humanize 'this greatest of machines, a great city'.[35]

John Dewey took Hull House as his 'working model' for social centres that provided for adult education and public forums. Boston's Ford Hall, founded in 1908, was geared to 'town meetings'. Frederic Howe directed the larger People's Institute in New York, where a thousand working-class men might debate topics from municipal socialism to feminism. Rochester, New York, used its schools for this purpose in 1907; within five years more than three hundred educational facilities were doubling as community centres for neighbourhood activism. Schools were undergoing a significant change, based in part on Dewey's ideas about multiple forms of learning. Needing to expand with millions of immigrant children, many unfamiliar with modern city life, hundreds of new urban schools were designed to train minds and bodies with more flexible classrooms, assembly halls, theatres, cafeterias and special areas for manual or vocational training and domestic science. Gymnasiums and playgrounds now became fundamental components of American educational facilities. The Chicago-based architect Dwight Perkins incorporated such facilities into more informal, single-storey suburban schools that often included open-air classrooms.

Other kinds of urban buildings also had to accommodate much larger, more diverse crowds of people and activities. Early twentieth-century business hotels like New York's Waldorf-Astoria and Chicago's La Salle were immense, and their disparate facilities carefully organized. Railway terminals were complex spatial systems behind their ornate Beaux-Arts façades. New York set the model with McKim Mead & White's Pennsylvania Station (1902–10), occupying two full city blocks. The new Grand Central terminal (1903–13) encompassed even more space and activities in every direction. A major accident in 1902 propelled the state legislature to require electrification and underground tracks. This prompted William Wilgus, the railroad's chief engineer and soon its vice-president, to carry out an ambitious double vision over the decade 1903–1913, all the while continuing service. The architects Reed & Stem and the engineers Warren & Wetmore designed a vast new station surrounded by 'Terminal City', a complex of adjacent hotels and offices interconnected via subterranean concourses and overhead traffic viaducts, as well as street access. In addition, by moving the noisy, polluting tracks to the north underground, Wilgus transformed 19 hectares of land into the prestigious Park Avenue.

Reed & Stem and Warren & Wetmore, Grand Central Terminal 'City', New York City, 1903–13, section.

LUNA PARK AT NIGHT, CONEY ISLAND, N.Y.

Luna Park at Coney
Island, Brooklyn,
New York, c. 1905,
postcard.

Electric power was essential to the new public architecture and to metropolitan urbanism. New York's Broadway was first called the 'Great White Way' in the 1890s, paying tribute to the electric lights and illuminated advertising that amazed visitors with new, ephemeral spectacles. As cities shifted from private to public ownership of utilities between 1900 and 1920, they extended electricity not only geographically but also temporally. An 'Architecture of the Night' encouraged entertainment-oriented businesses to stay open around the clock. Major firms collaborated to transform Main Streets around the country into 'White Ways', eager to create an aura of progress and glamour. With key 'sights' illuminated, both locals and tourists learned to comprehend the modern metropolis in terms of exciting architecture.

Animated and illuminated amusement zones anticipated today's notion of Modernism as spontaneous events. Rem Koolhaas's book *Delirious New York* (1978) praised Brooklyn's Coney Island for a 'New Technology of the Fantastic' in decidedly unserious, surreal settings where the audience became part of the performance.[36] Coney Island's kinesthetic pleasures attracted more than a million visitors a day, especially young people from every social class, eager to suspend conventional settings and rules of conduct'. George C. Tilyou opened Stepplechase Park in 1897, borrowing directly from the Chicago Exposition's Midway. Luna Park followed in 1903. Co-owner Frederic Thompson had studied architecture, which, he claimed, gave him 'all the license in the world' to create 'a dream world, perhaps a nightmare world – where all is bizarre and fantastic'.[37]

Most progressive reformers wanted wholesome forms of leisure and disapproved of idle pleasures like amusement parks, which nonetheless proliferated on the peripheries of many large cities. Fears about chaotic abandon misunderstood these settings, where the illusion of freedom concealed an elaborate system that carefully orchestrated technologies, spatial organization and desired effects. American modern environments often exhibit a double theme of control and liberation. Simon Paten, the pragmatist economist and social theorist, recognized that Coney Island was in fact standardized, disciplined and conformist beneath the gaudy veneer and titillating rides, providing a 'safety valve' in the volatile economies of contemporary life.[38]

chapter three

Electric Modernities, 1919–1932

The 'Roaring Twenties', the 'Jazz Age', 'Metropolitanism' – under these and other exuberant labels the United States became a potent cultural force in the world in the 1920s, matching its new-found military and economic dominance at the end of World War One. Sheldon Cheney's *The New World Architecture* (1930) described the American tempo of innovation: 'What seemed insurgent and revolutionary two years ago is now the accepted and standard . . . so fast moves "Modernism".'[1] The term *Modernism* was everywhere, from business and advertising to literature, painting, dance, music, photography and architecture. For the first time in American history the majority of the population lived in cities, and urbanity encouraged a delirious pace of experimentation, especially in New York. Everything was purportedly up-to-date in Kansas City and Cleveland, too, and certainly in Los Angeles. The suburbanite William Carlos Williams cried: 'Back into the city!/ Nowhere/The subtle! Everywhere the electric!'[2]

Like the metropolis with its dynamic, unpredictable amalgams of people and ideas, American Modernism tended to dissolve categories like High and Low, spurring lively debates about form and programme. Cosmopolitan American architects and artists embraced multiple Modernisms, eschewing any one true path or doctrinaire manifesto. *The Brickbuilder* became *Architectural Forum* in 1917, signalling the importance of debate as well as a shift from masonry details to business acumen. By 1930 the AIA convention was asserting a common ground among disparate tendencies by criticizing any 'crystallized vocabulary', whether the 'static and inorganic quality of tradition [or] the new European theology'.[3] Americans still tend towards such pluralism, an asset for engaging difference, but a hindrance when everything seems relative or purportedly equal.

The mood was confident, but not isolationist. 'Paris is no longer the capital of Cosmopolis', wrote one returnee in 1919. 'New York has become the battleground of modern civilization.'[4] Americans had become knowledgeable about contemporary European avant-gardes in

New York, photograph
by Walker Evans, 1929.

the arts with the 1913 Armory Show in New York. Architecture followed in the early 1920s. The *Journal of the American Institute of Architects* first showed Le Corbusier's work in 1923, the same year that *Architectural Record* reviewed his *Vers une architecture*. In 1927, Jane Heap, editor of the *Little Review*, one of many experimental 'little magazines' of the 1920s, sponsored a popular *Machine-Age Exposition* in a small Manhattan gallery which showed industrial objects and Russian Constructivist paintings alongside photographs of American and European buildings.[5]

Given the era's reverence for business, relatively few architects tried to challenge conventions or address problematic urban conditions. 'Our modern architecture is frankly commercial', contended the critic Edwin Park, part of 'the vulgar turbulent vortex of democratic industrial life'. As if anticipating Rem Koolhaas, Harvey Wiley Corbett expressed full confidence that consumerist values were inherently progressive. Keenly aware of competition from builders, construction-contractor firms and mail-order-plan companies, the profession emphasized skills in 'problem-solving' and design research, eschewing the pure incarnations of 'objectivity' – what the Germans called *Sachlichkeit*. This new generation knew how to compile the latest functional data on a given problem, explained the *Record*, how to 'systematize' it graphically, then '*translate these purposes into buildings*'.[6]

Américanisme, americanismo, Amerikanismus, even Soviet *amerikanizm* testify to Europeans' fascination with this business-oriented functionalism and their angst about its underlying values. Some outspoken Americans were equally critical. Frederick Ackerman, a socialist architect, studied economics with Thorstein Veblen at the New School in New York, then joined the short-lived Technical Alliance, whose members called themselves 'technocrats' – the first group in history to use the term, which to them meant an elite with advanced technological know-how. (Veblen was 'Chief Engineer' for this 'soviet of engineers' who hoped to overthrow capitalism through expertise aligned with 'the instinct of workmanship'.)[7] Ackerman criticized his fellow-architects' subservience to capitalism through 'profit-induced fashions', including that of the emergent modernist aesthetic. 'Commercialism is a new God,' he declared, one that 'destroys human lives, values and environments'.[8] Far from being an outsider, Ackerman voiced his opinions in major architectural journals. Despite the Red Scare that followed the Russian Revolution in 1917, American architects of the time were willing to discuss a full spectrum of political ideologies.

Imagery in every sort of medium responded to the changes wrought by the hyper-commercialism of the 1920s. American photographers, fas-

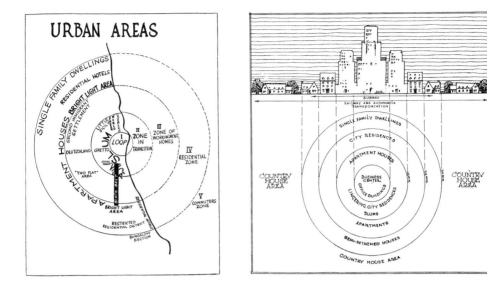

cinated by the fast-changing built environment, usually juxtaposed old and new or muted the abstraction of their European counterparts, occasionally experimenting with the simultaneity or 'interpenetration' of viewpoints in montages that supposedly captured the ambiguities of modern life. In any case, the professional architectural press confined almost all photographs to autonomous portfolios of soft pictorialism. Modern architectural drawings followed three prevailing trends. One emphasized dramatic angles and massing – notably Hugh Ferriss's smouldering images, which seemed to cry out for bold action. Another drew upon the syncopated rhythms of jazz for Art Deco and streamlined vehicles for Moderne commercial buildings. A third evoked the precision of statistics, charts and specifications captured in Le Corbusier's saying: 'The American engineers overwhelm with their calculations.'[9]

Diagrams, too, became increasingly sophisticated, using the virtual space of the page to relate intellectual and social propositions, another process of abstraction. Clarence Perry's Neighborhood Unit Plan defined such relations in terms of walking distance, while the Chicago School of Sociology used concentric zones to reify spatial theories that suggested how the flow of capital in real estate, industry and finance affected residential patterns.[10] Within a few years, *Architectural Record* would adapt these diagrams. *Architectural Graphic Standards* epitomized the scientific line. A compendium of data and simple drawings first published in 1932, it became an indispensable tool almost immediately, the bible of normative practice throughout the world. Frederick Ackerman had provided the vision for his two young associates. His foreword praised the translation of the 'simple language of facts' into images.[11] He used the term *data* in its technical sense to mean quantitative relationships between production, materials and human needs, urging architects to engage in materials production, programming, planning and regulations rather than passively accepting what already existed. Only later would some critics recognize that 'abstract visualization' dehumanized workers into mere statistics.[12]

Even mainstream journals now invoked science. *American Architect* added a Department of Architectural Engineering in 1917. *Architectural Record* began a 'new chapter' a decade later with the declaration: 'Modernism is an attitude of mind – the scientific attitude.' Readers were advised to adopt 'the research method of science – observation, hypothesis, deduction, experimental verification.'[13] The moving force was A. Lawrence Kocher, managing editor from 1928 to 1938, simultaneously a preservationist at Colonial Williamsburg and the architect of striking modern buildings, notably the Aluminaire House with his partner Albert Frey in Syosset, New York (1931). The editorial board included significant modernists like Knud Lönberg-Holm, Henry Wright, Henry-Russell Hitchcock and Douglas Haskell. The *Record* also inaugurated a 'Technical News and Research' section that analysed a new 'Problem' every month, providing extensive data about current materials, methods, costs and other 'performance-based' criteria. The Associated Business Papers awarded this feature and its creator, the architect Robert Davison, first prize for editorial excellence in 1929. Historian and critic Henry-Russell Hitchcock praised Kocher's work, predicting that America seemed ready to produce the 'most individual and characteristic new architecture'.[14]

Hitchcock's 1929 book, *Modern Architecture,* explored over a century of advances on two continents. He lauded Frank Lloyd Wright as the incarnation of a 'New Tradition', but saw the future in the bold formal experiments of three 'New Pioneers': Le Corbusier, Ludwig Mies van der Rohe and J.J.P. Oud. Increasingly disturbed by the wide-ranging diversity of architecture in the us, Hitchcock felt a need for one controlling style. Philip Johnson, a wealthy young aesthete who shared those concerns, contended that Europe had already achieved an architecture that was 'unified and inclusive, not fragmentary and contradictory'.[15] Johnson was searching for a cause. He would take up fascism and other right-wing movements in the late 1930s before going to architecture school and then continuously renewing his role as a polemicist, indeed a pundit. Few individuals anywhere have anticipated or directed the currents of change in architecture with his distinctive combination of power and impertinence.

Alfred H. Barr, Jr, Director of New York's fledgling Museum of Modern Art (MOMA), persuaded Hitchcock to revise his text into a short book and exhibition in collaboration with Johnson. They christened the project 'Modern Architecture' as if theirs was the only legitimate use of the term. Barr coined the catchier phrase 'International Style', an even more all-encompassing mantle. This was in part a reference to the International Congresses for Modern Architecture (CIAM), founded in 1928. European aesthetics also responded to social conditions, such as the rise of pacifism and social-democratic governments, intent upon remaking cities after World War One and providing services for working-class populations. The avant-garde were fascinated by modern construction technologies; 'laboratory' materials like concrete, steel and glass; and smooth, unornamented surfaces. Yet today's historians rightly question the inherent unity and progressive social agenda of what came to be called the Modern Movement. Some architects insisted that functional considerations, whether scientific or political, determined their designs, while others gave priority to artistic and emotional expressionism. Claiming to distill an incontestable worldwide phenomenon, the MOMA *Modern Architecture* exhibit of 1932 made its case by focusing exclusively on work that fit the curators' formal criteria.

Two official publications accompanied the MOMA exhibit: a formal catalogue entitled *Modern Architecture* and *The International Style: Architecture since 1922,* a pithy synopsis of ideas with the same illustrations. Both codified Modernism in terms of three 'principles': volume rather than mass; regularity without axial symmetry; and strict aversion to applied ornament – in other words, rigid formal rules based on abstract spatial relations. Hitchcock and Johnson believed that American architecture needed discipline, not individualism, and certainly not social purpose. They discreetly acknowledged that modern architecture was 'clearly distinguishable' from one country to another. Needing to include some American examples if only to legitimize the international claim, the selection favoured recent émigrés like William Lescaze and Richard Neutra. Although Barr detested Raymond Hood as a false, profit-driven opportunist, he made the cut. MOMA's high priests ridiculed almost all the skyscrapers of the 1920s and early 1930s as the 'crude' products of 'confused', 'half-modern' commercial 'impresarios' who would surely be hostile to aesthetic reform.[16]

Low-cost housing reform, a fundamental concern for most Europeans, was relegated to an addendum to the books and to a back room at the exhibition overseen by Lewis Mumford and Catherine

Bauer. Hitchcock would look back twenty years later, slightly embarrassed by the 'narrow . . . condescending . . . puristic' absolutism of that youthful polemic.[17] In fact, his second thoughts had appeared even earlier, when he had produced books and exhibitions on Richardson and Wright, nineteenth-century American 'vernacular' architecture and pattern books. These subjects, innovative in their own terms, had inspired Continental modernists. Hitchcock sought unsuccessfully to counter the myth, still firmly entrenched today, that a 'design migration' had brought Modernism from Europe to a backward nation.

For too long the 1932 MOMA exhibition has been lauded as the defining point in the history of American modern architecture. In fact, it had a limited impact on both the public and the profession. Most critics of the time complained that it was both narrow-minded and reductively formalist, exorcizing any social and political aspirations. The exhibition had several venues outside New York, often in department stores. Meant to be didactic, it was really just a label – indeed a 'fashion show', wrote Knud Lönberg-Holm in *Shelter*.[18] The curators expunged diverse experiments on every continent and reduced the US to a caricature, true in some ways but far too all-encompassing, that of an ignorant and purely commercial wasteland in desperate need of guidance. The 1920s were far more interesting than we have been led to believe.

Towering Commerce

The decade began with the *Chicago Tribune*'s announcement of an international competition for its new headquarters. This was above all a brilliant marketing strategy, especially since the site was one of the first properties in the expansion of the city's central business district along North Michigan Avenue, made possible by a 1920 bridge across the Chicago River. The newspaper's public-relations department proclaimed a lofty civic purpose of educating the public about architectural history and Modernism. They leavened the missionary zeal with occasional cartoon spoofs. Publicity continued for several years, even after the announcement of a winner in 1922. The businessmen who dominated the jury liked Howells' and Hood's Gothic-draped skyscraper. Its innovations – novel wind-bracing with diagonal structures, use of public-transit tunnels to free the street from excavation and storage – were independent of the architectural design. Many people, then and now, preferred Eliel Saarinen's 'enchanted mountain', which took second place. Far from a martyr, Saarinen immigrated to the US a year later, a move sponsored by the *Tribune*.[19] Americans eagerly absorbed his scheme as an expression of progressive design. *Western Architect*, based

in Chicago, adopted an abstracted version as its official logo. The competition was not a failure or a retreat, as has often been charged, for it stimulated local and international debate about multiple possibilities for skyscraper design.

Today's modernists no longer disdain commercial buildings. Many architects now acknowledge the pleasures of Art Deco undisturbed by its popular appeal, its florid surface ornament and its overt commercialism. (This certainly does not validate the recent surge of facile adaptations and outright copies.) Yet 'Art Deco' is a concept of recent vintage. 'Moderne', 'modernist' and 'modernistic' were the descriptive labels in the 1920s and '30s, first for decorative objects, then for a smooth, syncopated geometric architecture with visibly machine-made surfaces, typically adorned with polychrome ornament. The term 'Art Deco' only arrived in the 1960s with renewed interest in the legendary 1925 Exposition des Arts Décoratifs in Paris.[20]

American Art Deco was not mere imitation, since the first example predates the 1925 exposition: New York's Barclay-Vesey, designed by Ralph Walker and completed in 1923 for the New York Telephone Company. Cities all over the country (and soon all over the world) quickly set out to boost their images with brilliant new towers, such as Detroit's Guardian Building (1929), the Atlantic Richfield Building in Los Angeles (1929), Seattle's Olympic Tower (1931), and the Kansas City Power and Light Company Building (1931). Houston marked its new status as the largest city in Texas with a construction surge that included the Gulf Building (1929), based on Saarinen's second-place proposal for Chicago. Atlanta's City Hall (1930), another such appropriation, is one of several governmental skyscrapers of the decade.

These architects paid no attention to structural honesty or restraint, the hallmarks of orthodox Modernism. They took a different path towards modernity, exploring visual perception and ephemeral special effects, qualities of considerable interest to today's designers. Herbert Croly praised the 'Architectural Effects' that could be achieved through colour and light, especially the fantastic illusory settings that emerged at night. The experience may have disturbed the puritanical gatekeepers of

modern architecture, but it enthralled those in other arts. 'Here is our poetry,' wrote Ezra Pound, usually a critic of American culture, 'for we have pulled down the stars to our will.'[21]

Skyscrapers were money-making machines. Speedy construction and resonant imagery helped determine design. Then as now, corporate executives liked façades that called attention to themselves. Holabird & Root (sons of the Chicago School giants) adapted Saarinen's *Tribune* entry for the *Chicago Daily News* Building (1925–9), adding a public plaza that stepped down to the river. Raymond Hood's modern towers embraced New York's dense vivacity. He accentuated the height of his *Daily News* Building (1925–9) with the illusion of vertical stripes in white glazed brick offset by dark horizontal bands. The enigmatic black-glass lobby attracted so many tourists that another entrance had to be created. Hood's Radiator Building (1924) gleamed in black and gold, while his McGraw-Hill Building (1931) shifted from blue-green at the base to an ethereal blue at the crown, as if dematerializing into the sky. The 'spirited struggle' for 'experimental eclecticism' of Ely Jacques Kahn's dazzling glass-and-polychrome skyscrapers helped define corporations and specialized districts like the new central business district of midtown Manhattan.[22]

New York's Chrysler Building (1930) marked a new stage in Art Deco spectacles. William Reynolds, a speculative developer and the creator of

86

Coney Island's Dreamland, mounted an intense publicity campaign about William Van Alen's 77-storey design sheathed in expensive stainless steel. When the auto magnate Walter P. Chrysler bought the proposal in 1928, Van Alen added new ornament based on hubcaps and a magnificent crown of illuminated arcs. He saved the most dramatic gesture until the last moment in late October 1929. Everything seemed complete until a 'vertex' spire, 56 metres high, secretly constructed and hidden inside, rose over the course of a few hours to make this the world's tallest building, if only for a few months until the Empire State topped it with 86 storeys and a zeppelin mooring mast. Critics condemned the stunt, but the Chrysler became a beloved symbol of New York, recently dubbed 'Rhapsody in Chrome'.[23]

Walter Ahlschlager with Delano & Aldrich, Carew Tower and Fountain Square, Cincinnati, Ohio, 1929–31, postcard of illuminated night view.

The iconic skyscraper for modern historians is the 32-storey Philadelphia Savings Fund Society tower, a design that evolved over several years. George Howe started with a sleek tower in 1928. Then his new partner, the young Swiss architect William Lescaze, made the scheme more 'correct' – i.e., horizontal. When the frustrated client, James Willcox, demanded a resolution in 1931, the asymmetrical design brilliantly synthesized the horizontal banding of the floors and the vertical thrust of the tower. Materials and fenestration mark the different sectors inside. Advertisements declared that there was 'Nothing More Modern' than the building's numerous technological advances, such as dropped ceilings of acoustical tile that provide 'silver stillness' and hermetically sealed windows for 'complete environmental control'. The scarlet neon PSFS sign on the roof screens cooling towers for an early air-conditioning system. Willcox praised the 'ultra-practical' result.[24]

Immense mixed-use complexes were promoted as 'cities within a city' that benefited the public at large. Walter Ahlschlager built such enclaves in Chicago, New York, Memphis, Detroit and Oklahoma City. Cincinnati's Carew Complex (1929–31) featured a dramatic, almost Baroque sequence of public spaces leading from a huge hotel to an adjacent office tower, testifying to

Ahlschlager's experience as a theatre architect. A through-block shopping arcade made shopping up-to-date with links to department stores. The 25-storey parking garage was one of only two 'automated' facilities in a downtown skyscraper at that time.[25]

For many people New York's Rockefeller Center still embodies cosmopolitan American modernity, but it scarcely looked that way early on. A private donor, John D. Rockefeller, Jr, had assembled the midtown site in 1928, calling it Metropolitan Square for commerce enhanced by a new opera house. The multi-block complex required a team, the Associated Architects, that combined the reliable firm of Reinhard & Hofmeister with two more daring consultants, Harvey Wiley Corbett and Raymond Hood. Hood envisaged 'A City under a Single Roof' as a network of towers connected by upper-level walkways and subterranean tunnels, which soon became a more feasible underground concourse and rooftop terraces. The scene drew inspiration from nearby Grand Central's Terminal City. When the Metropolitan Opera withdrew in 1929, a more popular art form, the Radio Corporation of America (RCA), took its pivotal site with a thin, 70-storey office slab, and the site became Radio City.

The name Rockefeller Center came with the gala opening in 1932, evoking financial stability through its patron's name. The sequence of public and semi-public spaces had adapted to a series of unexpected economic contingencies and now seemed harmonious. Yet one centrifugal space came much later in response to the failure of the shops in the sunken plaza. Four years after the opening, Hood reconsidered the lower level and decided to create an open-air skating rink with restaurants to both sides. Public response remained mixed. Lewis Mumford attacked the 'organized chaos' for years, condemning the 'bad guesses' and 'grandiose inanities' of this 'paper architecture'. Then suddenly, like most people, he grew fond of Rockefeller Center, calling it 'a serene eyeful' in 1939. He never explained his change of heart and always lamented the private ownership of public space.[26]

Mumford was not alone in stressing the negative side of modern public spaces, housing and workplaces. Tensions built everywhere during the boom years of the 1920s. Upton Sinclair coined the term 'white-collar' in 1919 for the fast-growing stratum of office employees who distinguished themselves from 'blue-collar' factory workers and identified strongly with their companies. Professional managers continued to transfer the concept of work flow from the factory to the clerical pool, insisting that maximum visibility in a large open space increased production and loyalty. Lee Galloway used a photo of the atrium in Wright's 1906 Larkin Building as the frontispiece for his 1919 book *Office Management*. 'American plan' offices contrasted the central holding pens

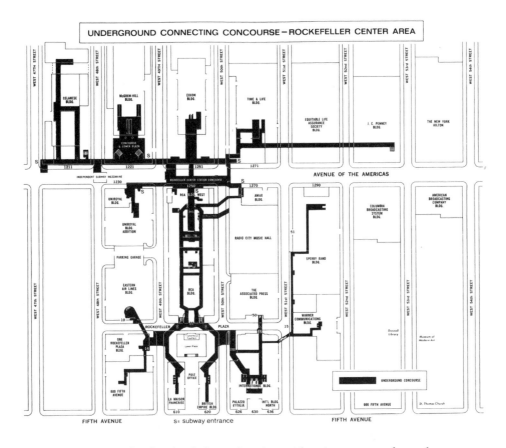

UNDERGROUND CONNECTING CONCOURSE – ROCKEFELLER CENTER AREA

Rockefeller Center, plan of concourse level of main complex.

Rienhard & Hofmeister with Harvey Wiley Corbett and Raymond Hood, RCA Tower and Rockefeller Center, New York City, 1928–32.

for female clerks and typists with private rooms for male managers, painstakingly gradated by size and status. New technologies also affected office buildings. Heating, ventilation and air-conditioning (HVAC) controls advanced with 'manufactured weather', internal systems that freed the façade from its role as mediator between interior and exterior environments.[27]

The 'Hawthorne Experiment' turned managers' attention away from environmental improvements. A team of social scientists set out to measure how illumination levels affected female workers at Chicago's Hawthorne Works in 1927. Confounded by inconclusive results, they brought in new consultants who experimented with other variables. In 1932 the Harvard psychologist Elton Mayo announced that ambient environments are not as significant for well-being and productivity as teamwork, learning and even the researchers' attention to the employees' responses. This came to be called 'the Hawthorne effect'.[28] While

Holabird & Root,
A. O. Smith Research
and Engineering
Building, Milwaukee,
Wisconsin, 1930.

there is still debate about the phenomenon, it prompted analysts to focus on work relations more than architectural reforms.

Industry too shifted towards scientific research in the 1920s. Albert Kahn helped expand Henry Ford's vision with a massive new plant on the River Rouge outside Detroit, near the original factory. First used during World War One, some 100,000 men soon worked on the sprawling 1,000-acre site that would eventually encompass almost 100 buildings, the largest and most famous factory in the world. Major advances in Ford's plate-glass factory (1922) would have repercussions in architectural windows, while the Engineering Laboratory (1925) helped control the production and processing for virtually every component. Recognizing that these iconic images of modernity helped promote his 'brand', Ford commissioned brilliant paintings and photographs of Kahn's plants.

Other companies engineered special research centres as well. Unlike earlier university-based facilities, corporate research and development (R&D) buildings were free to explore daring designs as a form of advertising. Engineering and chemical corporations promoted new research laboratories as expressions of scientific innovations, even as they tightened security over what happened inside. One of the most dazzling, the A. O. Smith Company's Research and Engineering Building in Milwaukee (1930), featured a bold façade in aluminium and glass. A parallel increase in scale in other fields tended towards blank façades, notably the parabolic steel shed for what was then the largest building in the world, the Goodyear Airship Dock in Akron, Ohio (1930). (Hitchcock belatedly praised it in 1951.) The unaesthetic aesthetics of this era were geared to expansion, flexibility and control, signalling the emergence of R&D in corporate science.

Ford plant at River
Rouge, Michigan, photograph by Charles
Sheeler, 1922.

Raymond Hood, 'City Within a City', 1929, aerial view. Drawing from *Contemporary American Architects: Raymond M. Hood* (1931).

CONTEMPORARY
AMERICAN ARCHITECTS

RAYMOND M HOOD

Visionary Cities

Seeking to press beyond commissions for individual buildings, many architects drew schemes for the modern cityscapes they hoped to see. Richard Neutra worked on his imaginary scheme for 'Rush City Reformed' between 1925 and 1930, taking Southern California as an archetype. Touting the slogan 'Ameliorate, not agitate', Neutra juxtaposed anonymous prefabricated housing slabs and towers with lively drive-in shopping. Fast-moving superhighways, bus stations and airports provided for the continuous 'transfer' of human energy, a major theme in the project's initial publication in his *Wie baut Amerika?* ('How Does America Build?') (1927). Reaction was broadly positive, including Hitchock's acclaim that 'Creation is again . . . a possibility, and nowhere more so than in America.'[29] Raymond Hood preferred a denser urban landscape based on New York's skyscrapers, which he imagined as a metropolitan concentration of towers or strung along a remarkable expansion of the city's bridges. Harvey Wiley Corbett envisioned

Manhattan's streets as multi-level traffic systems. All American visions of the future relied on far-reaching transportation infrastructures.

The Regional Plan Association of America (RPAA), founded in New York in 1923, was much broader in purview. This small multi-disciplinary group anticipated many of the environmental and social concerns of the early twenty-first century. The RPAA was sentimental about small-town America (as depicted in Mumford's 1939 film, *The City*), but it connected housing, social services, infrastructure and conservation as necessary factors in regional development. If Mumford was their prime spokesperson, the 'ecologist' Benton MacKaye embodied the RPAA's key ambitions. MacKaye was among the first to use the word *environment*, understood to extend from metropolitan centres to wildernesses and even virtual realms, a shifting 'flow' of ideas, images and activities that affected change at many levels. Influenced by the pragmatists, MacKaye spoke of 'visualizing' ongoing changes through various media.[30]

Another group with a similar name would continue to affect development. The Regional Plan Association of New York and Environs (RPA) enjoyed a full decade of research funded by more than a million dollars from the Russell Sage Foundation. Its conclusions and projections appeared in two hefty volumes illustrated by architects with divergent modern proclivities, and an eight-volume statistical survey of the region in 1929–31. Robert Moses and the Port Authority would implement many RPA proposals from the 1930s until the early 1960s: Manhattan as a global city geared to finance, luxury housing and culture; the gentrification of Harlem and the Lower East Side; the dispersal of industry outside the city; a dramatic increase in leisure facilities as the exemplars of modernity; and sprawling residential suburbs for specific classes. This last point remained vague since the RPA's pro-business vision led the group to drop a proposed ninth report on housing as overly controversial, since the data revealed class inequalities.[31] Those same ambitious but biased priorities drive today's RPA and other groups like it around the country.

The Many Faces of Modern Housing

The acute need for housing after World War One forced up costs. Presidents Coolidge and Hoover championed home ownership, hoping to stimulate the house-building industry, but without pressing it to be more rational or cost-effective. The resulting increase in production (8 million new units in the 1920s, mostly before 1926) saw the rise of large-scale 'developers' who relied on modern materials and mass production, usually hidden behind façades that evoked romantic myths of national heritage, aristocratic ancestry or exotic charm. The 1920s suburbs for the

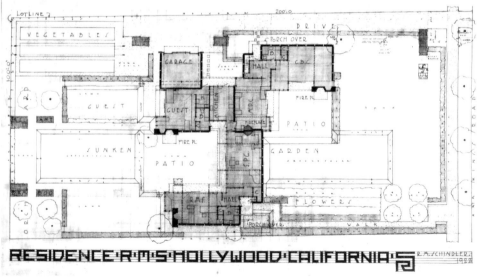

elite were often carefully planned, including public-transit systems, but the flood of inexpensive dwellings was usually plagued by shoddy construction and cramped spaces.[32] Uniformity and cacophony were less of an issue than the problems they obscured: laissez-faire municipal governments that tolerated poor construction; uncoordinated production and regulations that inflated costs; dreary house and site plans under the guise of economy; tensions about social and financial security that dramatically increased class and racial segregation. The astute Henry Wright of St Louis deplored the 'millions of cheap shoddy houses . . . very distinctive but all alike'.[33] Yet he believed that this idiosyncratic American pattern could generate alternatives by combining new technologies with careful site plans, staking a claim in between the two poles of European Modernism, its elegant custom villas and its *Existenzminimum* blocks of workers' housing.

Gifted modern architects won public respect for their private houses, nowhere more so than in southern California. R. M. Schindler, Neutra, Frank Lloyd Wright and his son Lloyd Wright worked in and around Los Angeles, sustained by an avant-garde culture of European émigrés and flamboyantly successful Americans.[34] Each one developed innovative concrete systems, adapted to normative construction processes since they were intended to be mass prototypes. Schindler's experiments were the most radical and varied, including tilt-up panels, 'slab-cast' and sprayed gunite. Neutra applied gunite to the delicate steel matrix of the Lovell Health House (1927–9) and developed a series of prefabrication systems that stressed 'lightness of construction' with concrete aggregates, as well as a 1930 tensile structure based on the circus tent.[35] Driven in part by the increased price of lumber, Wright took up cheap concrete-block, asking, 'Why not see what could be done with that gutter-rat?'[36]

Schindler arrived in Los Angeles in 1919 to supervise Wright's Hollyhock House (1921). Originally from Vienna, he had come to America at the urging of Adolph Loos, then apprenticed to Wright at Taliesin in Wisconsin. In 1921 Schindler built a communal dwelling on King's Road in Hollywood for his family and that of his friend Clyde Chace. The intricate sequence of shared and private spaces includes seven distinct outdoor zones. The materials, all left exposed, juxtapose thin concrete wall panels with redwood ceilings and taut expanses of lightweight canvas. Schindler described the house as a spatial marriage of the solid, permanent cave and the improvised, ephemeral tent. Socially it embraced his wife Pauline's hope for 'as democratic a meeting-place as Hull House'.[37] Schindler was a committed socialist, but few of his designs for workers' colonies or moderate-cost tract houses were ever realized. Hitchcock and Johnson were put off by his idiosyncratic

Rudolph Schindler, Schindler-Chace House, West Hollywood, California, 1921–2, outdoor patio.

Schindler-Chace House, plan of house and gardens.

balance of intuition, invention and social interventions, refusing him a place in their canon, a slight that wounded Schindler deeply. His principal reputation remained that of an artist-architect intrigued by ephemeral planes and interlocking volumes, although in fact his vision was much larger.

Schindler's Lovell Beach House (1925–6), another masterpiece of American Modernism, used five transverse frames in reinforced concrete to support the house, literally and figuratively. They generated its rhythm, provided seismic protection and lifted up the main living area for majestic views of the ocean. The textures of concrete and untreated wood were rough and tactile, for this was a primitive shelter, not a 'machine for living'. The 'play-court' in the sand beneath the house embodied site-specificity and even a primal hearth with its outdoor fireplace, offset by the asymmetry of a stair up and a ramp down to the sea. The interior revealed Schindler's concept of sculptural 'space forms' in a De Stijl-like play of minute details and broad expanses. Despite its sturdy materials and lavish budget, the house embraced impermanence, even cheapness, by adapting conventional builders' materials and methods. Schindler was initially inspired by the functional pile structures often found in beachfront dwellings – a fact that intrigued the editors of *Popular Mechanics*.[38]

Neutra, another Austrian, arrived in Los Angeles in 1925, also having apprenticed with Wright, and lived at King's Road for five years. He quickly understood that Modernism's fame – and his own – relied on

Richard Neutra at the
foot of his Lovell
Health House.

publicity. Neutra's magnificent Lovell Health House represents his first triumph. This was the same Dr Philip Lovell, the charismatic author of a popular newspaper column on physical and mental fitness, who turned to Neutra after Schindler had designed his beach house. Perhaps Lovell recognized a kindred charismatic spirit, since Neutra prescribed a 'full dosage of environment' for what he dubbed the 'Health House'.[39] Practical experience with American contractors helped Neutra appropriate materials and techniques from commercial buildings: an open-web steel frame, standardized steel casements, a dramatic double-height glass wall and slender steel cables from the roof to stabilize the balconies. European in its geometry, the relation with the landscape makes this an American house. The steep site was an essential component. The building proceeds down a rocky hillside, broken by small terraces and a path to the swimming pool, before terminating in a running track. The house immediately became the apotheosis of the International Style and a local landmark, even an advertisement for Lovell. When he invited readers to see it themselves in 1929, some 15,000 Angelenos took up the offer.[40] The experience profoundly affected Neutra, who continued to promote an ambient, open-air hedonism as the basis for physiological and psychological well-being throughout his career, a synthesis he would later call 'bio-realism'.

Frank Lloyd Wright relocated to southern California in 1917 and again on his return from Japan in 1923. Nature posed difficult challenges on the

Pacific Rim with earthquakes, floods, mudslides, brushfires and parched desert heat further inland. Wright adopted new materials, notably a technique his son Lloyd had used for the Bollman House in Hollywood (1922). Wright *père* named it the Textile-Block system in reference to the textured exterior patterns and the reinforcing steel set into grooves inside the blocks, weaving them together even under seismic pressure. He experimented with a variety of techniques for a 'kaleidoscopic' array of clients: the Hollyhock House for the wealthy theatre patron Aline Barnsdale; the Alice Millard House ('La Miniatura') for a widowed bookseller (1923); a proposed desert compound for the solitary A. M. Johnson; and several resort communities that disrupted conventional notions of domesticity.[41]

Housing research became more systematic all over the country. At one end were small collective enclaves like Schindler's and Neutra's Architectural Group for Industry and Commerce (AGIC), Frederick Ackerman's Technocracy groups, Buckminster Fuller's Structural Study Associates and Philadelphia's Housing Study Guild. At the other end

Frank Lloyd Wright, Alice Millard House ('La Miniatura'), Pasadena, California, perspective from the garden, coloured pencil and graphite on paper, 1923.

were major enterprises like President Herbert Hoover's Commerce Department, which standardized building materials, and the Department of Agriculture's Forest Products Laboratory, which developed stressed-skin plywood panels. *Architectural Record*'s Robert Davison became director of a well-funded housing division at the John B. Pierce Foundation in 1931, overseeing a large staff of designers and sociologists in the country's most far-reaching experiments with prefabrication. Eager to corner a new market, the Architects' Small House Service Bureau, founded in Minneapolis in 1921, generated 250 stock-plan designs, all historicist in style though adapted to different climates, available for $6.00 per room.

The architect Clarence Stein convinced a New York financier to form the limited-dividend City Housing Corporation, another group dedicated to modern housing – as this group understood the term, with an emphasis on site planning and cooperative financing rather than architecture per se. Respect for English Garden City ideals coalesced with an awareness of problems caused by the profit-driven American superstructure of financial institutions, real-estate developers and building industries. Stein and his partner Henry Wright designed the first venture, Sunnyside Gardens in Queens, New York (1924–8), together with Frederick Ackerman, all members of the RPAA. Lewis Mumford, who became a resident, called it 'pragmatic idealism with a vengeance', contending that the relatively banal architecture accentuated residents' connections to the collective garden-courtyards and social services.[42]

R. Buckminster Fuller, Minimum Dymaxion House, 1929.

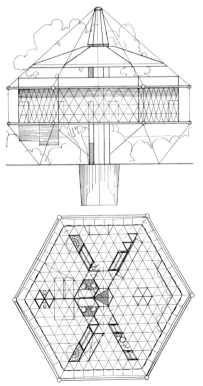

Stein and Wright also created Radburn, New Jersey, intended as a self-sufficient garden community, a 'Town for the Motor Age'. Begun in 1928, Radburn synthesized various progressive concepts: a greenbelt, spacious common greenswards, superblocks, a differentiated road system and pedestrian walkways that never crossed vehicular streets. Ackerman designed many homes and the town shopping centre. Radburn was planned for diverse social classes, work possibilities and housing types – all with attached garages. The Depression reduced these goals to a pleasant model suburb rather than a valiant alternative.[43]

Buckminster Fuller was not an architect, nor can his designs and polemics be easily classified. He emphasized 'shelter' as opposed to architecture and derided 'outdated' concepts like property ownership, convinced that he could transform the world by doing 'more with less'. The press touted his polygonal Dymaxion House design (1929) of steel and plastic as the prototype dwelling for the future. ('Dymaxion' meant 'dynamic' plus 'maximum efficiency'.) In characteristically obscure yet prescient language, Fuller described design as a 'Check list of the/Universal Design Requirements/of a Scientific Dwelling Facility–/as a component func- tion/of a world-encompassing service industry'.[44] His 1928 4D manifesto – a reference to time as the fourth dimension – envisioned an apart- ment-building variation with a stack of '4-D Utility Units' made of transparent plastic walls.

Displays of Fuller's prototypes were quite popular, but only the Dymaxion car and the prefabricated Dymaxion bathroom unit enjoyed even minor success. He rarely considered emotions or site planning, convinced that information and integral processes of change ('ephemer- alization') would lead to progress. His own reputation shows that process. The AIA rejected his offer of rights to the patents for the Dymaxion House in 1929, passing a resolution that condemned all pre- fabricated building as 'peas-in-a-pod reproducible designs'.[45] Almost forty years later, Fuller appeared on the cover of *Time* with a panoply of his inventions and the AIA awarded him its gold medal.

Some later historians have implied that single-family houses defined the 1920s, but the new large-scale residential developments also invested in apartment buildings for cities and suburbs. 'Rather than eliminating the home', explained one book, 'these new types of multi-dwelling houses offer a new type of home [based on] convenience.'[46] Cosmopolitan apart- ment buildings flourished, ranging from luxurious to livable, prized today as 'pre-war' buildings. The boom extended everywhere. Grand apartment towers transformed the character of Chicago, Manhattan and the Bronx. Nelle Peters became one of the most productive architects in Kansas City by specializing in apartment buildings. By 1928 multi-unit buildings con- stituted 53 per cent of new construction in Los Angeles, a region that according to *Architectural Record*, enjoyed 'the most promising new designs' for apartments.[47]

Urban apartment-hotels and 'bachelor hotels' attracted single people. Inexpensive hotels featured compact 'efficiency' units, later known as single-room occupancy (SRO); lodging houses were far more spartan with only cubicles or open floors. In contrast, low-rise, high-density 'gar- den apartments' were popular just outside the dense central areas of cities. (The self-trained architect Andrew J. Thomas apparently coined the term.) Chicago, Philadelphia, San Francisco and especially southern

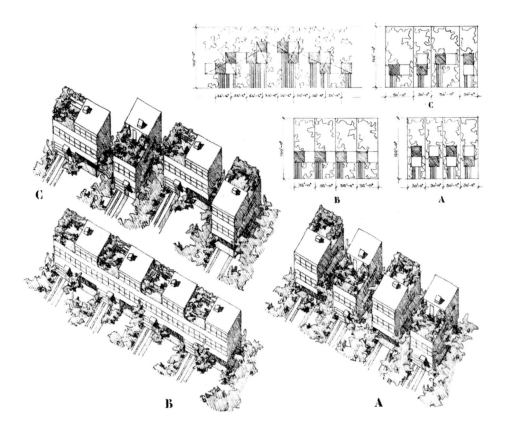

California developed many appealing variations on the type. Confronting a crisis in affordable housing, several states and municipalities helped unions and limited-dividend companies sponsor housing. Most were cooperative apartment complexes that included communal meeting rooms, laundries, childcare and expansive outdoor areas. The Amalgamated Clothing Workers' projects in the Bronx and Manhattan are among the most impressive. In 1931 *Architectural Record* distilled some of the ways to avoid monotony through staggered site plans for garden-apartment arrangements.[48] Unlike in Europe, all American housing had to engage client preferences, which meant an emphasis on irregular massing, soft landscaping, familiar motifs – and garages. All the same, alarmed about the perceived risk of transitory neighbours, many cities and elite suburban areas passed restrictive covenants and rigid zoning restrictions that banned everything but single-family houses.

Cars, Clubs and Cinemas

Automobiles redefined American public space during the 1920s. Every city carved out space for parking lots and public garages, also called 'automobile hotels'. Knud Lönberg-Holm undertook extensive research for an article on petrol stations in *Architectural Record*. Bypassing modernist polemics, he stressed the benefits of easy cleaning, visual unity, efficient movement and bright signs. Standard Oil of Ohio and Texaco commissioned standardized modern stations along these lines.[49] New kinds of stores were also geared to automobiles. The first supermarkets were extremely plain, clean designs that combined extensive parking with vast, non-directional, self-service space inside. Drive-in markets used eye-catching roofs and signage to grab drivers' attention. Wilshire Boulevard in Los Angeles became a new kind of linear downtown geared to automobile traffic. Bullock's Wilshire (1929) was the first department store to orient its main façade towards the parking. Meanwhile, suburban shopping centres used packaged themes to provide social and economic hubs that combined shops with landscaped areas and parking.

Modern hospitals also adapted to the car with extensive parking and patient drop-off areas, one piece of a profound shift in biomedical environments and clientele. Before World War One, hospitals had principally served the poor with open charity wards. Doctors saw paying patients in small offices or visited them at home. Boston's Lying-In Hospital (1922) was the first to medicalize childbirth. Now larger, yet compactly organized within multiple specialized departments, hospitals provided new models of expertise, efficiency and comfort to attract middle- and upper-class patients. These up-to-date facilities provided the familiar hygienic metaphors for modernist aesthetics: surgeries were small, specialized rooms, unlike the earlier teaching amphitheatres, and sanitized laboratories became a necessity.

New York's consolidated Columbia-Presbyterian Hospital inaugurated the diversified skyscraper facility as an interconnected 'medical centre'. Encompassing seven buildings on more than eight hectares in northern Manhattan, this complex combined a modern research facility, teaching hospital and general hospital for the surrounding area. The architect James Gamble Rogers used flow diagrams and technical data to address what he called the three functional problems for hospital design: control and collaboration in scientific research, improved hygiene and efficient circulation systems (principally to facilitate the doctors' ease of movement). The first stage, begun in 1921 and completed in 1928, drew praise for the 'size, simplicity and austerity' of the astylar towers.[50] Building

heights, window placement and rooftop solariums were based on thera-peutic, not aesthetic, considerations. The luxurious Harkness Wing drew elite patients and a strong donor base. This was the first hospital organized around modern laboratories, x-rays and technical monitor-ing. Within a decade most hospitals were devoting two-thirds of their floor area to such services.[51]

Other educational facilities followed the shift to clean lines, open spaces and specialization. The theories of John Dewey and Maria Montessori encouraged 'progressive' educators to adopt more flexible classrooms, while the San Francisco school architect John J. Donovan argued that schools should be geared to the emotional and intellectual needs of different age groups. Nursery schools and kindergartens for

Lloyd Wright, Yucca-Vine Market, Los Angeles, 1928.

middle-class children showed the strongest evidence of these theories. Elementary schools were informal and home-like, rarely more than one storey high, while high schools and the new junior high schools provided a degree of order and monumentality for adolescents.

The New School for Social Research in New York, founded in 1919, was oriented towards a progressive 'new social order'. When the economist Alvin Johnson became director, he popularized psychoanalysis, Marxism, modern dance and expressionist drama, commissioning a new building for continuing education in 1929. Joseph Urban, principally a theatre and set designer, adapted bold, abstract patterns with great economy of means. Urban used 90 colours for the interior, the choices governed by lighting, programmatic codes and what he termed empathetic studies of perception.

The electrifying architecture of entertainment enhanced urban nightlife. Prohibition encouraged an explosion of new venues for movies and theatrical performances. New York's most spectacular theatres and clubs were concentrated around Times Square, while Harlem was the epicentre of a 'Renaissance' in African-American culture – especially remarkable in music and dance – that resonated in

Joseph Urban, New School for Social Research, New York City, 1929–31, street façade.

other cities north and south. Some night-clubs fused modernist imagery with African motifs in their design as well as perform-ances. Disproving the idea that brilliant architecture generates progressive effects, the patrons were usually whites only. Hundreds of clubs, cinemas and perform-ance spaces around the country catered to segregated African-American audiences, some grand, others spare. One lavish ensemble opened in 1914 in Atlanta's Sweet Auburn district, variously called the Auditorium, Pioneer and Royal, alongside the Odd Fellows Hall. Then, as now, extrav-agance usually meant highly orchestrated performances rather than creative experi-mentation, but audiences were enthralled by the spectacles.

Vachel Lindsay's *Art of the Moving Picture* (1916) had challenged architects to seize this new medium as 'propaganda' to publicize new visions of 'a future Cincinnati, Cleveland or St Louis . . . Why not erect our new America?'[52] For more than a decade, that mandate generated flamboyant 'palaces' with fulsome orna-ment. Palaces legitimated movies as mid-dle-class culture, erasing the working-class origins of nickelodeons. A small coterie of architectural firms established distinctive styles to publicize particular Hollywood studios and their chains of theatres. Patrons were drawn to 'Wonder Theatres' and 'Atmospherics' – which created the illusion of being outdoors, 'to avoid being boring', explained the architect John Eberson.[53] Large cities built palaces with 3,000 to 6,000 seats, orchestra pits and elaborate stages for music and dance performances. The opulent lobbies, often as big as the audito-riums, might provide childcare, kennels, lounges and refreshments, while tall office buildings overhead made the multi-purpose complexes even more profitable. The introduction of sound in 1926 ended the variety of entertainment in favour of longer 'feature films'. (New York's Radio City Music Hall of 1932 was the exception.) Within a year the country had more than 17,000 movie theatres, often the most opulent and exciting buildings in town. As the Los Angeles architect

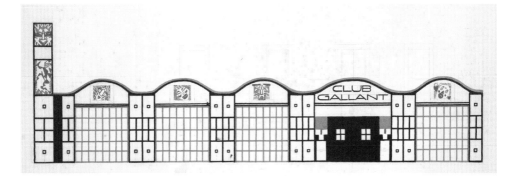

Winold Reiss, Club Gallant, New York City, 1919, side elevation.

S. Charles Lee explained, 'The show starts on the sidewalk.'[54]

Thousands of these lavish downtown palaces would close soon after the Depression hit in 1929, victims of financial pressures and a cultural turn against excess. An entirely new type now appeared, the neighbourhood theatre, a diminutive structure with 500–800 seats, unified from marquee to interiors with smooth industrial materials like steel, glass, concrete, chrome and Formica. An important early example of this shift had opened in 1929, as if on cue: the Film Guild Cinema in New York's Greenwich Village. Frederick Kiesler, yet another Viennese émigré, considered cinema an art form that required silence and darkness to help audiences concentrate on the flat screen. His screen-o-scope, shaped like the human eye or a camera lens, included auxiliary screens (on the sides and ceiling) to become a total, interactive realm. In Kiesler's view, 'The entire building is a plastic medium dedicated to the Art of Light '– what he and Buckminster Fuller called 'correalism', an integral relationship between each object and its environment.[55] The architects Ben Schlanger and John Eberson used a similar aesthetic for new movie theatres in the mid-1930s, eliminating the vestigial stage, the magnificent stairways, balconies and box seats. Schlanger also emphasized the individual experience of cinema and his opposition to class and ethnic divisions, a mood captured in the films of Charlie Chaplin.

Few American architects of the 1920s were as daring as Kiesler, who recognized theatricality as a means for unpredictable interaction, yet many engaged similar themes. Modernity was an intoxicating excitement based on 'mutability of environment', wrote Janet Flanner in *The Cubical City* (1926).[56] Despite its limitations, the private market experimented in many realms from skyscrapers and stores to housing, while non-profit institutions built model schools, hospitals and housing. Illusions of freedom and progress collapsed in disarray with the

Frederick Kiesler,
Film Guild Cinema,
New York City, 1929,
street façade.

Film Guild Cinema,
screening room.

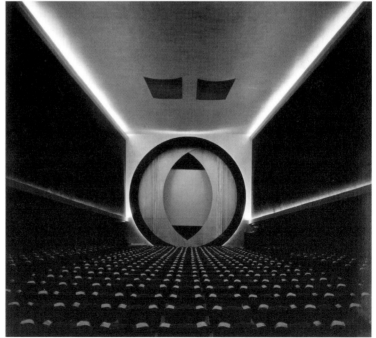

Depression. Real change would come in 1932 – not with the MOMA show, but with Franklin Delano Roosevelt's election as President. FDR promised a major federal investment in principles of equality and social justice, an ambitious goal often sustained by modern architecture. He chose the name for his campaign from a book, *A New Deal* (1932) by Stuart Chase, an economist in the RPAA, reminding us that seemingly minor or idealistic efforts to rethink the environment can have profound effects.

chapter four

Architecture, the Public and the State, 1933–1945

Franklin Roosevelt's three-term presidency sustained the US through the 'long decade' of the Great Depression and World War Two by *'politicizing* the whole of American life'.[1] The term *liberal* replaced *progressive* to characterize such interventions, determined in purpose, pragmatic in strategy, what FDR's first inaugural address called direct action to achieve dramatic results. The attorney Thurman Arnold first used the term 'welfare state' in 1937 to describe a fusing of 'spiritual government' and 'temporal government' dependent on cultural as well as political factors.[2] Modern architecture, so critical to the New Deal's goals, would be altered by its processes. Approximately 90 per cent of the country's architects and engineers were unemployed in the early 1930s, so even those few who never worked under governmental auspices were affected by the momentous changes.

Three issues of relational aesthetics from this era still affect American architecture. First is the ambiguous tension between centralized power and decentralization. Regionalist sympathies might derive from bullheaded backwardness, 'earmarked' Congressional funding or imaginative local knowledge. Second is an implied correlation between formal and political idioms – typically that Modernism is inherently progressive while neo-traditionalism or neo-classicism is intrinsically fascist, though sometimes the inverse – when in fact all governments employ a range of stylistic idioms.[3] Third is the rhetorical excess of polemics, starting off as conspicuous hyperbole, but soon taken as self-evident truths. For example, one critic disparaged the Public Works Administration (PWA), a federal agency, for having set back modern American architecture by not producing any masterpieces.[4] But is architecture a matter of exceptions or spectrums? And just *how* did thousands of PWA projects preclude innovation?

Established meanings in the arts came under challenge from every direction. The Popular Front called for intrepid graphic imagery that could rally the masses, while Ezra Pound demanded 'Make It New!' in 1934.[5] An experimental tone infused alternative magazines like *Plus:*

US Housing Authority poster for Lakeview Terrace, a PWA-sponsored housing project by Weinberg, Conrad & Teare, Cleveland, Ohio, 1934.

Orientations of Contemporary Architecture, sponsored by *Architectural Forum*, and *Task*, by students from several Boston-area architecture schools. Others switched their titles and timbre. Buckminster Fuller transformed Philadelphia's *T-Square Club Journal* into *Shelter* in 1932. The motto inveighed 'Don't Fight Forces; Use Them', focusing on social and ecological issues and occasionally showing a savage wit. The staid *Pencil Points* became *Progressive Architecture* a decade later. Despite the crises, the tone was surprisingly optimistic in all the journals. Joseph Hudnut, dean of Harvard's Graduate School of Design, declared that 'Form is an expression of faith' in a 1938 article entitled 'Architecture Discovers the Present'.[6]

Art museums new and old sponsored exhibitions on contemporary design, their first ventures into this realm. Rarely doctrinaire, they encouraged discussion about forms, larger environments and their implications. By 1936 the new architecture curator at MOMA was vowing to 'interrupt abstract arguments' and replace them with 'concrete examples of new construction which may be of vast significance in the future'.[7] An informal San Francisco group called Telesis, asked to mount an exhibition at the Museum of Art in 1940, supplemented familiar drawings of the generic urban environment 'as it is' and 'as it could be' with open-ended questions for the public: 'What is good housing?' 'Do you like where you work?' 'Is this the best we can do?'[8]

The extensive deliberations rarely cited Johnson's and Hitchcock's supposedly canonical exhibition. (*Shelter* ridiculed it relentlessly, and *Architectural Forum* declared that if the 'International Style' was not broad enough to include the diversity of recent American work, 'this is the fault of the term, not of the reality'.)[9] It was Catherine Bauer's *Modern Housing* (1934) that taught Americans about progressive architecture in Europe, which she described as 'new form [and] joyous, extravagant creative *élan*'. A young and outspoken reformer, Bauer rejected simple solutions and formal typologies. Her constructive criticism noted the weaknesses as well as the strengths of iconic European *Siedlungen*, the new modern housing estates. Cautioning Americans not to emulate work from abroad, she called for Modernisms in the plural, responsive to change, contingency and cultural diversity. Why not combine 'rational investigation' with the 'broad history of mass emotion and popular desires'? Bauer would be a formidable presence for three decades, challenging architects, museums and government agencies to experiment and then appraise the results, not just the intentions. Having helped draft the legislation that created public housing, she would lambaste the effects of 'towers-in-the-park' twenty years later.[10]

New Deal programmes embraced American history, including natural history, as 'a useable past' of wholes and parts, a resource for Modernism, not an opposition. Lewis Mumford's insightful study *The South in Architecture* (1941) stressed the need to respect 'the integrity' of regional elements based on local geographical and cultural conditions while always reaching for 'the universal element [that] transcends the local, the limited, the partial'.[11] The Historic American Building Survey (HABS) paid unemployed architects for measured drawings; the Historic Sites Act then provided funds to purchase, maintain and interpret some of these properties. The selection portrayed a diverse nation with multiple ethnic and regional vernaculars. New buildings did not have to emulate 'historic shrines'. The private sector followed a similar path. When the architect Mary Colter built dramatic sites for tourists crafted from stone rubble near the Grand Canyon (1922–37), she insisted that her structures were 'geological', not replicas or reproductions, even though they drew on Native American ruins. 'National Park Service rustic' all too soon replicated this direct aesthetic.[12]

The 1930s witnessed a convergence of social and ecological disasters that converted environmentalism, formerly an elite pursuit, into a collective necessity. The problems encompassed every kind of setting. Homeless city-dwellers erected Hooverville shantytowns; abusive farming and mining practices compounded the devastating effects of floods, droughts and erosion in the Midwestern Dust Bowl; developers' crude layouts had destroyed the promise of many suburbs. The idea of conservation in all these realms focused on large-scale environmental strategies. Indeed, the modern unit of design combined the region and the planned community, interconnected with larger infrastructural networks. Landscape architects now took a major role in design, notably Garrett Eckbo, Daniel Kiley and Albert Mayer, all self-described modernists. They emphasized 'multiple-use planning' that accepted flexibility and mobility, showing how every milieu relates to fluctuating social and environmental systems.[13]

The artist Wolfgang Born praised 'Geo-Architecture' as 'America's Contribution to the Art of the Future', a fusion of built forms with dramatic natural sites to highlight the power and fragility of the physical world.[14] Architects around the country experimented with permeable skins and exoskeletons that could be adapted in response to site and climatic changes. James Marston Fitch's *American Building* (1947) praised these 'environmental controls'.[15] Given the tumult of the era, the search for equilibrium connected environmental factors with a desire for political and social harmony.

The New Deal remains controversial in American political culture. Conservatives, aghast at radical interventions in a free-market economy, have recently tried to dismantle its welfare-state programmes like Social Security, disaster relief and housing assistance. Liberal Americans, once impatient with Roosevelt's 'middle way', are now fighting to preserve that legacy. The first hundred days of F.D.R.'s administration passed major legislation and created agencies like the PWA, the Civilian Conservation Corps (CCC) and the Federal Emergency Relief Administration (FERA). The principal goal was reducing unemployment, which hovered around 30 per cent in large cities. 'The PWA is essentially a creative agency,' declared one pamphlet; 'it creates jobs, and it builds'.[16] Build it did: over a six-year lifespan approximately 34,000 buildings, including schools, courthouses, hospitals, recreational facilities, airports and housing. Major names like William Lescaze, George Elmslie, Richard Neutra and Lloyd Wright joined the ranks, though most designers were lesser-known figures who favoured 'PWA Moderne'. Given Washington politics, all but two of the nation's more than 3,000 counties requested and received some new structure. *Life* magazine declared this the greatest public building programme in the history of humankind, even though costs ran to $4 billion.[17]

Work and Public Works

Samuel Wiener
(Jones, Roessle,
Olschner & Wiener)
for the PWA,
Municipal Incinerator,
Shreveport,
Louisiana, 1935.

New Deal agencies provided the nation with public services that are now too easily taken for granted. Three design tenets characterized the best work, all of them resonant in contemporary Modernism: skilful site planning, public access to virtually all projects and daring interventions that also engaged local cultures. Collaboration defined these endeavours, often to the point of anonymity within the 'alphabet agencies'. Architects worked closely with engineers and landscape designers to upgrade the nation's infrastructure, creating bold municipal incinerators, asphalt plants, water-treatment facilities and majestic parkways. Ancillary linkages for the highway networks included access ramps, toll booths, parking garages and bus terminals. Almost 20,000 bridges were constructed throughout the country, including the much-loved Golden Gate Bridge (1933–7) in San Francisco, designed by Irving and Gertrude Morrow.[18]

Ely Jacques Kahn and Robert Jacobs, Municipal Asphalt Plant, New York City, 1944 (now Asphalt Green Sports and Arts Center).

The PWA helped fund Robert Moses's vast system of 3 bridges, 9 parkways and 255 parks or recreational facilities throughout the New York Metropolitan Region. Here, too, results could be at once spartan and spectacular, for both individual structures and for the ambitious scale of the ensemble. When Aymar Embury II, Moses's favourite architect, completed the George Washington Bridge in 1931, he left the structure

Aymar Embury, Dwight James Baum, and J. Weisberg for Robert Moses, New York City Commissioner of Parks and the PWA, McCarren Pool entry pavilion, Brooklyn, 1936 (now the Joseph H. Lyons Pool).

CROSS-BRONX EXPRESSWAY

HENRY

87 Robert Moses's
New York, showing
the Henry Hudson
Parkway (1933–7)
(foreground) and the
Cross-Bronx
Expressway leading
to the George
Washington Bridge
(1927–31), rendering,
1955.

exposed, discarding the neo-classical sheathing. Le Corbusier would declare this 'place of radiant grace' his favourite building in the US, evidence of the nation's 'conviction and enthusiasm' for the new.[19] Moses too remains a subject of passionate debate. Admirers point to accomplishments that transformed New York, benefitting many middle-class citizens, and broke through bureaucratic roadblocks that usually stymie ambitious master plans. Critics cannot forget that Moses wielded political power like an omnipotent pharaoh, never elected to office and contemptuous of public opinion. Moses used his authority to demolish working-class neighbourhoods that stood in his way and further segregate African-Americans, who did not fit into his grandiose vision.[20] His example forces architects, developers and citizens everywhere to ask if the virtuous goals of Modernism justify the means by which it is realized.

Other government agencies also employed architecture and the arts. The Works Progress Administration (WPA) took the lead with 188,000 new and renovated public buildings and infrastructure services. Its Federal Art Project engaged all types of media. Writers were paid to tour their states and produce travel guides; musicians and actors to entertain every social group; graphic designers to produce posters; painters and sculptors to embellish public spaces. Although the goal of 'art for the millions' favoured easily comprehensible documentaries, social realism and stripped-down classicism, the post-war caricature of insipid representational art is exaggerated. Many administrators were cautious about any Modernism that seemed coded or self-consciously difficult. Yet modern architects designed important buildings, and major abstractionists like Stuart Davis painted striking murals. The subtle distortions of 'dynamic realism', 'social surrealism' and recycled materials (a favourite for WPA theatres) critiqued entrenched power and artistic fashions.[21]

The Tennessee Valley Authority (TVA) received considerable national and international praise. Extending across a 1,500-kilometre-long swath of land and waterways, the TVA provided residents of seven impoverished Appalachian states with an integrated system of electrical power, flood control, communication, conservation, employment and recreation. Director Arthur Morgan wanted an 'architecture of public relations' to fulfill his vision of a 'laboratory in social and economic life'.[22] He appointed the young Hungarian émigré Roland Wank as principal designer after hearing him criticize the Army Corps of Engineers' designs for folksy buildings and ornamented dams. Wank called for prefabricated housing and forthright volumes as more in keeping with the spectacular natural settings. An exhibition of 1941 at MOMA featured Wank's seven majestic hydroelectric dams, eleven

Roland Wank for the TVA, powerhouse and gantry crane, Kentucky Dam, 1939–44.

Prefabricated trailers
near Fontana Dam,
Tennessee, c. 1939.

tributary dams, powerhouses and gantry cranes. Three years later another MOMA exhibition asserted that the TVA's structures 'combine[d] to form one of the monuments of our civilization'.[23]

The project was orchestrated from each detail to the totality, 'one unified machine, one organic whole', in the words of the TVA economist Stuart Chase.[24] Every aspect was geared to impress the press and the public. Each dam incorporated adjacent sites for recreation. A sequence of views along new roadways built expectations, and the striking visitor centres orchestrated enticing spectacles. Careful site planning softened the monotony of prefabricated trailers and standardized permanent dwellings in the new town of Norris, Tennessee. Nonetheless, the 'socialist' premises of public ownership curtailed the ambitious goal of the TVA as a prototype for cooperative ecological settlements elsewhere. Nor were all the locals so content. Lewis Hine, hired to document the dramatic changes to a 'backward' way of life, observed that most people resented 'the rapid and, to some, shocking transition to a new era'.[25] Norris would later be criticized as a suburb in the wilderness.

Industrial designers conjured up products at all scales, including buildings at world's fairs that drew consumers by recasting technological fantasies as voluptuous modern power. The role of the media continued to expand as radio stations multiplied with the popularity of FDR's 'Fireside Chats'. Crowds in Los Angeles flocked to two rival networks on Sunset Boulevard: William Lescaze's sleek 'International' broadcast station for CBS and the Austin Company's glass-brick Moderne building for NBC. Film production concentrated in Hollywood, where studios built new headquarters, but the real excitement occurred on the back lots. A major studio now produced some 40 films a year with extravagant sets typically designed by young architects with a penchant for cosmopolitan modern decor, high-tech imagery and lavish fantasy settings. The art director Stephen Goosson combined the urban visions of Le Corbusier and Hugh Ferriss for *Just Imagine* (1930). His utopian Shangri-La for *Lost Horizon* (1937) mixed Europe's cubic volumes with an elegant horizontality and landscaping reminiscent of Frank Lloyd Wright.

Wright's own Johnson Wax Administration Building in Racine, Wisconsin (1936–9), embodied the New Deal's call for enlightened work

Frank Lloyd Wright,
Johnson Wax
Administration
Building, Racine,
Wisconsin, 1936–9,
view of the Great
Hall.

relations. The commission conveyed a sense of redemption: a sudden economic surge for a company that had refused to fire employees; a last-minute shift by chief executives who had first commissioned a prosaic design; proof of the phoenix-like revival of Wright's career. The daring structural system used mushroom-columns made of concrete reinforced with steel mesh, expanding at the top like lily pads some 6 metres in diameter, then tapering down to delicate bases set in hinged 23-centimetre metal supports that Wright called 'crow's feet'. The Wisconsin Industrial Commission was highly suspicious and demanded proof that this system could carry the weight of the roof. Wright complied, ever the virtuoso performer, loading the test column with 60 tons of sandbags and rocks, five times the required weight, to the delight of reporters who covered the event.

Equally inspired was the use of standard Pyrex-glass tubing to fill the interstices between the lily pads and within the red-brick walls. The workspace is suffused with natural light during the day; the exterior is luminous at night. As in the Larkin Building, mezzanines looked out over the main workspace as they connected a multi-level assemblage of offices, laboratories and other facilities. In another prophetic gesture, the lobby flowed directly into a cave-like garage. When the entire city was invited to the opening in 1939, over a third of the population came to marvel at the Great Workroom. Wright considered it as inspiring 'as any cathedral'. *American Business* acclaimed the 'uplifting repose', and *Life* called the project a harbinger of things to come, more prophetic than the New York World's Fair.[26]

Housing in Hard Times

Now in his sixties, Wright imagined himself reinventing every aspect of American society. Broadacre City captures the scope of that ambition. The idea had emerged in the late 1920s, but remained purely rhetorical until the *New York Times* asked him for a counter-proposal to Le Corbusier's *Ville Radieuse* in 1932. 'Ruralism as distinguished from *Urbanisme*', Wright declared, describing an immense harmonized plan that would, he hoped, encompass the entire nation – or any other country that might be interested. A 1.1-metre-square model, a prototype utopia for some 4,000 people, was displayed at Rockefeller Center in 1935 and then travelled to other cities. Broadacre celebrated the automobile as the vehicle for freedom and a return to the land, 'minimum of one acre to the family'.[27] Occasional towers and malls provided points of concentration for commerce, culture and government within the vast dispersed landscape. Megalomaniac and environmentally unsound, an artistically coordinated sprawl, Broadacre paradoxically sought to harness the forces of mass production, automobiles and telecommunications – a decentralized but synchronized vision of modernity that still remains potent for many Americans.

It was not this grand project, but an extraordinary country house, Fallingwater, that ensured Wright's fame. Edgar Kaufmann, scion of Pittsburgh's largest department store, commissioned the family hideaway at Bear Run, Pennsylvania, late in 1934. He supposedly did so at the behest of his son, who had just become an apprentice at Taliesin (working on the Broadacre City model), although the opposite may be true. In any case, Fallingwater, completed in 1937, soon became the most famous modern house in the US and probably in the world. A drawing of it hangs behind Wright on the 1938 cover of *Time* magazine. A Wrightian myth suggests that he designed Fallingwater in only two hours, although he visited the site many times. In any case the design never changed after the initial proposal, which surpassed all possible expectations even in its location, straddling and possessing the small waterfall rather than merely looking out upon it. Like so many of Wright's designs, the structure transcends oppositions. It seems at once a natural formation, anchored to the earth by vertical piers of local sandstone, and a daring tour de force. Reinforced-concrete slabs cantilever out 4.5 metres from the rock shelf, then realign with the streambed. Those floating planes make this relatively small dwelling feel expansive. They suggest that Wright had studied the European modernists he so disdained, although Fallingwater is unquestionably site-specific even in its cultural location, at once enhancing nature and wrestling with it. The experience is magical, encompassing both the permanence and the impermanence of creativity and the natural world.[28]

Wright continued to advocate high-quality affordable housing with a new moniker, 'Usonian', alluding simultaneously to the US, to the technocratic acronyms of New Deal agencies and to his friend Buckminster Fuller's Dymaxion schemes. Like other modern dwelling types, Usonians maximized economy and reduced area. Wright experimented with several basic modules, typically a grid of rectangles offset by diagonals, but also circles and hexagons. Shallow concrete-slab foundations contained radiant heating, which also prevented frost heaves in cold climates. External structure and internal finish became a single layer, usually brick or wood-frame, left exposed and reinforced with built-in storage to stiffen single-storey walls. Wright nestled some delightful spatial experience in every dwelling, what he called 'essential Joy', perhaps simply dappled sunlight through geometric fretwork on a thin plane of inexpensive plywood. Each house balanced ecological and social harmony with individuality and even hedonistic delight.

The Jacobs House in Madison, Wisconsin, designed for two 'common sense' young professionals, was the archetypal Usonian (1936–7). Its inclusive modernity maximized economy and flexibility without sacrificing familiarity or comfort. 'What are the essentials in their case, a typical case?' Wright asked readers of *Architectural Forum*.[29] He then specified three experience-based criteria for the modern dwelling: a transparent wall of glass to connect the living area with a small enclosed garden; a compact 'work-space' (aka kitchen) to form a service core, replacing the hearth as a spatial fulcrum; and a carport to shelter the automobile, now fully integrated into the family dwelling. All three would become norms for the best post-World War Two suburban houses.

Wright's houses remind us that residential building continued despite the Depression. Indeed, government subsidies focused overwhelmingly on the private sector, seeking to revive and modernize this critical segment of the economy. The Federal Housing Administration (FHA), created in 1934, guaranteed mortgage loans for banks and improved the terms for owners. As hoped, housing starts quickly rose for the first time in eight years. The FHA soon financed almost half the

Frank Lloyd Wright,
Herbert Jacobs
House, Madison,
Wisconsin, 1936,
living room.

Jacobs House,
floor plan.

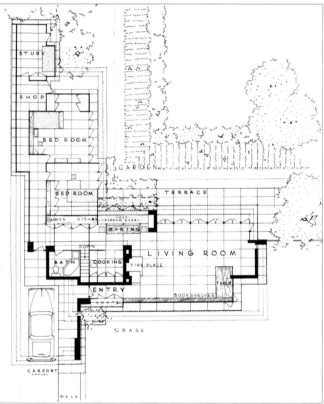

country's mortgages, investing more than $4 billion in the next six years and prompting most banks to follow its guidelines.[30] Both the numbers and the architecture have usually been ignored. Local FHA officials were often cautious about the re-sale value of 'non-traditional' styles or pro-grammes, but a shift in public taste saw modern houses become increasingly popular, 'no longer the frigid white symbol of a small cult' in the words of *Architectural Forum*.[31] Far more problematic was the FHA's endorsement of racial segregation as part of sound 'neighbour-hood planning' – a position that lasted until 1968.

Modern American dwellings shared an attitude towards domesticity more than a stylistic idiom. An open flow of space on the ground floor reinforced informality and the continuities of an 'indoor–outdoor house'. Industrialized systems of construction joined with simple, tactile natural materials, often drawn from the local landscape: wide cedar and spruce planks in the Pacific North-west, blank stucco walls in the South-west, rough fieldstone in Pennsylvania, clapboard siding in New England. *The Modern House in America*, a popular compendium, emphasized such regional adaptations, dismissing the International Style as a misnomer for copyists. One of the editors, Katherine Morrow Ford, insisted that 'modern architecture cannot be reduced to a precise formula.'[32] Hybridity rather than purity seemed the fitting expression of American culture, unpredictable amalgams of tradition and innovation, local and universal, personal and collective.

Walter Gropius had been intrigued by the idea of 'light construction, full of bright daylight' since his early days at the Bauhaus in Germany.

Walter Gropius with Marcel Breuer, Gropius House, Lincoln, Massachusetts, 1937, garden façade.

Harwell Hamilton Harris, Havens House, Berkeley, California, 1939, photograph by Man Ray.

After the Nazis seized power, he emigrated to England and then, in 1937, to the US, where he was invited to chair the Architecture Department at Harvard. The next year he designed his own house in suburban Lincoln, Massachusetts, partnering with the Hungarian Marcel Breuer for this and several other residences. If the Bauhaus remains present in the white planes, transparent glass walls and flat roof, which caused squawks from neighbours, the two colleagues eagerly incorporated local clapboard and fieldstone,as well as that all-American vernacular element, the screened porch. 'There is no such thing as an "International Style"', Gropius insisted. 'The fusion . . . produced a house that I would never have built in Europe with its entirely different climatic, technical and psychological background.'[33] Gropius asserted a more stringent philosophy in his teaching. Quoting Ralph Waldo Emerson on 'Self-Reliance', he urged students to break with architectural history in order to become leaders for the future. Since Modernism was by now accepted, even triumphant, in most American schools by the late 1930s, the Gropius crusade fostered missionary zeal rather than the 'humanistic' or 'democratic' aspirations for 'diversity' of his writings.

American Modernism remained strongly regional throughout the 1930s. California continued to foster exceptional creativity. Neutra and Schindler in Los Angeles were joined by a second generation that included Gregory Ain, Raphael Soriano and J. R. Davison. Cliff May reinterpreted local history with the vaguely modern, low-lying ranch house, while Albert Frey cultivated cosmopolitan flash at the desert resort of Palm Springs. Cohorts in the Bay Area interpreted their region's informal, nature-infused 'simple life' with redwood siding, abundant glass and dramatic angles. The San Francisco Museum of Art held special exhibitions in 1942 and 1949 to promote 'Bay Area Domestic Architecture' by William Wurster, Harwell Hamilton Harris, Gardner Dailey, John Funk and others. Less well known outside their locales are Pietro Belluschi and John Yeon in the Pacific North-west; Kraetsch & Kraetsch and Alden Dow in the upper Midwest; Harris Armstrong in Missouri; Victorine and Samuel Homsey in Delaware; and Igor Polivitsky, Robert Law Weed and Lawrence Murray Dixon in Florida.

Climatic adaptations determined Weed's Florida Tropical Home in Chicago's 1933 Century of Progress exhibition. The house's solar orientation, cross-ventilation and concrete canopies ('eyebrows') to shade windows remained mainstays of modern houses in that state until the mid-1950s. George Fred Keck's path was more indirect. He realized that the glass walls of his House of Tomorrow at the 1933 Chicago exhibition kept the workmen comfortable despite the bitter Midwestern winter. Keck and his brother William immediately began to experiment with passive solar orientation and flexible louvres in houses and apartment buildings, keenly aware of aesthetic as well as physical effects. When local developer Howard Sloan commissioned a home just outside Chicago in 1940, the Kecks enlisted producers to meet their specifications for radiant floor heating, ventilation louvres, insulation materials and Thermopane windows. Two years later Sloan renamed his development Solar Park and required that all new architecture be 'modern' – that is, architect-designed with climatic adaptations.

Fortune magazine now defined American modern housing as 'inventive, industrially produced, and resourceful' about environments.[34] The editors clearly saw a business potential that has returned in recent years. The appearance and purpose of windows changed when the Libbey-Owens-Ford Glass Company launched 'The Picture Window Idea' in the early 1930s, emphasizing large, unobstructed expanses of glass to frame views of the outdoors.[35] The popular shelter press hailed this 'Modern Miracle', and

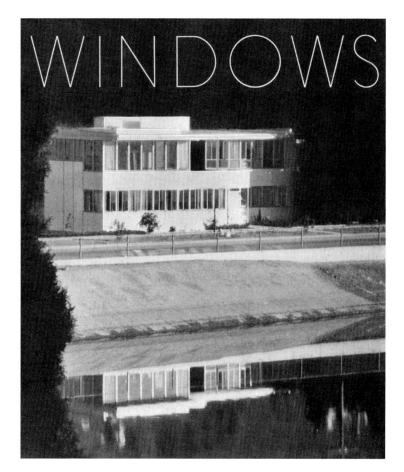

architects experimented with solar orientation. Two of the most significant
were finished just after the war. Eleanor Raymond and Dr Maria Telkes,
director of MIT's solar laboratory, collaborated on a Solar House with early
photovoltaic panels (1948). That same year, Frank Lloyd Wright finished
another home for the Jacobs family in Middleton, Wisconsin, named the
Solar Hemicycle for its arc of windows facing a sun-catching sunken basin.
The earth for the basin became a protective berm that blocked north winds
in the winter. Ingenuity balanced wizardry.

The Depression gave considerable impetus to prefabrication – a
catchword for an array of processes and products. Innovative research
was often affiliated with universities and government agencies such as
the Forest Products Laboratory. By 1935, 33 private companies had generated unique systems based on stressed-skin plywood, modular steel

Robert McLaughlin for American Houses, Inc., Moto-Home, New London, Connecticut, 1933–4.

frames or steel frames with asbestos-cement panels. Two architects founded major firms: Howard Fisher's General Houses and Robert McLaughlin's American Houses, known for its steel-frame Moto-Home, purportedly easy to expand or move and equipped with a 'mechanical core'. Marketing for modern houses routinely evoked the automobile industry, which continued to expand without major advances.

Collaboration was an ideal if not a reality. Robert Davison linked the Pierce Foundation with Columbia University's Institute for Housing Research. He hired sociologists to analyse changing patterns in consumerism and family life at Pierce Heights near Hightstown, New Jersey, and building-materials companies to help develop products like Cemesto (thin sandwich panels with layered asbestos-and-fibre insulation), soon a standard material. Buckminster Fuller's second Dymaxion dwelling was one of several mast-houses during the 1930s. Many architects were drawn to 'shape engineering' (a term derived from the curve of an aircraft fuselage), such as Corwin Willson's Eggshell trailer-house, Martin Wagner's Iron Igloo and Wallace Neff's Bubble House, produced by spraying concrete over inflated rubber balloons. None of these went beyond a few prototypes since inventive forms trumped issues of production. Konrad Wachsman and Walter Gropius set out to make a 'packaged house' for the General Panel Corporation, but Wachsman kept redesigning the purpose-made components, aiming for an ideal system, so that after four years not one house had been completed.

Wherever possible, modern dwellings were organized into enclaves with careful attention to landscaping. The most powerful examples were the New Deal's three Greenbelt Towns, begun in 1935 as self-sufficient suburban towns surrounded by 0.8-kilometre-wide protective greenswards in the tradition of English Garden Cities and Radburn. Greenbelt, outside Washington, was the most ambitiously modern in its clusters of attached housing and communal outdoor areas. It provided an important model for New Towns in the 1960s and early 1970s.

Miami and Miami Beach filled with blocks of simple Art Deco garden apartments, carefully sited for sun-control and cross-ventilation. Privately owned low-rise garden apartments in Los Angeles included Neutra's Strathmore and Landfair, as well as Gregory Ain's Dunsmuir Flats in Los Angeles (1937), admired for the varied façades that adapt to

Gregory Ain,
Dunsmuir Flats
garden apartments,
Los Angeles, 1937,
garden façade.

the site. Smooth horizontal planes faced one street, garages another, while step-backed façades opened onto small private gardens, providing abundant light on three sides of each unit. Even mass-market builders like Fritz Burns of southern California emphasized the need to think of streetscapes and 'architectural sequencing'.

Housing the 'Common Man'

The New Deal also saw the first federal efforts to address the injustice of 'one-third of a nation, ill-housed', in the words of FDR's second inaugural address in 1936. The total numbers are small: just over 21,000 units in 51 projects under the PWA; 2,200 in the three suburban greenbelt towns;

and another 120,000 units under the Housing Authority (USHA) before World War Two – many fewer than planned and meagre in comparison with some 4.5 million new units in Europe.[36] American housing usually incorporated familiar tropes from local surroundings, in part to deflect public suspicion about such interventions. Pressure from realtors and reformers required slum clearance, demolishing at least one existing unit for every new one. Few of the evicted families could afford the new government housing, which was geared to the 'middle third', the out-of-luck 'deserving poor'. With this combination of reforms the nation's poor often saw their housing options plummet.

All the same, the architectural quality and site plans of the best PWA housing remain inspiring. A commitment to jobs brought high-quality craftsmanship in a range of materials. Realizing that 'Housing Is More than Houses', Washington added facilities for leisure, recreation and social services. Designers engaged the landscape, drawing on trends in Swiss and Scandinavian housing, as well as Ernst May's work in Frankfurt, Germany. The site plans accentuated four qualities: irregular super-blocks with low-rise, low-coverage building groups; continuity with surrounding streets and buildings; adaptation to the distinctive contours of the landscape; and inviting spaces between buildings. Educators debated the relationship between the rigorous minimalist aesthetic of Europe's Modern Movement and a more 'humanized' informal variety in the US. Harvard Dean Joseph Hudnut, responsible for bringing Gropius to the design school, now implicitly criticized him when Hudnut derided 'plumbing, fresh air and prophylactic calm' as sanitized ideals imposed on working-class families. In the ultimate insult, he called Gropius' approach to Modernism more suburban than urban.[37]

The Carl Mackley Houses in north-eastern Philadelphia remain appealing more than 70 years later. Adaptation to circumstances characterized the project from the start. Catherine Bauer represented the client, a local branch of the hosiery-makers' union. The principal architect, Oskar Stonorov, a recent émigré from Germany, presented one version of the project for the Philadelphia venue of MOMA's *Modern Architecture* exhibition in 1932. In keeping with recent avant-garde trends, this model featured ten-storey *Zeilenbau* rows – rigid diagonal slabs orientated to maximize sunlight and fresh air. Stonorov knew enough not to show this version to union officials. His partner, Alfred Kastner, oversaw the massing and site layout, converting the unrelenting shapes to irregular three-storey blocks. The buildings rise and fall with the gently sloping site, punctuated by passageways, balconies and small recessed spaces around stair landings. Even colour softened as Stonorov's original white walls gave way to industrial tiles in autumnal

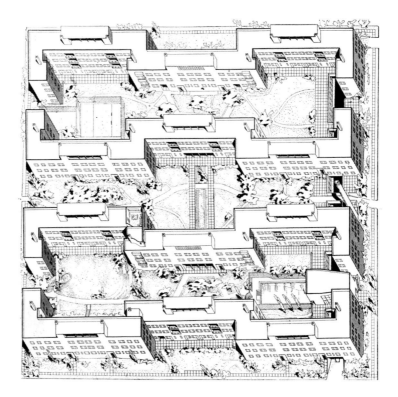

Oskar Stonorov and Albert Kastner for the PWA, Mackley Houses, Philadelphia, 1932–5, axonometric drawing from *Architectural Record* (February 1934).

Mackley Houses, photographed in 1985.

shades of orange, tan and mauve, consistent with the multi-hued brick of Philadelphia's row-house vernacular. The unit sizes were meagre, but generous public amenities included childcare facilities, a swimming pool, meeting rooms, an underground garage and rooftop laundries.[38]

New York experimented in multiple veins. Frederick Ackerman's First Houses alternated rehabilitation and demolition along one dilapidated block of East Village tenements. The Williamsburg Houses in Brooklyn (originally the Ten Eyck) comprised the largest and most costly PWA project. William Lescaze, chief designer under R. R. Shreve, organized the ten-block site into three super-blocks with *Zeilenbau* slabs set 15 degrees off the grid. Bravado overruled climate studies, since the court-yards become wind channels in winter and block summer breezes. Nonetheless, the bold horizontal stripes and handsome community services cultivated a sense of local pride. Harlem River Houses responded directly to local residents' demands, articulated by the Consolidated Tenants League. Designed by Archibald Manning Brown with John Louis Wilson, an African-American architect, the series of walkways and courtyards connects the project with the surrounding streets.[39] Another African-American architect, Hilyard Robinson, enlivened flat-roofed International Style buildings at Langston Terrace (1938) in Washington, DC, with bas-relief ornament and informal placement around a central courtyard on a naturally terraced slope.

'New groups and classes are knocking at the door,' explained a 1936 article in the *Record*, 'asking as of right what used to be the privileges of the few.'[40] Good intentions to be sure, but when American public hous-ing became official in 1937 with the Wagner-Steagall Act standards plummeted. USHA set policy and funding in Washington while local authorities chose locations and interpreted the guidelines. Unlike the

Burton Cairns and Vernon DeMars for the FSA, migrant workers' housing at Chandler, Arizona, 1936.

PWA most projects were not so much restrained as resentful, even mean-spirited. This was not the fault of 'Modernism', but of specific repressive policies. Congressional pressure imposed draconian restrictions on construction costs and standards to make it clear that public housing was inferior to the lowest-quality private housing.[41]

The Farm Security Administration (FSA) was the most radical and unequivocally modern federal housing agency. The FSA built 95 communities for migrant farm workers from California to Texas. The justly famous photographs of the migrants by Dorothea Lange and others dramatized the poignant dignity of these impoverished families that fled the Midwestern Dust Bowl. The architecture, while far less well known, parlayed similar emotions into redressing some of the problems. California's regional office insisted on considerable autonomy for its principal designers, Burton Cairns and Vernon DeMars, who mixed sources from European housing estates and Israeli *kibbutzim* with American garden-apartments and local vernacular traditions.[42] Inexpensive materials predominated by necessity and predilection: plywood, asbestos cement, prefabricated aluminium panels and traditional adobe bricks.

FSA layouts varied as well, using *Zeilenbau* rows, hexagons, culs-de-sac and differing combinations from neighbourhood to neighbourhood. Interviews generated multi-bedroom units for extended families at the end of large rows and designated spaces for baseball, weekend dances and teenagers' drag races. The landscape architect Garrett Eckbo placed schools, childcare, health centres and other community buildings near existing groves of trees. Cross-ventilation, walls of windows and covered walkways provided further relief from oppressive heat. The architectural media were resoundingly enthusiastic, as was the Swiss critic Albert Roth, who included the FSA camp at Chandler, Arizona, in *Modern Architecture* (1940), the quintessential text for European modernists. Two decades later, *Architectural Record* declared that these FSA images were part of 'the collective subconscious of the Modern Movement'.[43]

Public Spaces of 'Better Living'

Some private businesses prospered as ad men of the mid-1930s invented two still-potent phrases 'Better Living' and 'American Way of Life'. Southern cities began to promote their assets, laying foundations for the Sunbelt's post-war growth. Los Angeles continued to thrive in myth and fact, a new breed of modern city, seemingly amorphous in its far-flung dispersal. Aircraft and automobile factories appeared on the city's

Arneson River Theater at Paseo del Alamo Riverwalk, San Antonio, Texas, Robert Hugman for Works Progress Administration (WPA), 1929–41, photograph c. 1960.

periphery even before the war, along with planned housing enclaves. Popular tourist attractions multiplied – drive-ins, motor inns, the Farmer's Market, Crossroads of the World – while cosmopolitan shops and department stores flourished along Wilshire and other major boulevards.

Government agencies funded the most important public buildings of the 1930s, often combining structures with sites to bring citizens together for a variety of activities, planned and spontaneous. Some were grand, like the Red Rocks Amphitheater near Denver (1941), with its excellent natural acoustics for 9,000 people at a spectacular site carved from sandstone monoliths. Most projects were comparatively small, sheds for classical-music festivals and infill community centres in urban neighbourhoods. Waterfront development on ocean and river sites combined ecological adaptations with public recreation. City and state parks added swimming pools, field houses, playgrounds and band shells to serve large crowds. Resort towns like Stowe, Vermont, improved their ski trails at public expense.

San Antonio's Paseo del Alamo, or Riverwalk, has its origins here in a process that illustrates similar ventures elsewhere. Aware that the river in the centre of town had become an open sewer prone to dangerous floods, the local architect Robert Hugman had first envisioned a plan in 1929. A decade later, a newly elected Democratic mayor secured generous federal funding from the WPA. By 1941 the city had a bypass channel for flood control, 21 blocks of landscaped walkways, 31 stairways to the river's edge, 21 handsome bridges, shops and a large amphitheatre across the river from a stage for plays and films. O'Neill Ford restored the nearby La Villita, centre of the original Mexican settlement, under the auspices of the National Youth Administration (NYA), which soon became Lyndon Johnson's first political base.

The New Deal dramatically increased the number and quality of American schools and modernized their pedagogies, giving assertive architectural expression to theories of progressive education. Modern pre-schools were both rational and lyrical. Neutra's prototype ring-plan school from 'Rush City Reformed' remained on paper until a school

Saarinen and
Saarinen with
Perkins, Wheeler
and Will, Crow Island
School, Winnetka,
Illinois, 1940.

Crow Island School,
plan.

principal in Bell, California, campaigned to see it realized in 1935. Crow
Island School (1940) in Winnetka, Illinois, a suburb north of Chicago,
became a nationwide model for decades to come. The design was a collaboration between Eliel Saarinen, his son Eero, the Chicago firm of
Perkins, Wheeler and Will, and Carleton Washburne, the school super-
intendent whose influential Winnetka Plan loosened strict separations

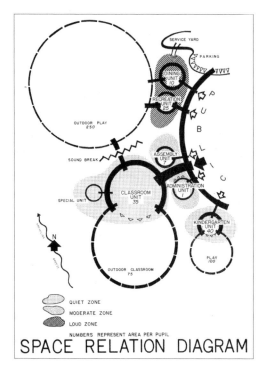

SPACE RELATION DIAGRAM

'Space Relation Diagram' from William Caudill's pamphlet 'Space for Teaching' (1941).

between grades and between curricular subjects. 'Activity classrooms' encouraged various pursuits and flowed into age-grouped outdoor spaces. Simple brickwork and local wood reinforced the spirit of joyful resourcefulness. John Dewey provided the philosophical grounding: these schools were social centres for the entire community, their indoor and outdoor facilities open round the clock.

High schools were more imposing structures. While some held fast to the neo-Georgian style, many New Deal schools combined modern functionalism with Moderne streamlining. A MOMA exhibition on schools in 1942 featured examples that had also appeared, without the architects' names, in PWA publications. Lescaze's Ansonia High School in Coldspring, Connecticut (1939), was a resolute steel-framed structure articulating the separation of three units (auditorium, classrooms and gymnasium), with smooth bands of glass block and salmon-colored brick to enliven the façade. Architectural design became more abstract with an early bubble diagram about school activities in William Caudill's pamphlet 'Space for Teaching' (1941). But rhetoric about straightforward plainness and functional plans sometimes disguised class and racial prejudice. Since the construction and maintenance of American schools are tied to property taxes, poor districts suffer calculated cutbacks in architecture and educational services, while prosperous suburbs enjoy good facilities.

Several independent architecture schools took up the modernist cause while asserting distinctive philosophical goals. Frank Lloyd Wright's Taliesin West in Arizona is at once a formal statement with its diagonal geometry and an informal ensemble determined by topography and site. After a three-year search during respites from the harsh Wisconsin winters, Wright found the site in Paradise Valley. Planning evolved *in situ* beginning in January 1938. Apprentices made the walls of 'desert rubble stone', mixed with cement and cured in wooden moulds, creating a textured material that seems primeval. Regular rows of rough-sawn redwood trusses are angled to echo the mountains in the distance and support the roof, much of it originally covered in taut canvas. One terrace

138

Frank Lloyd Wright,
Taliesin West,
Scottsdale, Arizona,
1938–59.

Taliesin West,
interior of studio.

incorporated a petroglyph boulder found nearby, suggesting archaic creative forces as well as modern innovations. Like Taliesin East in
Wisconsin, this 'desert compound' encompassed home, work, school and
community life for the Taliesin Fellowship and their visitors. It would be
a formative place for many creative architects who were apprenticed
there, including John Lautner, Alden Dow, Paolo Soleri, Henry Klumb
and the iconoclastic MOMA curator Elizabeth Mock.

Mies van der Rohe,
Illinois Institute of
Technology (IIT),
1943–7, photo-
montage with model
of campus.

Mies van der Rohe,
Alumni Memorial Hall,
IIT, 1947, corner detail.

Mies van der Rohe's Illinois Institute of Technology (IIT) represents a seemingly opposite but parallel approach to education and environments. If Wright connected to myth and place, so did Mies with his timeless classical abstraction. Both shut out the inconsistencies of reality. This commission brought Mies to the US in 1937, when Chicago's Armour Institute, soon renamed IIT, hired him to direct its School of Architecture and create a prestigious new campus. He sketched the rigorous site plan of parallel rows the next year, then set it on a plinth and slightly modulated the uncompromising uniformity during the war years. Mies's devotion to *Baukunst*, a famously untranslatable German term, elevated customary skills and well-established rules to attain a spiritual ideal. IIT gave substance to his declaration, paraphrasing Thomas Aquinas, that 'truth is the significance of facts'.[44]

Seemingly oblivious to the site, Mies in fact sought to evoke the 'material and spiritual conditions' of Chicago's grid.[45] Fascinated by American building methods, his reiterated materials celebrated commonplace stock items. The Minerals and Metals Research Building (1941–3) established a basic prototype of large-span interiors with low brick-and-glass curtain walls. The strategically exposed I-beams were in fact welded to the corner columns, a symbolic expression of structure that Mies continued to use in later buildings. Despite protests neither Mies nor the IIT trustees worried that construction forced demolition of the Mecca, an apartment building that had been at the heart of Chicago's African-American cultural 'Renaissance'. This provided another layer of what Sarah Whiting has called IIT's 'bas-relief urbanism', simultaneously figural and abstract, sitting lightly on the ground yet incised into the city fabric. In all these ways IIT anticipated post-war redevelopment.[46]

Deploying Modern Architecture

The American economy rebounded in 1939 as the government and major industries geared up to help the European Allied powers fight the Nazis. The American 'Arsenal of Democracy' doubled the output of aircraft and munitions factories even before the US officially entered the combat. The nation declared war in December 1941, the day after the Japanese attack on Pearl Harbor. First 10 million, then 20 million Americans enlisted. Almost as many joined the war effort at home by helping produce ships, planes and munitions in 46 different locations. Flight schools and air stations proliferated. Fighting on two fronts, across the Atlantic and the Pacific, required a coordinated national effort, one that would have an extraordinary effect on the post-war economy and, by extension, on architecture.

HOUSING: AN INTEGRAL PART OF TOTAL DEFENSE

ENVIRONMENTS FOR PEOPLE

FACTORIES FOR DEFENSE MATERIALS

BOTH MUST BE CAREFULLY COORDINATED WITH THE DEFENSE PROGRAM TO AVOID OVER EXPANSION AND BOOM BUILDING

'Housing: An Integral Part of Total Defense', *Pencil Points* (February 1941).

The scale and coordination of wartime production altered every industry from weaponry to building materials. A hundred major corporations received two-thirds of government contracts, names like General Electric, Chrysler, Boeing, Westinghouse and Kaiser. Nearly a thousand automotive plants converted to war work. The military commissioned new factories, port facilities, supply depots and airports, most of them colossal. The world's largest aircraft plant, the Dodge engine factory in Chicago, designed by Albert Kahn and constructed by the George Fuller Company (1943), had an area of 600,000 square metres, almost half as much floor space as the entire industry in 1940.[47] As plants grew exponentially larger, engineers calibrated the fabrication of tanks and bombers down to the square centimetre of space. The Austin Company, famous for its industrial buildings, designed and built 'blackout' factories with 'breathable' walls and luminous surfaces that could function on minimal electric light.

With several billion dollars allocated to scientific research, universities and industrial consortiums built sophisticated laboratories to study radar, rocketry and jet propulsion. New synthetics replaced critical *matériel* like steel, aluminium and rubber, leading *Newsweek* to proclaim a 'New Era in Plastics' in 1943.[48] Sponsored-research laboratories at the Dow and DuPont chemical companies invented fibreglass, styrofoam foam cores and clear acrylics for pressure-sealed aircraft radomes. New resins made plywood more durable, while laminated-timber columns and trusses extended across astounding distances. Navy airship hangars used prefabricated wooden arches to break previous records for timber spans. Since wartime culture 'made do' with scarce resources, recycled debris became Homasote, a wallboard of wood pulp and ground newspaper bound with resin.

The Navy Seabees included more than a thousand architects. (The word *Seabees* spells out the acronym for their official name, *Construction Battalions*). They designed ingenious systems and unique structures that made a virtue of necessity by improvising with the materials at hand. Quonset huts represent a similar team effort, created by a team of Navy architects in just one month, April 1941, at Quonset Point

Austin Company, climate-controlled Consolidated-Vulvee Aircraft 'Blackout' Plant, Fort Worth, Texas, 1942, partial view of interior.

Naval Air Station in Rhode Island. Made of lightweight corrugated steel, Quonsets were stackable, easy to assemble and highly adaptable. More than 170,000 were produced in over 80 different plans and sizes during the war, for use as hospitals, hangars, housing and storage units around the world. Even the earliest schemes featured insulation layers and connecting units.

The Quonset hut's success can be attributed in part to its corporate producers. George Fuller, a leading Chicago contractor, initiated the process, while Stran-Steel was a well-known manufacturer. Buckminster Fuller invented something remarkably similar in 1941, the Dymaxion Deployment Unit, a minimal mobile dwelling that went on display at MOMA. A few hundred were produced before restrictions on sheet steel were imposed. Quonsets were even more versatile, however, especially in the hands of imaginative designers. Bruce Goff joined the Seabees and used them extensively, most famously to renovate and build new structures at Camp Parks, a Seabee base near San Francisco, in 1944. The Seabee Chapel combined two 'elephant huts' with masonry walls and surplus or scavenged

Bruce Goff, Seabee
Chapel, Camp Parks,
California, 1945.

materials.[49] 'Any materials were fair, old or new,' he explained; 'we had to
reevaluate them to use them in ways that seem fresh and valid'.[50]

Some 9 million people moved to the booming coastal cities and new
war-towns to help the war effort. Desperate to meet the housing needs
of defence workers, Washington passed the Lanham Act giving lucrative
subsidies to private developers. The leaders formed a lobby, the National
Association of Home Builders (NAHB), and restructured their mode of
operations. By 1942 the private sector had built nearly a million
dwellings, 80 per cent of the wartime total. Mass production and prefabrication facilitated fast-track schedules for barracks, trailers,
demountable units and permanent housing. (The NAHB insisted this
housing had to be taken off the market, either demolished or sold after
the war ended.) Gunnison's conveyor belts led to the firm's slogan 'Press
a Button, and You Get a Home'. Henry Kaiser's Aluminum Company
used factory-based systems to create plants and housing for 45,000 ship-
yard workers and their families, including the 'miracle city' of Vanport,
Oregon, soon known as Kaiserville. William Levitt adopted labour-
saving on-site techniques from southern California developers to
build 750 naval officers' homes at Oakdale Farms in Norfolk, Virginia,
which became the prototype for Levittown in 1947, the low-cost,
mass-produced housing project that epitomized post-war suburbia.[51]

A third of these defence workers were women – known generically as
Rosie the Riveter – which raised questions about the relations between
home and work, especially since three-quarters of them were married.

Although women with young children were encouraged to stay at home, Kaiser provided 24-hour daycare services staffed by experts, and 3,000 such centres were constructed around the country.[52] Pietro Belluschi's McLoughlin Heights in Washington state put daycare in an arcaded shopping centre around a pedestrian green, an amenity lauded in the press as a new kind of community centre. But most defence towns adopted FHA standards for 'planned communities' with limited social services. As large numbers of African-Americans migrated from the South seeking factory work, racial segregation became more entrenched, and 'incursions' led to riots in several cities. When American local governments looked ahead to a new phase of growth, most of them took these self-contained, segregated satellite communities as the prototype for post-war suburbia and urban redevelopment.

Once again, some notable alternatives merit close attention. Herbert Whittemore, director of the Division of Defense Housing, hired a number of prominent modern architects. Indeed, he specifically called for 'Unusual materials, designs, and methods of fabrication not used in normal times'.[53] A small British pamphlet, 'Homes by the Million', praised the results, proof that standardization did not have to be monotonous, that site plans were as important as architecture.[54] Construction technologies and site plans received far more attention than social services in all these projects. Antonin Raymond called for 'small laboratories of housing with the architects as chief scientists', such as his project at Bethlehem, Pennsylvania.[55] Neutra's Channel Heights near Los Angeles arranged four different house types in a bold abstract pattern, making an asset of the rugged terrain cut by a deep ravine. Gropius's and Breuer's Aluminum City Terrace in New Kensington, Pennsylvania, softened prefab units by adding wood siding and following the contours of difficult terrain. William Wurster produced 1,700 demountable houses at Carquenez Heights at the Vallejo shipyards north of San Francisco in a record 73 days, half the units in plywood, the other half in Homasote. Ever the pragmatist, Wurster insisted on experimentation along with results, convincing the government to allocate 25 units for him to try other methods – skeleton frame, bentwood frame, masonry walls – each of which proved less expensive than conventional modular systems.[56]

Inspired low-cost housing was important to Louis Kahn, who formed a partnership with George Howe in Philadelphia to complete five war-housing projects. Oskar Stonorov often joined them, and Catherine Bauer's 'office' occupied a corner of the collective workspace. Their most ingenious and well-publicized design was Carver Court, a 100-unit township for African-American steelworkers near Lancaster, Pennsylvania (1944). Here Kahn first articulated what he called 'Essential

Kahn, Howe &
Stonorov, Carver
Court housing for
African-American
defence workers,
Coatesville,
Pennsylvania, 1944,
community centre
(left) and housing.

Space', a concept and formal expression he would sustain until his death. The initial drawings and the term *ground-free* alluded to Le Corbusier's *pilotis*, but Kahn's scheme anticipated changes. Bold concrete forms raised the living areas off the ground plane to provide spaces that residents could use for the rituals of their ordinary lives – protecting a car perhaps, or enclosing a play area or an extra room. A handsome community centre was another essential, a simple yet unmistakable 'social monument' to forge collective identity.[57]

Wars often initiate specialized environments for destruction. The Army sent the émigré architects Antonin Raymond, Konrad Wachsman and Erich Mendelsohn to Dougway, Utah, to create replicas of typical Japanese and German villages for incendiary bomb tests. Far more potent was the vast, once-secret world of the Manhattan Engineer District (MED), which oversaw atomic weapons at four locations eventually known as Hanford, Washington; Oak Ridge, Tennessee; Los Alamos, New Mexico; and Alamagordo, New Mexico, where the first atomic-weapon bomb was tested.

Plans for Oak Ridge came first and grew most quickly, despite utmost secrecy. The choice of a fledgling architecture firm, Skidmore, Owings &

Merrill, with only 25 employees, shows the military's strategic decision-making and the long-term implications. Louis Skidmore and Nathaniel Owings founded a partnership in 1936, then worked on the New York World's Fair of 1939 with John Merrill. They affiliated with the Pierce Foundation to produce a prefabricated Experimental House, which became the basis for 600 new dwellings at Albert Kahn's Glenn L. Martin Aircraft Factory outside Baltimore in 1941. Plans for Oak Ridge began in June 1942, but six months later MED officials expressed frustration that the initial firm lacked any 'originality or modern innovations'.[58] A secret committee contracted the Pierce Foundation and its architects. Only when hostilities ended would the world learn about the 75,000 people who lived and worked in Oak Ridge, with every building designed and supervised in secret by the 650 employees of a firm that now called itself SOM, an acronym first used in 1949.

There was nothing architecturally significant about Oak Ridge, but the architects' teamwork and all-encompassing organization impressed both government and corporate leaders. As Ambrose Richardson, an

Skidmore, Owings & Merrill, K-25 gaseous diffusion plant for U-235 bomb material, Oak Ridge, Tennessee, 1944.

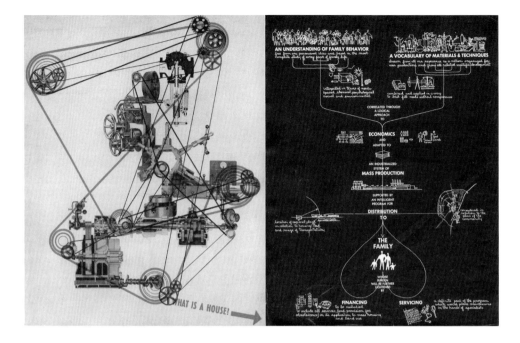

SOM architect, later explained: 'We were no longer the starry-eyed young designers who wanted to rebuild the world in the Le Corbusier, Mies mold. We did still seek that, tempered by the pragmatism born of an extraordinary, immediate need. We matured a lot.'[59]

Progress had been the goal for New Deal and wartime architects, defined by an amalgam of rigour and risk-taking. Roland Wank put it clearly in 1941: 'We seek fulfillment in action.'[60] As concerns shifted from Social Security to national security, government agencies increased the scale, cost and complexity of their endeavours across the country and then around the world. Modern ambitions resided in the chillingly beautiful factories, the vast house-building industry, the scientific-research organizations, the planned leisure activities. The integrated networks of institutions and companies that made key decisions during the war would then commission the most significant post-war architecture. The media baron Henry Luce recognized this when he used his editorial page in *Life* to proclaim the war as the dawn of the 'great American century'.[61]

As always, there were alternative voices in politics, intellectual life, the arts and in architecture. The most vivid came from the two coasts. The drawings of Charles and Ray Eames captured their enthusiasm about wartime knowledge. Ray's covers for *Arts & Architecture* in the 1940s used vivid abstract shapes to encourage open-ended interpretations. Citing Buckminster Fuller, Charles emphasized that 'the miracle of industry in war would revolutionize the peacetime world', especially in much-needed new housing. The sterile parameters of functionalism had to give way to more personal, sometimes even ephemeral concepts of human 'needs'.[62] Both of the Eameses anticipated a more cohesive yet still joyful and individualized national agenda.

The Museum of Modern Art synthesized the varied ideas and ambitions of the New Deal and the war years with a series of exhibitions under Elizabeth Mock. Also Catherine Bauer's sister, Mock served as acting director of Architecture from 1941 until Philip Johnson ousted her in 1945. Her popular 1944 exhibition and catalogue, *Built in USA since 1932*, provided a 'creative synthesis' of overlapping currents during that remarkable decade. The title suggests both a sequel and an antidote to the famous International Style exhibition of 1932. Mock's show celebrated the TVA, the FSA, Dunsmuir Flats, Johnson Wax, several Usonian houses, Taliesin West, New York's Municipal Asphalt Plant, the Crow Island School, Carver Court and many of the buildings discussed in this chapter. Her brief text spoke eloquently about the need for 'humanizing' modern architecture, embracing the challenges of science and industry without neglecting those of environmentalism, emotions and community life. Those themes are again resonant today.[63]

chapter five

The Triumph of Modernism, 1946–1964

Americans felt justly proud when their decisive role in World War Two catapulted the nation to superpower status. Immediate post-war realities were difficult, however, with the country plagued for several years by severe inflation, housing shortages and job scarcities. The 'GI Bill of Rights' promised generous education, health and housing benefits for 11 million returning veterans, but facilities were sorely lacking. The horrors and deprivations of the war made a safe middle ground seem especially appealing. Commentators touted social and political consensus – what Arthur Schlesinger, Jr, called 'the vital center' in 1949 – as the basis for a fundamental national character, an American Exceptionalism. The ascendancy of modern architecture became a central tenet of this accord throughout the country and the world.

All sorts of angst underlay the 'nifty fifties'. A cheerful outlook was always shadowed by the risk of failure, falling from grace by having made the wrong choice. With the first references to the Cold War in 1948, the government initiated a military and propaganda campaign of preparedness. Officials promised protection in underground bomb shelters and curvilinear architectural surfaces that supposedly deflected radioactive fallout. Senator Joseph McCarthy's virulent attacks on supposed Communist infiltration made any criticism seem potentially dangerous. Competition between companies, cities and neighbours was all the more intense for being discreetly hidden. The transparency of curtain walls and picture-windows could not assuage ever-present fears about contamination, subterfuge, spies and secret lives.

Architecture did not escape the ferocity of these tensions. Lewis Mumford's 1947 essay 'The Bay Area' in the *New Yorker* attacked the International Style as placeless and inhumane, then extolled an alternative Modernism, a 'free yet unobtrusive expression of the terrain, the climate, and the way of life'. His title clearly referred to northern California, past and present, although Mumford resisted provincialism, lauding similar predilections from Latin America to New England. Philip Johnson, once again MOMA's Curator of Architecture, quickly counter-

I. M. Pei, Alcoa's Washington Plaza Apartments, Pittsburgh, Pennsylvania, 1964, view from a 'blighted' neighbourhood, from *Fortune* magazine (October 1964).

attacked, staging a 1948 symposium with an alarmist title: 'What Is Happening to Modern Architecture?' Even a sensitive designer like Marcel Breuer mocked Mumford's appeal to humanism. 'If "human" is considered identical with redwood all over the place or with imperfection and imprecision,' he sneered, 'then I am against it.'[1] The vituperative tone and aftermath of this event forced the discipline into polarized camps, contemptuous and soon ignorant of each other: East Coast versus West, universalism versus regionalism, radical avant-garde innovations versus adaptive pragmatist experiments.

As if to finalize the break, a 1952 MOMA exhibition, *Built in USA*, acclaimed pristine office buildings, elegant apartment buildings and suburban dwellings along with one glass-walled industrial structure in Texas in deference to the 1920s European Modern Movement. Curators Arthur Drexler and Henry-Russell Hitchcock proclaimed that the 'quality and significance' of post-war American architecture was 'more nationally standardized – in a good sense' and also 'more luxurious – and not to balk at a word – beautiful'.[2] To buttress the implied comparison they appropriated the title from Elizabeth Mock's 1944 show, thereby erasing its legacy of popular, multifaceted Modernisms.

Modern art was central to the post-war commercial world and to intellectual resistance against the pervasive influence of 'mass culture', typically attacked as a form of totalitarianism. The avant-garde saw themselves as outsiders to an establishment that often cultivated them as it explored a wide range of aesthetics. Clement Greenberg's 'Avant-Garde and Kitsch' became a mantra, affirming the intellectual difficulty of 'genuine art' by heroic individuals whose rigorous formalism probed the distinctive medium of their art, whether painting or architecture. 'The essence of Modernism,' he told a Voice of America audience, lay 'in the use of characteristic methods of a discipline to criticize the discipline itself.'[3] Critics like Dwight McDonald condemned all aspects of 'middlebrow' or 'midcult' taste. Television soon extended the pervasive and seemingly pernicious realm of popular culture to a mass audience. Whereas only 5 per cent of households had televisions in 1950, this escalated to almost 90 per cent by the end of the decade. To artists and intellectuals, the built environments and social worlds on the screen seemed unspeakably vulgar.

President Harry S. Truman's Council of Economic Advisers assured the nation of permanent prosperity so long as American capitalism experienced continuous growth, regulated by fine-tuned governmental interventions. Government agencies helped the private sector expand dramatically, especially producers of building materials and the real-estate industry. The gross national product soared 250 per cent between

1945 and 1960, while expenditures on new construction multiplied nine-fold. A prescient 1947 article by Hitchcock dared to suggest that 'the Architecture of Bureaucracy' in large, anonymous firms might be appropriate for most needs in post-war society. He acknowledged the usefulness of an 'Architecture of Genius' for monumental structures, but warned of 'pretentious absurdity'.[4]

In principle, all Americans were middle class or almost there. The unprecedented affluence of the 1950s created the world's first mass middle class, roughly half the population by most indicators, with race a major factor in the split. Real incomes rose for most socio-economic groups, as did home ownership, while the advent of credit cards and new consumer goods provided a bounty of comforts known as 'the good life'. 'Fitting in' was a prime goal, and most groups ostracized those who did not abide by their norms. In many ways the country was more democratic than at any time in its history, but also more materialistic and intensely conscious about status. C. Wright Mills's *White Collar* (1951) described businessmen assuming the trappings of professionals, including their titles, claims of highly specialized knowledge, and assertions of public interest. Professionals, including architects, became even more concerned about their own authority and prestige. Modern architecture was a cornerstone of these ambitions, whether in civic facilities, office buildings or houses. Vance Packard's *The Status Seekers* (1959) compared blue-collar suspicions of Modernism with its 'snob-appeal' for those with aspirations. 'Eggheads have enough self-assurance so that they can defy convention', he contended, 'and they often cherish the simplicity of open lay-out.'[5]

Businessmen and politicians saw the modern metropolis in terms of orderly development and deplored the dynamic, disorderly world of city streets. Urban renewal – a generic term taken from 1954 federal legislation – remains the most controversial aspect of post-war American growth. The 1949 Housing and Urban Redevelopment Act joined federal and local governments to 'modernize' downtowns and boost property values by clearing blighted properties to create large parcels that would attract investors. As experts looked for problems they could 'solve', they fixated on recent African-American migration to major cities, which increased dramatically during the 1940s and '50s with the decline of Southern sharecropping. A major tax liability, this demographic shift also fuelled 'white flight' to the suburbs. Title 1 of the 1949 Act gave re-development agencies two-thirds of the funds to eradicate blighted areas. Only 20 per cent of a designated area had to be declared 'blighted' for the entirety to be demolished.

Urban renewal dispossessed more than 400,000 families between 1949 and 1967, federally aided urban highways an additional 330,000. The writer James Baldwin called this 'Negro removal', although small-scale commerce and homes in stable white ethnic neighbourhoods also fell to the bulldozers. Low-income African-Americans lost the equivalent of one of every five homes. Replacement or public housing provided for less than one half of 1 per cent of those displaced. White ethnics scattered fairly widely, although many experienced a sense of 'grief' as they were cut off from the ties of family and friends, but racial segregation limited options for African-Americans, which in turn increased rents and over-crowding. Black ghettos and all-white suburbs became far more permanent and pervasive features of American life, what one Soul song called 'a chocolate city with vanilla suburbs', although there were some all-black suburbs.[6]

The results transformed American cities almost as radically as their bombed-out counterparts in Europe and Japan. New building sought to keep or lure wealthy residents and increase urban tax bases. Construction standards in Title 1 housing for middle-class tenants were notoriously shoddy and favoured small units, making them unsuitable for families with children. Luxury apartments and corporate office towers predominated, along with convention centres, stadia and tourist mon-uments like the St Louis Arch (1947–66). Pittsburgh's Gateway Center by Otto Eggert and Daniel Higgins was the nation's first completed redevel-opment (1948–53). Mayor David Lawrence then appointed himself head of the Redevelopment Agency and continued major projects. The 1954 Urban Renewal Act encouraged cities to combine historic preservation with large-scale new building. Almost 1,600 urban-renewal projects would be in place by 1965. Highly visible examples include Denver's Mile High Center (1952–60), Philadelphia's Penn Center and Society Hill (1955–64), San Francisco's Golden Gateway and Embarcadero Center (1957–67) and Boston's Prudential Center and Government Center (1960–68). By 1960 *Fortune* magazine could proclaim a revised model of the American city as 'a control tower'.[7]

Scientific and social-scientific discourse helped legitimate architects' desire for leadership, especially in urban transformations. MIT's Norbert Wiener, author of *Cybernetics* (1948), extrapolated from the 'feedback' conditions of new information-processing machines. Harvard's Walter Gropius favoured the social sciences, cellular biology and nuclear physics. The main result was analogies about social cohesion, organic growth and dynamic power in architecture. The Social Science Research Council sponsored a conference in 1951 about these trends, but quickly withdrew from the topic in frustration about the vague methods. This did not curtail architects' enthusiasm.[8] References to quantitative surveys generated vague norms about the 'typical office' or 'average family'. Facile

Elaine de Kooning in the de Koonings' Soho loft, New York City, c. 1958.

'liveability' studies evoked psychoanalytic theories and sociological data to prove the potent effects of home environments.

The familiar story of post-war Modernism gives the illusion of a common purpose which has obscured significant experiments and variations in all the arts, including the peripheries of architecture. Some were created by inspired 'outsiders'. Simon Rodia completed Watts Towers in Los Angeles in 1954 after 33 years of inspired, ad hoc construction. Elusive 'underground' artists transgressed boundaries, while small journals explored broad cultural terrains. The Walker Art Gallery in Minneapolis created the *Everyday Art Quarterly* (renamed *Design Quarterly* in 1951). J. B. Jackson's *Landscape* explored 'new architectural forms' in the 'ordinary realm', including builders' houses and drive-in restaurants. The first semi-programmed, mixed-media 'happenings' and live electronic music were staged; bebop dissonance spurred virtuoso riffs; and painters incorporated tattered fragments of mass culture. New York artists unintentionally suggested a new approach to space, beauty and time when they began to transform industrial lofts into live/work spaces in the late 1950s. Faced with abandoned buildings when industries moved out of the city, landlords were willing to rent cheaply, if illegally. The artists honed necessity into an aesthetic, transmuting the gritty open spaces of industrial modernity into a harbinger of future trends in design. Within a decade, these aesthetic principles would play a visible role in architecture, and three decades later in real estate.

Corporate Modernism

Post-war finance and business launched a 'systems' revolution. The economist and management consultant Peter Drucker led the charge with his influential book *The Concept of the Corporation* (1946). Transferring military strategies to private business, he hailed a rational model of centralized management and decentralized operations, each entity a holistic 'social institution'. In principle, both individuals and units would identify themselves as interchangeable parts in a corporation's large-scale, standardized yet more flexible system. Financial and marketing specialists calculated tactics for continual growth, in part through 'planned obsolescence' – a term coined in 1954, although the basic principle had emerged in the 1920s. A parallel set of human-relations experts sought to build employee morale and company loyalty. Prestigious architecture firms synthesized these goals with new kinds of office buildings based on the subtle distinctions of a statistical Sublime. Large architect-engineering-construction companies built generic modern structures with higher capacities and more 'flexible space' – converting a wartime idea to peacetime prosperity.

Skidmore Owings &
Merrill (Natalie de
Blois and Gordon
Bunshaft, principal
designers), Union
Carbide Building, New
York City, 1960,
typical office interior.

Interior spaces helped reorganize the day-to-day world of advanced capitalism after World War Two. Modern paintings and sculpture adorned the transparent ground-floor lobbies, suggesting lofty principles. Isamu Noguchi created biomorphic lobby ceilings for two of Harris Armstrong's 1947–8 corporate headquarters in St Louis, although most lobbies were self-consciously understated. Noguchi and other modern sculptors soon collaborated with architects to design outdoor plazas for major corporate clients. Art served to humanize business calculations. Office floors were much larger in the raw space of their footprints and the 'modular coordination' of perfectly uniform arrangements. Designers replicated the physiognomy of the exterior building modules, subdividing internal grids with lightweight standardized office partitions, visible signs of order and flexibility – even if changes were rare. Control extended to micro-grids of luminous ceiling panels and sealed windows to ensure a uniform temperature with central air conditioning. The furniture designer Florence Knoll collaborated with major architects to provide evidence of good taste and orderly employee diligence for elite corporations. A new profession called 'space planning' helped balance strong public image with efficiency in ordinary offices.

Architects mostly obsessed about façades, especially the transparent curtain wall, a thin, non-load-bearing cladding 'hung' on the structural frame. The term honed Modernism's focus on surface or skin, combining visible transparency with the minimalist elegance of construction details. Executives shared architects' beliefs that impeccably coordinated building systems communicated directly to employees and the public. The building committee for the Inland Steel headquarters in Chicago spoke of investing in a 'unique institutional identification', or corporate image; its chairman compared the façade to 'a man with immaculate English tailoring'.[9]

Pietro Belluschi, Equitable Building, Portland, Oregon, 1944–8 (today the Commonwealth Building), main street façade.

Two precedents were clear at the time: Mies van der Rohe's unbuilt Berlin project for a glass skyscraper (1921–2) and Pietro Belluschi's Equitable Insurance Company Building in Portland, Oregon (1944–8). Belluschi had first conceived the latter project for *Architectural Forum*'s 1943 series, 'New Buildings for 194x', so he was ready when a pre-war client approached him the next year for an office building. Sheathed in thin war-surplus aluminium, the Equitable rose all of twelve storeys, but its concrete frame and aluminium spandrels were virtually flush. Slender ground-level piers clad in pinkish marble maintained the street wall and a protected walking corridor for pedestrians. The absence of parking revealed pre-war origins, but the interiors were decidedly up-to-date with open floor plans and exacting climate controls. The immense glass windows were tinted, insulated and sealed, washed by an ingenious system suspended from the roof (soon a standard device around the country). Initially greeted with resounding praise, the Equitable's provincial location then hid it from view until a restoration in 1988 as the Commonwealth Building reaffirmed its significance as the first all-glass office tower.

Curtain walls and open, grid-based interiors became trademarks of Skidmore Owings and Merrill (SOM) and New York's Lever House (1949–52) assured their reputation for prestigious corporate statements. The structure comprised two gleaming asymmetrical frames: one hovers, a horizontal two-storey plane traversing the site; the other ascends 24 storeys. Gordon Bunshaft, chief designer in the New York office, convinced the client to create magnanimous public spaces, a broad 'plaza' under the *piloti* supports and an exhibition area in the tower's glass-enclosed lobby. A provision in the municipal zoning regulations permitted towers with small footprints to rise as sheer volumes without the setbacks required of 1920s skyscrapers. Bunshaft also understood architectural symbolism: the transparent façades celebrated cleanliness for a producer of soaps; lightly green-tinted glass reduced glare; spandrel glass between floors made the building seem to float unobtrusively. Its immediate success solidified the shift of New York's business and finance from Lower Manhattan to Midtown that had begun during the 1920s, while glass revolutionized a district defined by limestone.

SOM soon acquired four regional offices and high-status international commissions. Each office balanced collective anonymity with talented individuals. Natalie de Blois was another chief designer in the New York office, bringing an incandescent lightness to the Union Carbide and the Pepsi-Cola buildings (both 1958–60). Walter Netsch provided the schematics for the Crown-Zellerbach Building in San Francisco (completed by Chuck Basset in 1959) and then moved to Chicago. Netsch's Inland Steel (1954–8) gave prominence to gleaming steel columns rising the full height of the façade and clearly differentiated internal functions with a set-back windowless box for elevators, stairs and the HVAC system. *Fortune* contended that 'SOM took Mies's stainless-steel standard, warmed it up and sold it as a prestige package to the US businessman.'[10]

For most architects nothing surpasses New York's exquisite Seagram Building on Park Avenue, diagonally across the street from Lever House. Another narrative of redemption helped build its mythic status. Samuel Bronfman, president of the corporation, an international whisky-distribution company, announced a grand new building to celebrate its centennial in 1954 and selected an architect. His daughter, Phyllis Lambert, convinced him of the need for higher aspirations. Mies van der Rohe seemed the pivotal figure who was creating a 'grammar' and a 'poetry' for modern architecture. 'You might think this austere strength, this ugly beauty, is terribly severe', Lambert explained. 'It is, and yet all the

more beauty in it.'[11] Assertive individual interventions seem a leitmotif in American corporate Modernism.

Completed in 1958, the Seagram Building reduced modern architectural form to its simplest, most perfect elements. Clad in sumptuous travertine and topaz-tinted glass, this sleek box redefined the slab. A double-height glass entry lightened the massive structure. A grid of bronze I-beams is welded to the curtain wall at close intervals to evoke the ideal of structural expression. As with Lever House, the public space transmuted zoning regulations to permit a perfect rectangular volume and extended a grand gesture of *noblesse oblige*. The granite-paved plaza occupies 48 per cent of the site, raised on a plinth, if only two steps off the sidewalk. This grand forecourt distances the 38-storey tower from the street. The interiors are finished with exacting attention and opulent materials. Every aspect of the building is faultless and therefore neutral, leading to frequent comparisons with a Greek temple. Lewis Mumford considered the Seagram Building the 'Rolls Royce' of contemporary buildings, while Manfredo Tafuri spoke of its 'aloof' character, 'tragically . . . self-aware' of its superiority.[12]

The quality of Mies's building encouraged architects to believe that singular artworks allowed them to operate within a commercialized world, uncontaminated by commercial influences. Critical analysis focused on nuances of intellectual and formal rigour. Colin Rowe's 1956 essay, 'Chicago Frame', sought to distinguish unique works of art by master architects from the standardized veneers of buildings by commercial architects. Yet the inevitability of inexpensive copies raised a critical dilemma, given modern architecture's inherent drive towards replication. Every society confronts differences in economic leverage and technical skills. Rather than simply deploring inevitable copying, how can modern architects help improve urban streetscapes?

Many companies moved their headquarters to suburban locations where inexpensive land facilitated rambling low-rise facilities and easy expansion. Most industrial or business parks of the 1950s were haphazard groupings of bland structures with insipid landscapes, but some corporate 'campuses' were impeccably elegant. The General Motors Technical Center outside Detroit, commissioned in 1945, set a high standard even as it drew on the audacity of popular culture. Having overtaken Ford as the industry leader, GM's chairman, Alfred P. Sloan, Jr, took up Drucker's corporate programme of centralized policy-making and decentralized operations. Recognizing the pent-up demand for exciting new automobiles, he added vibrant stylistic imagery to the package, appointing GM's chief stylist, Harley J. Earl, as the first Vice-President of Design of any corporation. Earl initiated a series of remarkable changes, not just tail fins

Mies van der Rohe and Philip Johnson, Seagram Building, New York City, 1954–8.

and two-tone paint, but the annual model change, which he called 'dynamic obsolescence': the creation of desire for the latest styling.

Although Eliel and Eero Saarinen's design for the GM Center began as a joint project, Eero took over after his father's death in 1950. His appearance on a 1952 *Time* cover celebrated the Center's rigorous engineering, especially the early curtain-wall sections and the 1.5-metre modular system. Thomas Church's landscape design accentuated the ordered horizontality of the composition, offset by a tall, elliptical water tower and a sleek, low dome for Earl's exhibition extravaganzas. Building mock-ups allowed for systematic development, replacing the hagiographic ideal of aloof genius with models of collaboration and feedback. Eleven vibrant colours of glazed ceramic-brick walls distinguished various research functions, carried through to details, furnishings, even the colour of push-pins inside each building. Eero soon delved into American car culture with Neoprene gaskets and sleek glass, all specially produced by GM. He paid homage to Earl's famous spokes and tail fins in the main public lobby. Some custodians of high culture sneered at Saarinen's 'immoral' styling as an assault on the dignity of 'true' Modernism. He seemed too comfortable with big businessmen, his designs too appealing to the popular press. When the GM complex opened in 1956, *Life* called it a 'Versailles of Industry'.[13]

Office buildings were often staid glass boxes, but sometimes startling. Suppliers encouraged adventurous applications to promote their

products: Harrison & Abramowitz glorified one material at the Corning
Glass Center in New York in 1951, another in the Alcoa Aluminum
Company offices in Davenport, Iowa, and in the clip-on diamond-
faceted panels of the company's Pittsburgh headquarters in 1953. A court
ruling that aluminium, the first man-made metal, had to allow competition prompted the rival companies to commission audacious new
corporate structures and scores of other uses from parking garages to
housing. One of the most surprising is surely Minoru Yamasaki's 'architecture of delight' with gold-anodized aluminium screens on the
Reynolds Metals Regional Office in Detroit in 1961.

Exuberant vivacity was more common outside the East Coast. Even
banks, usually quite sedate, invested in eye-catching architecture. Three
Oklahoma City banks are still surprising. The eponymous Gold Dome
(1958), the undulating concrete shells of the drive-through facilities at
Central National Bank (1960), and the State Capitol Bank (1963), known
locally as the 'flying saucer bank' and often featured in the national
media, were all designed by the hometown firm of Roloff, Bailey, Bozalis,
Dickinson. Enrique Gutierrez's Bacardi USA (1963) in Miami translated
Mies's Seagram Building into a Latin idiom, decorating two walls with
resplendent murals in glazed-ceramic tiles from Spain. Commercial
architecture in Miami seemed to dance as the strong relief on its façades
(today known as Mi-Mo) accentuated colour, texture, shadows and other
sensual delights.

Roloff, Bailey,
Bozalis, Dickinson,
State Capitol Bank,
Oklahoma City,
Oklahoma, 1963.

The physics historian Peter Galison has highlighted the emergence of 'Big Science', typically dispersed away from major cities, during the post-war era. Post-war federal agencies funded scientific research and facilities in every field from atomic energy to zoology. The National Science Foundation, created in 1950, would see its influence soar after the Russians launched Sputnik in 1957. Large generic buildings proliferated for major chemical companies, pharmaceuticals, the energy industry and aeronautics during the Cold War. Galison links these spatial practices with modern art and architecture, as well as with the emergence of the 'military-industrial complex', a term first used in President (former General) Dwight Eisenhower's 1961 farewell speech to the nation.[14] Modern architecture was closely linked to defence contracts as well as to corporate power.

Silicon Valley emerged in the farmland between San Francisco and San José just after World War Two. Stanford University Vice-President Fred Terman established the Stanford Industrial Park in 1946 to encourage industry collaboration in high-tech research. Hewlett-Packard joined immediately since Terman had helped his former graduate students Hewlett and Packard set up a workspace in a Palo Alto garage in 1938 – now revered as a national landmark. The site was soon given a more stately name: Stanford Research Center. The landscape architect Thomas Church designed the 265-hectare site plan, while Terman himself established regulations about informal low-rise buildings and helped choose architects. Some were major figures, notably Erich Mendelsohn, who designed the headquarters for Varian Associates, and John Warnecke, who designed General Electric's microwave division. A similar, if less cohesive approach, took hold elsewhere, most conspicuously along Route 128 outside Boston, Massachusetts.

The embryonic information-technology industry sometimes sponsored notable modern architecture. O'Neil Ford, the architect of the
Texas Instruments Semiconductor Building in Richardson, Texas
(1956–8), invited the Mexican architect-engineer Felix Candela to collaborate on the hyperbolic paraboloid shapes supported by pre-cast
concrete tetrapods. Recognizing that this emerging industry required
continuous technology upgrades, Ford created the first full interstitial
floor between working floors. To encourage employees' collaboration, he
accentuated landscaped areas and hand-crafted wooden screens in
abstract patterns, both integral to his Modernism.

Meanwhile IBM's Thomas Watson, Jr, began a complete makeover
geared to computers in 1952. Watson hired Eliot Noyes to oversee the sleek
'new look' that encompassed product design, flexible 'horizontal' management and architecture: 150 plants, laboratories and office buildings
throughout the world in the succeeding fifteen years.[15] Noyes gave Eero
Saarinen several important commissions, notably the Watson Research
Center (1957–61) in Yorktown Heights, New York, an enormous arc – 300
metres long, 45 metres wide and three storeys high – with sleek glass prom-
enades on the front and rear, echoed by interior corridors. Saarinen kept the
sight lines under 30 metres to avoid vertigo. Saarinen also designed a
research structure for Bell Laboratories (1957–62) in Holmdel, New Jersey,
using dark mirrored glass to reduce heat gain, ensure security and provide
another signature façade. Such distinctive architecture has now set preservationists against the companies as they seek to replace their outdated
research buildings.

Healthcare followed a similar pattern. The National Institute of Health
sponsored multi-purpose hospitals for veterans while an emergent corporate medicine combined federal research funds with private-sector profits.

O'Neil Ford, Texas
Instruments
Semiconductor
Building, Richardson,
Texas, 1956–8, con-
struction photograph.

Louis I. Kahn, Salk Institute for Biological Studies, La Jolla, California, 1959–65, view of studies and courtyard.

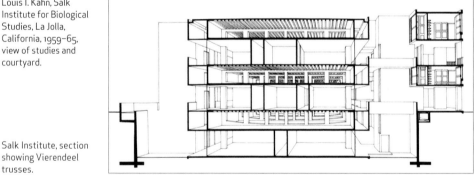

Salk Institute, section showing Vierendeel trusses.

The Texas Medical Center in Houston became world-famous when its 1947 campus added nine specialized hospitals in the succeeding six years, along with adjacent education and medical-office buildings. The centrepiece, the M. D. Anderson Cancer Center (1951–4) by MacKie & Kamrath, set new standards for oncological surgery, treatment, research and teaching. In the words of *Architectural Forum*, the building synthesized 'a complex industrial plant' with Wrightian 'organic architecture'.[16] The multi-level integration of landscapes added visual richness and therapeutic calm.

If Houston provided the model for recombinant expansion, Louis Kahn created two architectural monuments for medical research with two laboratory settings. The Richards Medical Research Building

(1957–61) at the University of Pennsylvania in Philadelphia replaced impersonal corridors with clusters of small labs in three eight-storey towers. Kahn's humanistic systems analysis differentiated 'served' spaces for human work from 'servant' spaces for mechanical equipment, relegated to a fourth tower, although some scientists complained that symbolism trumped functionalism. Kahn's Salk Institute for Biological Studies (1959–65) in La Jolla, California, took these ideas about order to a transcendent plane. A thin channel of water slices the spare central court, leading towards the Pacific and seemingly towards infinity. Two rows of four-storey concrete towers, open at ground level and angled for views of the sea, contain private studies and collective labs. Full interstitial service floors of pre-stressed Vierendeel trusses afford seismic support. Cloistered bridges, staircases and courtyards link the workplaces with chalkboards set into the walls at the junctures to encourage impromptu exchanges. Unpainted teak panels have weathered to soft antique patinas. Kahn's attention to minute details evoked scientific precision. The fundamentals of biological research and architectural systems entered the realm of the Sublime.

'Good-life' Modernism

'Like them or not,' announced *Time* in 1949, 'modern houses are here to stay [with] practicality and sometimes spectacular good looks.'[17] New houses for all classes came fully equipped with status, individuality, high-tech amenities and the natural Sublime. It took some time, however. Five years after the armistice the Housing Act of 1949 finally generated a long-awaited surge. An astounding 2 million dwelling units went up in 1950, and a total of more than 13 million between 1950 and 1960 – 11 million of them in the suburbs, which grew six times faster than cities. The elusive promise of security in the suburbs drove private emotions and public policy. Washington endorsed suburban decentralization as protection against a Russian nuclear attack. Indirect federal subsidies included income-tax benefits and expanded mortgage programmes, each costing the government at least five times more than it spent on housing subsidies for the poor.

A formidable cultural apparatus promoted modern suburban houses. Art museums in New York, San Francisco and Minneapolis sponsored full-scale model homes for general audiences, as did popular magazines and television programmes. The houses varied, of course, given the national desire for individual expression, but Modernism triumphed, especially in systems of production and spatial organization. Structural components were highly visible. Wartime synthetics like acrylic skylights, durable laminates, sandwich panels and new kinds of plywood became standard. Advanced technologies for comfort included insulation (rare before World War Two), automatic heating, passive solar orientation – and then a rush to air conditioning in the early 1950s. Built-in facilities and storage walls provided for a conspicuous increase in consumer goods.

The flow of space emphasized 'zones' rather than rooms, in part to cope with reductions in size. A 'master bedroom' was separated from children's bedrooms, and two new spaces appeared, an outlying utility/laundry room and the 'family room' at the centre. First awkwardly called a 'don't-say-no' place for children and teenagers, it linked the open kitchen and outdoor patio. The architect-authors of *Tomorrow's House* and the editors of *Parents' Magazine* christened the newborn space almost simultaneously in 1946–7. Architecture magazines lavished attention on open living areas and attention-getting roofs, including alternatives to the flat roof, much-maligned for its orthodoxy and its tendency to leak, but gave little attention to site.[18] Shelter magazines like *House Beautiful* defined 'the American Style idea' in similar terms: honest use of simple materials, comfort not show, privacy and view,

Jones & Emmons for Eichler Homes, family room in a model house in Sunnyvale, California, 1955. First Award of Honor from the AIA and the National Association of Home Builders.

Richard Neutra,
Kaufmann House,
Palm Springs,
California, 1946–7.

indoors and outdoors 'perfectly integrated'. These articles also stressed more overtly political references to 'freedom of choice' and the 'drive for something better'.[19]

Two well-known modernists became popular heroes at this time. *House Beautiful* editor Elizabeth Gordon lauded Frank Lloyd Wright's 'greater principles' as emblematic of American values. *House and Home*'s article 'Frank Lloyd Wright and 1,000,000 Homes a Year' (1953) explained how speculative builders could adapt specific techniques to make small houses seem more commodious. Richard Neutra was equally well received, the evangelist of therapeutic houses that increased psychological and physiological well-being. A *Time* cover story from 1949 praised his ability to merge spaciousness with compactness, exemplified in the magnificent Kaufmann House in Palm Springs shown behind him in the cover photo. *Time* praised Neutra as a leader in the movement to 'humanize and domesticate' the International Style.[20] Each of his domestic landscapes was highly specific; the house plans stretched out lithely, often dematerializing into their surroundings, especially where

sliding glass doors opened onto heated terraces. Neutra explored gestalt psychology to affect illusions of infinite space. He also worked diligently on possible mass prototypes, seeking to convert consumerism into progressive environmental design – indeed into *Survival through Design*, the title of his well-received 1954 book.

Arts & Architecture's Case Study Program helped popularize modern houses for a limited audience. The editor John Entenza issued a call for innovation in January 1945, then marketed 36 model dwellings over the next eighteen years, hoping to stimulate cooperation with industries (notably in metals) and to influence speculative housing. House #8 (1945–9) by Charles and Ray Eames was an epiphany for architects around the world. The Eames House literally captured the post-war sense of open possibilities since it transformed an initial neo-Miesian scheme, its foundation already poured, into a serendipitous assemblage with off-the-shelf industrial components set in an exposed steel frame. Structural rigour joined with a joyful interplay of colour and light, seemingly impromptu yet carefully staged. The overlapping social spaces extended into small niches with designated bedroom and studio areas, providing a flexible live/work environment for this husband-and-wife team, a distinct contrast to the exaggerated gender roles that defined most houses. Yet even this remarkable prototype remained a one-off.[21]

Suburban mass housing went modern for many reasons, including scale. Whereas a typical builder might have put up five houses a year before the war, speculative builders now generated instant subdivisions with thousands of tract houses, mostly indistinguishable from one another, which soon accounted for 80 per cent of American production.[22] The phenomenon of mass builders cannot be isolated from modernist dreams of standardized mass production. Architecture magazines assured readers that Modernism could happily coexist with merchant builders and the American mass market. For several years they promoted collaborations, offering useful design advice and pleading for alternatives to what was already recognized as sprawl.[23]

Most builders simply bulldozed greenfield sites to make the terrain uniform, then mixed conventional post-and-beam construction with factory production to cut costs. Levitt & Sons converted a potato field in Long Island, New York, into the first Levittown between 1947 and 1951. By 1950 the company's offsite factory was producing one four-room house every sixteen minutes. Like GM, Levitt produced a new model every year with special 'built-in' features that quickly became commonplace for other builders. Behind the traditional façades were modern amenities: radiant-heated concrete slabs replaced basements; double-glazed sliding windows and doors that extended onto patios; three-way fireplaces that

provided a centrifugal focus for open plans – a device borrowed from
Frank Lloyd Wright. Modernism endorsed standardization, which
extended to homogeneity of class, race and religion as suburbs grew
increasingly segmented.[24]

Modern architects had a significant effect on some impressive, racially
integrated white-collar developments. In 1948 the developer Robert
Davenport hired Charles Goodman to craft an idyllic progressive suburb
outside Washington, DC. By 1952 Hollin Hills had almost 500 homes,
variations on Goodman's fourteen different models. The landscape
architect Dan Kiley maintained the existing topography, kept most of the
trees and avoided visible references to property lines. The AIA considered
it exemplary American design. The architecture critic Michael Sorkin,
who grew up in Hollin Hills, remembers it as 'one of the truly happy
experiments in modernity'.[25]

Joseph Eichler built some 12,000 California houses between 1949 and
1968, all resolutely modern, economical and still appealing. Anshen &
Allen designed early prototypes for subdivisions in the Bay Area. In 1951
Eichler turned to Quincy Jones, an innovative young architect in Los
Angeles, after both received *Architectural Forum* awards. Expanding into
the southern California market, Eichler commissioned prototypes from
Jones & Emmons, Raphael Soriano and Pietro Belluschi. Jones and
Eichler designed a Case Study neighbourhood project of 200 small eco-

logical houses in 1961, never built because of opposition to fees for the community services.

Several architects challenged normative models by insisting on purity, occasionally to the point of didactic all-glass houses. Mies's house for Dr Edith Farnsworth in Plano, Illinois (1945–51), exposed yet sealed off from the outside world, proved so expensive and frustrating that the client sued the architect unsuccessfully. Philip Johnson's 1949 Glass House copied Mies's with 'a form of exhibitionism' that launched his own career. It also helped breed some 80 flat-roofed 'Harvard boxes' near the staid town of New Canaan, Connecticut.[26]

Regional Modernism flourished from Oregon to Florida, engendering softer variants on the glass box. Igor Polivitzky's Bird-Cage House in Miami (1949) encased a glass-and-steel-frame dwelling in plastic screens, providing almost total integration with the environment. The Sarasota wunderkind Paul Rudolph took a slightly different path. His glass houses used wooden jalousies drawn from Southern vernacular traditions that allowed residents to change the walls in line with their personal responses to climate and desires for privacy. The thin inverted-catenary roof of his 1950 Healy Guest House, known as the 'Cocoon House', was stabilized like a tent with cables and steel straps, then sprayed with a thin coat of Saran-vinyl 'cocoon' invented to protect battleships. The peripatetic Harwell Hamilton Harris, Dean at the University of Texas in the 1950s, distinguished the parochial, backward-looking 'Regionalism of Restriction'

Paul Rudolph, Healy Guest House ('Cocoon House'), Sarasota, Florida, 1950.

Best because each one is a well-loved style of architecture, beautifully adapted . . . because each is planned to fit a particular way of life . . . because each makes the most of the money it cost . . . because one, we think, could serve as the model for the best house for you

63

BEST SMALL HOUSES FOR **1954**

Lars Bang, Bendit House, Houston, Texas, 1954, from *Good Housekeeping* (1954).

from this 'Regionalism of Liberation' or locally based experiments that explored 'emerging ideas'.[27]

Government agencies enthusiastically supported another kind of experiment, prefabrication, seeking technological solutions for problems of affordability. Many such companies collapsed, Lustron most notoriously, beset by financial irregularities, restrictive local building codes and exaggerated promises, but some 300 firms were producing factory-built houses by 1956, accounting for 10 per cent of the nation's total output. Innovations required testing and small-scale production, so thoughtful designs by Edward Barnes, Henry Dreyfus and Charles Goodman reached only a small market, as did Carl Koch's series of inventions that began with folding stressed-skin panels on the Acorn House (1948). Koch later reflected that architects find it difficult to consider site plans, ongoing adaptations and marketing, preferring 'to focus on completely new prototypes'.[28]

The country saw many variations on basic types. Houston, Texas, enjoyed a decade of flat-roofed, steel-framed Miesian courtyard houses of all sizes and price tags. *Good Housekeeping* chose a design by Lars Bang as one of ten 'Outstanding Small Houses of the Year' in 1954. Esther McCoy noted that 'architectural misfits tripled during the 1950s', especially in the West, encouraging an engagement more experiential than cerebral.[29] Iconoclasts experimented with biomorphic forms and unusual materials. Bruce Goff favoured plastics and corrugated metal. John Lautner shaped concrete and added surprises like 750 drinking glasses set as skylights in the coffered concrete ceiling of the Sheats-Goldstein House in Los Angeles (1963). Several Lautner houses have starred in blockbuster movies, iconic expressions of audacity and divergence from conventional norms, akin to the *Playboy* Bachelor Pad of the era.[30]

Multi-family housing was fairly restrained in comparison with the experimentation of pre-war examples. Insurance companies and hospitals used redevelopment funds to finance huge urban enclaves, some fortunately relieved by thoughtful landscaping. Mies again provided the ideal model with two luxury towers at 860–880 Lake Shore Drive in Chicago

John Lautner, Sheats-
Goldstein House, Los
Angeles, 1963, as
shown in the movie
*Charlie's Angels: Full
Throttle* (2003).

(1949–51), so inexorably uniform that they make no accommodations to sun or wind conditions. MOMA praised the immaculate pair as 'Metropolis defined', precisely because these 'formidable urban objects' provoked an emotional response to urban life 'so well described by Franz Kafka'.[31] The young Herbert Greenwald developed the project, recognizing Mies's towering talent and the need to keep it in check by providing conventional rooms rather than completely open spaces for the apartments. A decade later, Bertrand Goldberg's cylindrical towers at Marina City (1959–64), also in Chicago, offered a more flamboyant prototype and a mixed-use programme.

Low-rise garden apartments re-emerged in the mid-1950s. Herbert Greenwald decided to acquire Gratiot, a large urban-renewal site in Detroit that had laid dormant since the initial clearance in 1950. The IIT faculty began the first section, called Lafayette Park, planned by Ludwig Hilberseimer with a relatively informal landscape by Alfred Caldwell and an extraordinary collection of Mies's architecture, including two-storey townhouses, single-storey courtyard houses and three high-rise apartment towers. Unfortunately, Greenwald died in 1959, leaving the eight other parcels uncompleted; they were sold off separately. As at other renewal sites, former residents could not afford the new accommodations, but the project was racially integrated and may embody a rare success, both spatially and socially.

Charles Goodman collaborated with the Reynolds Metal Company on River Park Mutual Homes (1959–62), which stand out amid the largely failed renewal area of south-west Washington, DC. Two nine-storey apartment buildings and barrel-roofed townhouses share common spaces. Both showcased aluminium with patterned screens that cast lyrical shadows. Similar qualities pervade the wooden geometries of St Francis Square, a San Francisco union cooperative by Marquis & Stoller, completed in 1961. This unusual super-block combined four city blocks into housing and a school. The 299 apartments are stacked three storeys high, arranged as seven groups around three major open spaces. The limited budget forced restraint, so the hilly site provides variety, accentuated by the interplay of decks, balconies and pathways. Lawrence Halprin's landscape plan accentuated vistas, pedestrian connections and various areas for sitting or children's play, relegating parking to the periphery. This remains one of the country's finest examples of affordable housing.

Mies van der Rohe, 860–880 Lake Shore Drive, Chicago, 1949–51.

860–880 Lake Shore Drive, site plan and initial floor plan.

Mies van der Rohe,
Lafayette Park,
Detroit, Michigan,
1955–8.

'Mid-Century Modernism' housing now commands attention in lavish architecture books, popular magazines and specialized real-estate firms. Even the moderate-cost, small-scale urban housing of the post-war years is again finding favour, especially when informal compositions are merged with environmentally conscious site-planning. Smaller garden-apartment complexes in Miami, Chicago, and San Diego merit reconsideration. So do the two-storey stucco apartment buildings of Los Angeles – dubbed 'dingbats' by Reyner Banham in reference to the prevalence of starburst ornamentation that resembled the asterisk-like printing symbol.[32] James Marston Fitch remarked that 'one of the most curious problems facing the architectural editor of a national magazine is trying to keep good West Coast dwellings from monopolizing its pages'.[33]

Public housing represents a small but controversial aspect of 1950s Modernism. Most officials and architects embraced the high-rise super-block as economical, even beneficial, convinced that it protected residents from 'contamination' by the surrounding slums. The costs of the Korean War compounded with Congressional antagonism against services for the poor to slash funding and obliterate many good intentions. Pruitt-Igoe in St Louis (1950–54) is a case in point. Both critics and the architect, Minoru Yamasaki, ignored the fact that the original plans had been scuttled. The descent from ideals to actualities shocked reformers like Elizabeth Wood, then Director of the Chicago Housing Authority (CHA). In 1945 she called for planning to be 'bold and comprehensive – or it is useless and wasted'.[34] The next decade revealed how concentrated locations aggravated problems of racial segregation. When Wood tried to integrate and disperse Chicago's housing, she was immediately dismissed. She went on to write *Housing Design: A Social Theory* (1961), a thoughtful argument for better alternatives and more resident involvement. Meanwhile, CHA's Robert Taylor Houses by Shaw Metz & Associates (1960–63) packed 27,000 residents into 28 virtually identical 16-storey towers on a 3.2-kilometre-long super-block – the largest such project in the world, now mostly demolished for a mixed-income HOPE VI enclave that depletes much needed housing for the poor.

The 1950s also saw a rise in second homes at ski and beach resorts, including modern icons like Neutra's Kaufmann House and Rudolph's Cocoon House. Wartime values of mobility, restraint and climatic adaptation remained strong for a decade with informal open plans and playful shapes, mostly in wood. 'Vacation houses' could be small and flimsy, thereby legitimizing poor construction standards, especially in Miami and other fast-growing southern cities. Government propaganda insisted that all American workers enjoyed holiday homes like the one displayed at the 1959 American Exhibition in Moscow, designed by Andrew Geller for the All-State Development Corporation. Made famous as the site of the famous Kitchen Debate between Richard Nixon and Nikita Khrushchev, it quickly became a prototype for several hundred 'Leisurama Homes' sold through the department store Macy's. Although Geller's custom-designed beach houses remained economical and whimsically adventurous, the country's 3 million second homes

Charles Goodman, River Park Mutual Homes, Washington, DC, 1959–62, night view.

Marquis & Stoller,
St Francis Square,
San Francisco,
California, 1960–61,
view of housing from
courtyard.

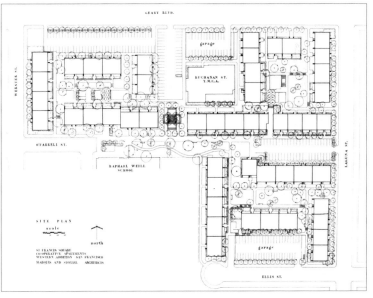

St Francis Square,
site plan.

would gradually become more elaborate and expensive in the early
1960s.[35]

Spaces for Leisure and Learning

The problem of monuments preoccupied post-war architects and critics,
who wondered how to represent unity in contemporary democratic societies. Neo-classicism virtually disappeared in civic buildings as private
architects replaced bureaucratic designers. The first great example was
the United Nations. Nelson Rockefeller donated a prime parcel of land,
determined to make Manhattan the world capital for trade and diplomacy.
A stellar team of international architects was assembled to create the
'Workshop of Peace' under the leadership of the Rockefeller favourite
Wallace Harrison.[36] The contentious design process began in 1948; by
1954 it was complete: a horizontal Assembly Building with a curved roof
line (and a dome as well, to entice a loan from Congress) alongside a tall
curtain-wall slab for the Secretariat.

Buckminster Fuller's geodesic (great-circle) domes were non-specific
solutions to any building task, based on a universal, tetrahedral cosmos
of tensegrity mathematics. Fuller both criticized and exemplified
Americans' romance with techno-science. Each invention was a simulation of natural and social systems, a means for ongoing exploration,

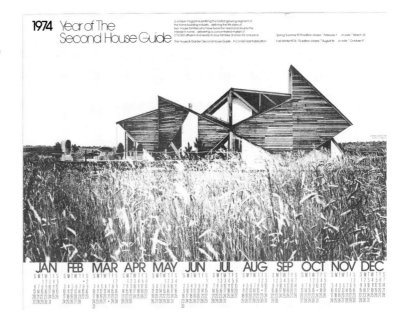

although both he and his disciples tended to take them as higher truths. The lightweight demountable dome was omnipresent for almost two decades. The Marines deployed them in the early 1950s. The United States Information Agency (USIA) took a portable dome to international trade fairs and exhibitions, eager to tout American ingenuity and technological prowess around the world. Fuller built a giant aluminium dome for the Ford Motor Company headquarters in Dearborn, Michigan, and others for a railway company in Shreveport, Louisiana, for Miami's Seaquarium and for the Climatron at St Louis's Botanical Garden. Architecture students around the country constructed domes outside their schools, confident of a spiritual and technological revolution. Over 300,000 geodesic domes based on Fuller's patents were erected between 1954 and his death in 1983.[37]

Embassies, military installations and other international buildings were equally significant representations of democracy and free enterprise. The State Department's Foreign Buildings Office oversaw more than 200 projects in 72 countries, determined to enhance America's prestige and underscore its technological prowess. Most of the structures were emphatically modern. SOM designed several incarnations of an Amerika Haus in Germany, all variations on the rectangular glass houses intended to 'sell America'.[38] The best known embassies were modern too, notably those in New Delhi by Edward Durell Stone (1959);

in Baghdad by Josep Lluís Sert (1961); and in Athens by Gropius/TAC (1962).

Flashy modern buildings for leisure were a conspicuous sign of American well-being in the post-war era. As flashy automobiles kept people on the move, Douglas Haskell acclaimed what he called 'Googie Architecture' in a 1952 article, taking the name from John Lautner's brilliant collision of fragmented planes on a 1949 Los Angeles coffee shop.[39] Commercial architects of the post-war era delighted in mixing synthetic materials, bright colours and startling shapes, often derived from engineering advances like 'cheese-holes' in steel-webs, rippled or folded-plate roofs, concrete-shell vaults, and exaggerated diagonal or free-form ('woggle') supports. The razzmatazz had a broad popular appeal that soon extended to franchises like McDonald's parabolic Golden Arches, designed in 1952 by Stanley Meston. In contrast, most post-war modern artists and intellectuals deplored the honky-tonk quality of the strip, resort hotels and middle-brow buildings like coffee shops or bowling alleys. Lautner insisted that the connection with 'Googie' hurt his career as a serious architect. As with Team X in Europe, the ideal vernacular was far away and exotic, not the commercial world close at hand.

Car-oriented suburban developers invented the regional shopping centre just after World War Two. Seattle's Northgate by John Graham set the basic formula in the years 1947–50: a freeway-intersection location, underground tunnels for deliveries, ample parking and fixed

R. Buckminster Fuller, portable US Trade Pavilion, Kabul, Afghanistan, 1956.

182

Douglas Honnold,
Biff's Coffee Shop,
Panorama City, San
Fernando Valley,
California, 1950.

layouts, albeit increasing in size. Suburban shoppers found a semblance of community life – privately owned with every detail calibrated to encourage consumerism as the emblem of American happiness. Victor Gruen's Southdale (1954) outside Minneapolis introduced the first 'mall': fully enclosed, climate-controlled, landscaped, evoking European gallerias in a lively, two-level central court. 'Integrated planning' considered everything from financing to human scale and visual surprises. Gruen soon appropriated these elements for pedestrian malls – he called them 'community leisure centers' – seeking to revitalize main streets in small cities. But larger shopping centres grew rapidly and, like housing, increasingly segmented to draw different socio-economic classes.[40]

More Americans could afford vacations at exotic resort hotels representing the 'tropical Modernism' of sensuous Caribbean retreats designed by Toro & Ferrer, Edward Durell Stone and Igor Polivitzky. Miami Beach had an astounding concentration of these, notably Morris Lapidus's eight

'flabbergast' hotels, as he rightly called them, drawing on his previous experience in theatre and retail plus a few tricks from Baroque Rome. He was sincerely convinced that 'the new sensualism' fulfilled fundamental 'emotional cravings'.[41] The word 'motel' (from motor and hotel) entered American dictionaries and lives after World War Two. Some were glamorous, even voluptuous, like Paul Lundy's Warm Mineral Springs Motel in Venice, Florida (1958) and Paul Williams's La Concha in Las Vegas (1962).

Las Vegas hit the limelight in 1946 with the Flamingo, its first modern (as opposed to cowboy-themed) hotel-casino. Spectacular competitors soon lined the Strip, most designed by car-oriented architects from Los Angeles, notably Wayne McAllister, Welton Beckett and Douglas Honnold. A major shift occurred in 1957 with the emergence of Young Electric Sign Company (YESCO). This specialist *extraordinaire* in neon and flashing lights designed signs for the 1957 Mint Casino and 1958 Stardust Hotel, the latter billed as the largest hotel in the world with 1,000 rooms. This changed basic relationships along the fabled Strip, where brilliant signs now upstaged the cheap and basic architecture.

A Boeing 707 carried Pan-Am's first non-stop flight to Europe in 1958, inaugurating 'jet-age' culture. Airports needed much larger runways and enticing modern structures for the surge in travel. Minoru Yamasaki's Lambert-St Louis Airport Terminal (1956) had already suggested a new idiom with its soaring, thin-shell groin vaults. The New York Port Authority then proposed the novel idea of separate structures for each airline, seemingly more efficient and a sight-seeing attraction as well. The original 'Seven Wonders' at New York's Idlewild (now Kennedy) Airport were glorious; the most spectacular was Eero Saarinen's TWA terminal, which opened in 1962. Saarinen's 'form-world' entailed a total environment. This one extended from the beak-like canopy entrance and upward-soaring wings to voluptuous interiors, even to details like stair railings and heating ducts. Douglas Haskell fondly called the structure 'Eero's "big bird" in concrete'. Within a few years several mass-market magazines were noting the build-up of auxiliary buildings, the 'Airport City' as a hub for travelling businessmen who became 'corporate gypsies'.[42] No longer adequate by the 1990s, even the famous TWA Terminal was threatened with demolition. A preservation movement has convinced Jet Blue to use it for some flights, thus lending cachet to budget travel.

New cultural institutions re-energized the experience of public space.

Morris Lapidus, Americana Hotel, Bal Harbor, Florida, 1957, drawing of entrance.

Museums embraced contemporary art and architecture for new buildings and extensions to City Beautiful temples of the early twentieth century. Louis Kahn's 1953 addition to the Yale Art Gallery in New Haven, Connecticut, was his first significant building, an open grid around a massive round stairwell with an exposed space-frame of concrete tetrahedrons to maximize flexibility for installations. The bravura of other structures generated early conflicts about the 'edifice complex'.[43] Frank Lloyd Wright's

The Las Vegas Strip. The 1958 Stardust Hotel and Casino with neon sign by Kermit Wayne of YESCO (Young Electric Sign Company) is on the right (imploded in 2007) and the 1961 La Concha Motel by Paul R. Williams on the left. Photograph c. 1975.

Eero Saarinen, TWA Terminal, Idlewild (now Kennedy) Airport, Queens, New York, 1956–62, interior of waiting area.

Solomon R. Guggenheim Museum in New York was immediately controversial, especially the spiralling ramp and the 'great-room' lobby, which he likened to being inside a seashell. Wright began the first design in 1943, modified the concept in 1952 with a change in client and patron, then completed the museum in 1959. Originally intended solely for 'non-objective', or abstract, painting, the curved walls of the galleries were meant to 'liberate' each picture, allowing it be seen independently and in the changing conditions of natural light. Critics, including many artists, reviled the building's 'egomaniacal' upstaging of artwork. But the public loved the dramatic spatial experience from the day it opened.

As high culture became more democratic, it often lost the vivacious exuberance of nineteenth-century theatres that had connected actors and audiences. Guthrie Theater in Minneapolis (1959–63) was an exception. Ralph Rapson, the architect, kept the interior spaces animated yet intimate with irregular acoustical 'clouds' and a moveable stage closely surrounded by small asymmetrical seating areas. The dynamic façade with its cut-out screens heightened changing perceptions of light and shadow, inside and out, surface and depth, all to convey the layers of meanings in all performance.

186

Frank Lloyd Wright,
Solomon R.
Guggenheim Museum,
New York, 1943–59,
interior view from
upper galleries to
base of the ramp.

The 'baby boom' generated thousands of new schools in suburbs and small towns, mostly single-storey elementary schools that emphasized 'day-lighting' and flexibility. Educators wanted to help children focus more effectively, while school boards tried to keep costs under control and plan for expansion. A bare-bones facility for West Columbia, Texas, completed in 1952 by the Houston architect Donald Barthelme, was widely admired. A 'roller-coaster' entry canopy for buses enlivened the inexpensive industrial materials, while 'neighborhoods' of classrooms faced landscaped courtyards. When the Supreme Court's momentous 1954 decision, *Brown v. Board of Education*, outlawed 'separate but equal' facilities, school districts in the seventeen Southern states continued to build segregated facilities. Paul Rudolph's Sarasota High School (1959) is one such example. Its gravity-defying concrete screens, stairs and cantilevers dramatize teenage social life while shielding classrooms from the sun – and from black classmates.[44] Formal brilliance can sometimes short-circuit social change.

Ralph Rapson,
Guthrie Theater,
Minneapolis,
Minnesota, 1959–63,
demolished 2006.

Several firms now specialized in educational facilities, notably John Lyon Reid in northern California and Caudill Rowlett Scott in Bryan, Texas, and Oklahoma City. Caudill's 1941 pamphlet, 'Space for Teaching', now became a major influence on modern schools. Committed to research and teamwork, CRS developed ingenious devices to control the elements and reduce costs, as well as planning strategies for better learning. Schools Construction Systems Development (SCSD) focused on packing all mechanical equipment into a roof system. The Ford Foundation's Educational Facilities Laboratory (EFL) sought to centralize and distill many such innovations.

A 1947 Presidential Commission report had declared mass higher education a national mission as returning GI students dramatically increased enrolments at major research universities and small liberal-arts colleges. The University of Miami, hailed internationally as the first modern university, completed its first buildings in 1948–9, based on wartime designs by Marion Manley with credit shared by her post-war associate, Robert Law Weed. Critics praised the flexibility, informality and climatic adaptations, and the daring engineering of rigid bents and cantilevers – using timber salvaged from military installations. In a similar vein Henry Klumb built nineteen magnificent tropical-modern buildings for the University of Puerto Rico between 1946 and 1966, drawing in part on his work with Frank Lloyd Wright.

Yale University President A. Whitney Griswold commissioned a wide range of expensive, daring modern buildings, beginning a trend that

continues into this century. Architects fostered 'identity' and 'community' with distinctive shapes and textured finishes, the most visible and notorious being the rough-textured Brutalism of Paul Rudolph's School of Art and Architecture (1958–64). By 1963 Richard Dober's *Campus Planning* had distilled a 'scientific' approach to the 'multiversity' based on 'modules' for continuous growth softened by greenery – two fundamental principles of American college campuses since Colonial times. Expansive modern dormitories were imperative for the expanded student bodies, including apartments for married GIs.

New kinds of educational institutions explored innovative environments for different kinds of learning. When SOM was selected from 260 applicants for the 'future-oriented' Air Force Academy in Colorado Springs (1954–62), the design overcame Congressional resistance by placing a thin classical veneer of limestone over disciplined industrial Modernism – using computers to analyse the structural loads. Ernest Kump's Foothill College (1957–60) in Los Altos Hills, California, provided a model for community colleges with 44 modular pavilions knit together by a informal site plan and wide overhangs that sheltered circuitous pathways. Edward Larrabee Barnes's 1961 Haystack Mountain School at Deer Isle, Maine, embraced nature with its bold roof lines on interconnected pavilions covered in cedar shingles. At the other end of the spectrum, major foundations raised funds for advanced research and conference centres in the social sciences at Princeton and Stanford. Despite similar dates and programmes, each was visibly distinctive.

If post-war intellectual life was deeply secular, the larger culture experienced a religious revival. Liberal congregations derived spiritual inspiration from abstract forms and dramatic incarnations of space and light – qualities the Protestant theologian Paul Tillich characterized as

'holy emptiness' and 'majestic simplicity'.[45] Three 'gathered churches' built between 1948 and 1951, when wartime restrictions remained in effect, mark a first stage of this shift: Eliel Saarinen's spare Lutheran Christ Church in Minneapolis; Pietro Belluschi's numinous wood-frame First Presbyterian Church in the lumber town of Cottage Grove, Oregon; and Lloyd Wright's Wayfarers Chapel in Palos Verdes, California, with panes of glass set in delicate redwood arches inviting communion with the sea and woodlands. Peter Blake's *An American Synagogue for Today and Tomorrow* (1954) dismissed 'meshugothic' historical styles and praised modern synagogues by Percival Goodman, Harrison & Abramowitz, Erich Mendelsohn, Philip Johnson – and the ever-present Frank Lloyd Wright, whose Beth Shalom (1953–9) in the Philadelphia suburb of Elkins Park has crystalline walls of lustrous corrugated fibreglass.

The scale and visual drama of religious architecture soon escalated. Marcel Breuer's first buildings (1954–61) for St John's Abbey and University in Collegetown, Minnesota, highlighted mammoth concrete plates, folded or honeycombed, and a massive trapezoidal bell-tower. Another kind of mega-church now emerged in the suburbs, epitomized by Neutra's Community Church (1962) in Garden Grove, California, for the evangelist Robert Schuller. Its fan-shaped area for 1,400 cars gives drive-in and walk-in worshippers alike a view of the nave. Schuller's success led him to collaborate with Philip Johnson on the nearby Crystal

Cathedral, completed in 1980, calling it a '22-acre shopping center for Jesus Christ'.[46]

By the end of the 1950s, more architects and critics were breaking out of strait-laced propriety. *Progressive Architecture* endorsed plasticity and 'emotional and sensual delight' in 1958; a 1961 series lauded the benefits of 'chaoticism'.[47] Most of the nation came to realize the limits of post-war promises as people confronted the entrenched problems of racism and poverty throughout the country, especially the deplorable condition of cities. *The Death and Life of Great American Cities*, Jane Jacobs's riveting assault on the destructive realities of urban renewal, became a best-seller in 1961; a year later came Michael Harrington's *The Other America: Poverty in the United States* and Rachel Carson's *Silent Spring*, an attack on chemical pollution. The shock of John F. Kennedy's assassination in 1963 affected the country deeply. The first large-scale urban riots broke out in Harlem and Los Angeles. Martin Luther King's March on Washington culminated with his 'I Have a Dream' speech – then his own assassination in Memphis. Modern architecture joined the ranks of social reform once again, this time offering incremental improvements rather than redemption through master plans.

In such circumstances, the slick, futuristic architecture of the 1964 World's Fair in New York did not seem worth its unprecedented cost, over a billion dollars. Robert Moses' elaborately orchestrated control now appeared heavy-handed. Professional and popular magazines savaged the New York Pavilion by Philip Johnson, the gigantic IBM logo-building by Saarinen with Charles Eames, and the House of Good Taste (in fact a pluralistic choice of Modern, Contemporary and Traditional houses along with an Underground Home). Two very different authors commented indirectly on choices. Susan Sontag's 'Notes on Camp' evoked the emerging realm of pleasure and theatricality, unconcerned about moral or aesthetic judgements. These very attitudes led the architecture critic Peter Blake to blast contemporary American culture and its landscapes as *God's Own Junkyard*. In any case, to paraphrase Bob Dylan, the times they were a-changin' – and so was architecture.

chapter six

Challenging Orthodoxies, 1965–1984

Modernists typically strive for radical alternatives to accepted norms. This certainly happened with the myriad attacks on the Establishment of the 1960s and '70s – including assaults on Modernism itself. The early years of hope saw violent protests in American cities, yet it still seemed possible to make the world a better place.[1] Youth culture confronted the nation with the exuberance of drugs and rock 'n' roll, the anger of anti-war and civil-rights protests. Young architects, sometimes still at college, affected the profession as never before, united in resistance to conventional curricula and clients, intrigued by emergent lifestyles – a key neologism of the era. Seizing the gerundive to signal continuous processes, they were 'doing architecture' in multiple unprecedented ways: free-form hippie communes; advocacy groups committed to helping the poor; environmentalist experiments; lighthearted, camp playfulness; fantastical megastructures; proudly unbuilt 'paper' or 'cardboard architecture' based on complex theoretical systems.[2]

Modern architects of all ages turned to historical precedents, seeking to ground their designs in scholarly knowledge – or at least intuitive associations. MOMA in New York helped launch this voyage. *Architecture without Architects*, Bernard Rudofsky's popular 1964 book and exhibition, celebrated the vernacular housing of Mediterranean and African villages, hoping to re-energize Modernism with visual proof that standardized forms could sustain meaningful communities. This romanticized universal vernacular ignored cultural variations and historical change in favour of 'timeless' roots. Drawn to the appealing imagery, architects eagerly incorporated similar 'precedents' or 'justifications', at least in presentations, especially for housing. MOMA then published *Complexity and Contradiction in Architecture*, Robert Venturi's 'Gentle Manifesto' of 1966. 'I am for richness of meaning rather than clarity of meaning', explained Venturi. 'I prefer "both-and" to "either-or" . . . the difficult unity of inclusion rather than the easy unity of exclusion.'[3] The book's rich and erudite historical archive was chosen for visual impact. Italian Mannerist distortions predominated, but American examples held their own, from

Sandy & Babcock (Diana Crawford, project architect), for the UDC, University Park Apartments, Ithaca, New York, 1973.

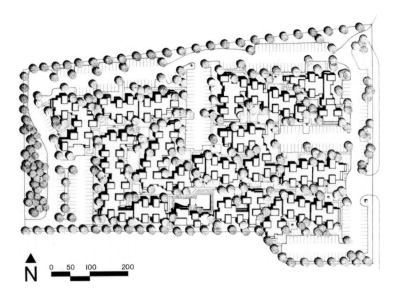

N 0 50 100 200

Thomas Jefferson to Main Street – judged 'almost all right' on the last page.

When Peter Eisenman founded the Institute for Architecture and Urban Studies in New York in 1967, he, too, looked to history, uniting a formalist fraternity around the legacy of European avant-gardes from the 1920s and '30s with no regard for political affiliations. The Institute then launched an exploration of *longue durée* typologies based on Italian neo-rationalist theories about abstract essences that provide the *ur*-roots of cultures. 'Theory' emerged, trans-coding or borrowing ideas from rarefied historical, literary and philosophical sources. The Institute's journal *Oppositions*, published from 1973 to 1984, proclaimed theory a 'critical agent' of destabilization, revealing the alienation of human subjects, the virtuality of objects. Its dissent focused solely on a hermetic architectural world.

Language, often baffling, was crucial to this and other tendencies. The New York Five (Eisenman, Richard Meier, Charles Gwathmey, Michael Graves and John Hejduk) emerged with a 1969 conference and exhibition at MOMA, followed by a 1972 book, *Five Architects*, with Judith Turner's elegantly abstract photographs of details in their houses. They also marketed themselves as the Whites, signifying a shared penchant for texts and white villas or, more precisely, axonometric drawings of such villas, a representational technique that looked back to Le Corbusier's interlocking planes of the 1920s. Drawings became an ideal – architectural expression uncompromised by clients or construction – and a new commodity sold in galleries.

Peter Eisenman, House VI, West Cornwall, Connecticut, 1972–6, axonometric drawings.

The group that came to be known as the Grays never coalesced as a collective entity with a manifesto. The name signalled a counterpoint to the Whites and a shared interest in ambiguous allusions. Robert Venturi, Denise Scott Brown, Charles Moore, Robert Stern and Romaldo Giurgula received the most attention, but many fellow-travellers were likewise intrigued by the nuances of everyday speech, the power of familiar narratives, the richness of architectural history and the brash honky-tonk world of popular culture. Questioning 'orthodox modern architecture' without discarding it, eschewing visionary utopias, the Grays wanted to re-enchant the world. They celebrated the modernity that already existed, especially in cities. Venturi and Denise Scott Brown argued that the commercial strip of Las Vegas was analogous to the Roman *piazza*, so architects should try to understand and 'enhance' it. Moore described his quest for 'strange and revolutionary and mind-boggling and often uncomfortable [possibilities] but only using the ordinary pieces'.[4]

Other forms of culture were also dissolving boundaries. Architects linked up with friends in the visual arts, theatre, dance and performance art who shared their euphoric, multi-sensory quest. The composer John Cage was a hero to young designers who sought an 'open-ended' exploration of possibilities, while Ann and Lawrence Halprin taught them to think of space in terms of improvised choreographies. Marshall McLuhan was admired for his vision of media-based 'allatonceness'. Environments were key to 'happenings', earthworks and site-specific sculpture. Young designers created ephemeral sets for avant-garde theatre performances and special-effects 'total environments' for explosive rock-music concerts at discos, clubs and coliseum performances.

Mothers of Invention concert with the Joshua Light Show at the Mineola Theater, Long Island, New York, 1967.

Numerous public forums took up these issues. Ada Louise Huxtable became the first architecture critic for the *New York Times* in 1963, defending and expanding the scope of Modernism while engaging in valid critiques. Other newspapers and magazines would follow, renewing the role of the public intellectual that Lewis Mumford and Herbert Croly had played earlier in the century. A surge of books and scores of 'little magazines' appeared around the country, most espousing cultural breadth and social relevance. Steven Holl's *Pamphlet Architecture* in New York, *Design Book Review* in San Francisco, *Oz* from the University of Kansas School of Architecture and other now defunct journals explored the intricacies of real and imaginary worlds.

Historic preservation briefly united all the factions. Modern architects protested unsuccessfully against the demolition of McKim, Mead & White's magnificent Pennsylvania Station in Manhattan in 1963. Giorgio Cavaglieri (who purportedly invented the term 'adaptive reuse' for his sensitive, visibly modern alterations) led the campaign to create New York City's Landmarks Preservation Commission, empowered to save other monuments from ruthless real-estate development. The 1966 National Preservation Act quietly signalled a momentous cultural shift. Whereas Americans had previously defined themselves as forward-looking, this act contended that the 'spirit and direction of the Nation are founded upon and reflected in its historic heritage.'[5]

Architects also took an active role in the political activism unleashed in the late 1960s. Preservation took a different form in efforts to protect and improve impoverished inner-city neighbourhoods, inverting urban renewal's efforts to eradicate them. The path-breaking 1965–6 legislation of Lyndon Johnson's Great Society provided funds for housing, health-care facilities, schools and other community buildings in low-income neighbourhoods. Harlem, Brooklyn and Pittsburgh initiated the first community design centres (CDCs), followed by some 2,000 others. Paul Davidoff coined the term *advocacy* to describe this embryonic move-ment of students and dissident professionals who worked directly with neighbourhood groups.[6]

Some young architects joined the counter-culture, hoping to under-mine conventional American homes, family life and professional practice by withdrawing from the mainstream. They favoured ephemer-al structures that sat lightly on the earth. Ant Farm, a radical collective based in San Francisco and then in Austin, Texas, mixed the freedoms of 'nomadology' and nudity with didactic agitprop performances. Huge inflatable PVC 'air pillows' sounded the alarm about dangers like air pollution. Hippie communes were fond of geodesic domes, seen as metaphors of cosmic and ecological harmony. Drop City, Colorado, founded in 1965, adopted Steve Baer's 'Zomes', exploded rhomboid dodecahedral domes fabricated from salvaged materials, principally junked car tops, then equipped with high-tech solar collectors and wind turbines. These and other alternative practices were media-savvy about maintaining networks and astutely marketing spontaneous events. The 1970 special issue of *Progressive Architecture*, 'Advertisements for a Counter Culture', described the importance of new technologies – a biosphere, domes, pneumatics, media and computers – in the transformative world of 'radical discontent and innovation'.[7]

Ant Farm, Clean Air Pod, pneumatic installation and Earth Day 'event' at Sproul Plaza, University of California at Berkeley, 1970.

Some of the most significant experiments of the era concerned the environment. Ian McHarg's *Design with Nature* (1969) and Reyner Banham's urban parable *Los Angeles: The Architecture of Four Ecologies* (1971) emphasized the power and potential dangers of another history, natural history, warning architects against hubris. The first Earth Day in 1970 fused biomorphic shapes, advanced technologies and public participation. James Wines and Alison Sky founded Sculpture in the Environment (SITE) that year, recasting architecture as public art that criticized modernist disregard for environments. Their 'de-architecture' installations revealed inevitable processes of change and decay. Best known are the eight showrooms for BEST Products, a profitable mail-order merchandiser. These include the crumbling Indeterminate Façade in Houston (1975), the Rainforest Showroom in Hialeah, Florida (1979) and the Forest Building in Richmond, Virginia (1980), where trees on the suburban site seem to have taken their revenge on the banal 'big box' structure.

Paolo Soleri's 'arcology' – architecture respectful of ecology – was an apocalyptic vision of gigantic mixed-use structures that preserved vast surrounding landscapes. These dense urban environments, some to be a mile high and housing 500,000 people, would reduce pollution and prevent sprawl. A 1970 book and coast-to-coast museum exhibitions of exquisite Plexiglas models won converts to the cause.[8] Soleri began the first prototype town, Arcosanti, in 1971 in the Arizona desert near Taliesin, where he had been apprenticed with Wright in the 1940s. The construction, still ongoing, is mostly hand-crafted by volunteers. The

OPEC oil embargo of 1973 helped spur the diffuse, but more down-to-earth Alternative Technology movement, which experimented with hybridized strategies like solar panels and earth-sheltered houses.

The dizzying simultaneity of the era sustained multiple groups and experimental perspectives, all passionate if quixotic. A 1971 cover story on 'New Architecture' in *Newsweek* featured Louis Kahn and Paul Rudolph alongside Arcosanti and Drop City – but not the New York Five.[9] The space programme, Moog synthesizers, Mod fashion trends, computer graphics and television blurred categories like 'radical' or 'Establishment'. Indeed, government agencies appropriated domes, pneumatics and sophisticated multimedia for spectacles like world's fairs, notably Fuller's immense geodesic dome at Expo '67 in Montreal.

When postmodernism came into American architecture in the mid-1970s, it failed to engage most of these permutations.[10] Charles Jencks translated the term from literary criticism with *The Language of Post-Modern Architecture* (1977), emphasizing 'multivalent' meanings, metaphors and syntax. In codifying the new trend he proposed an elaborate stylistic genealogy. Jencks also suggested a lighthearted approach and inferred that Modernism was a puritanical restriction on postmodernism's visual liberation. But Modernism had changed as well, of course. Recognizing that it was no longer possible to transform the world through design, many modern architects withdrew into their own esoteric games and brandished the idea of autonomy from the larger culture. The shift fit a national mood that Vernon Jordan, President of the Urban League, called 'antisocial negativism'.[11]

Modern architecture had indeed fallen from grace, and for many reasons. Radicals lambasted its close connections with the destructive forces of modernization, capitalism and the Vietnam War, while conservatives denounced the fundamental belief that it could remedy social problems. Architects responded to the fracas in myriad ways, but only two received extensive media attention, making them seem the only options. The wide-ranging eclecticism that rejoiced in symbolic allusions, personal experience and historical continuities was what came to be called postmodernism. In the opposite corner of the ring, post-structuralist critics of the profession demanded intellectual rigour and 'autonomy'.[12] Whatever their bent, most architects of the late 1970s retreated to issues of style – and discourse. 'Today's architects do not just build; they comment', noted Ada Louise Huxtable in 1980.[13] The discussion usually ignored the emergent post-industrial, 'post-Fordist' service economy, despite a major recession that cost jobs and unsettled lives, including those of many designers. Factions instead turned against each other in an impassioned religious war, ignoring their shared if contentious beliefs.

Retrofitting the Corporate Workplace

The sleek glass-box office buildings of the 1950s exploded in the late 1960s, an aesthetic detonation set off by an aggressive global economy. Corporations had to keep expanding their operations and dominate over competitors to succeed in this high-risk world. The same held for philanthropic organizations and governmental bureaucracies. Almost half of the nation's workers were 'service sector' employees in large offices. American CEOs wanted to oversee every aspect of their workforces, often making compliance the basis for advancement, even when the methods were cooperative.[14] American and European office buildings diverged in the 1970s, one geared principally to economic growth and control over employees, the other to environmental innovations and employee well-being.

The atrium lobby captured the new entrepreneurial spirit in the USA. These tightly guarded jewel boxes of corporate strength accentuated central power. Atriums also redefined urban 'public space', much of which now came indoors under private auspices. The earliest and most positive example was the Ford Foundation headquarters designed by Roche & Dinkeloo and completed in 1967. Officials for this ambitious international philanthropy wanted an inspiring work environment for their staff and an uplifting public presence in New York. Municipal zoning laws passed in 1961 had called for a plaza open to the public, so the indoor garden required a variance or waiver. The court, just 0.1 hectare, seemed immense, terracing down from 42nd to 43rd Streets and rising to a skylight. The structure was almost perfectly square, the offices arranged in an 'L' to look out onto and across the luxuriant garden. A grid of Cor-Ten steel encased glass doors and windows in a 1.8-metre module (0.6 metres larger than the standard size), which amplified the sense of spaciousness and collective purpose. Passers-by shared some of these pleasures, enjoying a sun-dappled marvel during the day and a luminous beacon at night.

Peachtree Center, a multi-block mixed-use development (MXD) complex in Atlanta, Georgia (dubbed Rockefeller Center South by local boosters), also opened in 1967. John Portman placed an immense gilded atrium at the core of this high-tech citadel. There is unmistakable energy in the 21-storey lobby of the Hyatt Regency Hotel, 'like Bernini on an acid trip'.[15] The restless negative space pulsates with illuminated waterfalls, glass-capsule elevators and bowered terraces of rooms rising above awe-struck spectators. Peachtree Center was ideal for the tens of thousands of newcomers to Atlanta each year, eager for an urbanity that provided the order of suburbia, what upbeat books on the city specified as 'only . . . the beautiful, never the ugly or depressing'.[16] Its popularity

Kevin Roche, Ford
Foundation, New York
City, 1966–7, atrium.

Ford Foundation,
section.

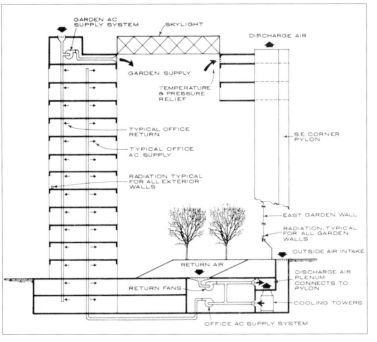

spurred an expanded complex of some twenty buildings within a decade, all interconnected by sky bridges, hermetic and controlled – an instant and artificial city.

Portman had flouted AIA conventions by combining the roles of architect and developer. He first insisted this gave him freedom as a designer. His 1976 manifesto, *The Architect as Developer*, audaciously claimed an even higher purpose: he could save declining downtowns by assembling land and capital for large-scale complexes to attract lots of people. The AIA soon concurred and elected him a Fellow. The Hyatt hotel chain launched a boom in glitzy downtown establishments, and Portman was invited to build 'power architecture' in cities from San Francisco to Shanghai, each with a grandiose atrium. The most colossal offspring was the Renaissance Center in Detroit (1973–8), a vast riverside complex in mirrored glass fortified by concrete ramparts and raised on a plinth. Portman opened the way for today's savvy architect-developers, who recognize that architecture begins with the design of financing and property. Another legacy is more unsettling. His Modernism created two architectural and urban realms, one inside and carefully packaged, the other outside and left to decline.

Office-building in the 1970s celebrated bold, imposing façades. A 1979 MOMA exhibition, *Transformations in Modern Architecture*, curated by Arthur Drexler, observed that now 'the object is to conceal rather than reveal.'[17] *Brutalism* was the inauspicious term for blank concrete surfaces, a reference to Le Corbusier's rough-textured sculptural concrete, *béton brut*. Corporate CEOs, still fearful of urban riots, felt assured by the fortress-like solidity of heavy walls with exaggerated roofs and parapets. Windows took unusual forms like slits or portholes, often configured in irregular patterns. Corporations vied for attention with the mastodontic cylindrical corners of Kevin Roche's Knights of Columbus headquarters in New Haven (1970), William Pereira's pyramidal Transamerica Building in San Francisco's Embarcadero Center (1972), and Hugh Stubbins's Citicorp Building in New York (1977), the last's sharp-angled crown seemingly cut by a knife. Virtuoso structures rotated, gyrated and turned askew with frantic gestures that quickly became clichés.

Mirrored glass was another favourite 'skin', a distinctly American fad using inexpensive materials to create the appearance of glamour. Cesar Pelli's bulging Pacific Design Center in Los Angeles (locals call it the Blue Whale) inaugurated mullion-less 'shaped glass' in the years 1970–75. Colin Rowe's and Robert Slutzky's article 'Transparency: Literal and Phenomenal (Part 2)', written in 1955–6 but published only in 1971, undermined simple arguments in favour of transparent glass, providing an intellectual pedigree for more opaque façades. Most architects simply enjoyed the amalgam of calculations and accidents of light. Some argued that large glass buildings were rendered invisible because they reflected the sky. No one bought the sell. Films like *The Towering Inferno* and *Earthquake* (both 1975) sensationalized legitimate fears about civic disasters with shards of glass raining terror on pedestrians. One local catastrophe delayed the opening of the John Hancock Tower in Boston (1971–6), designed by Henry Cobb for I. M. Pei, when the large windows were mysteriously sucked out of their frames, crashing down on Copley Square. (Pressure differentials with the double-paned windows seem to have caused the problem.) The energy crisis gave impetus to tinted or reflective glass, but workers in neighbouring buildings complained that mirrored surfaces caused severe glare, heat gain and disorientation. Drexler dryly acknowledged that the trend 'conveys an indifference to human presence most people interpret as hostile'.[18]

Philip Johnson returned to the limelight with such a building, trading his early International-Style rigour for an eclectic, 'less boring' redefinition of Modernism. He formed a partnership with John Burgee to design the IDS Center in Minneapolis, headquarters for a large financial-services firm, completed in 1972. The original programme of a glass tower became four prismatic buildings of different heights and diverse uses, filling a downtown block. Dizzying zigzag shapes (Johnson called them 'zogs') made of thousands of small re-entrant angles enlivened the façades. The centrifugal focus is a multi-tiered space frame with skyway links to surrounding buildings. Below is a giant retail complex called the Crystal Court, open to the street on all sides, but still resolutely private space.

Texas soon beckoned with a series of grandiose corporate and cultural commissions for Johnson. Pennzoil Place (1976) became an instant icon for Houston's new petroleum-based wealth, its two skewed trapezoidal towers of ominously dark glass rising alongside a 3-metre slit. The impresario-developer Gerald Hines found that 'extra quality in buildings would make our product stand out [for] a better class of client', clients willing to pay between $3 and $4 per square metre more than the going rate, even in a depressed market.[19] Pennzoil was part of a city-within-a-city that expanded earlier concourse networks. Richard Ingersoll has predicted that the 'fifth largest city in the United States [i.e. Houston] will someday be famous among urbanologists as the first modern city without streets' since there are only elevated freeways and tunnels which connect over 50 downtown buildings extending for a total of seven kilometers.[20]

Height remained a premium in this economic climate. Sears, Roebuck, and Company commissioned SOM to design Chicago's Sears

Tower. With 110 floors it held the title of the world's tallest building from its completion in 1974 until 1997. Construction technology could still generate a dramatic public presence. The SOM partners Bruce Graham and Fazlur Khan (a structural engineer) developed a system they called 'bundled tubes' that tied together nine glass skyscrapers of different heights into one building with interlocked exterior tubing for lateral wind loads. The MOMA curator Drexler classified this under the rubric of 'cages', seemingly oblivious to the parallel with Max Weber's 'iron cage' of capitalist bureaucracy.

Most New Yorkers resented the gargantuan size of the World Trade Center, which would only achieve iconic status with its tragic destruction in 2001. Conceived in 1960 in an effort to bring international businesses

Johnson/Burgee, IDS Center, Minneapolis, 1969–72, Crystal Court.

to Manhattan's flagging financial district, the WTC signalled the power of the emerging global economy. Construction took a decade, 1966–76. The site encompassed 65 hectares and more than 930,000 square metres of office space. Excavation for the foundations would provide the landfill to build Battery Park City. All this was too much for an architect like Minoru Yamasaki with no experience in skyscraper design, so Emery Roth was brought in as an associate. Yamasaki transformed the modern glass skyscraper into two towers with a historicist façade of inverted Venetian Gothic arches at their base, shown on a 1963 *Time* cover. But hubris was the major complaint. 'The World's Tallest Fiasco', opined *The Nation*. 'The ultimate Disneylandfairytaleblockbuster', declared Ada Louise Huxtable. 'It is General Motors Gothic.'[21]

Meanwhile, the rise of the Sunbelt intensified the fiscal crisis for the north-eastern Snowbelt and Midwestern Rustbelt cities like Detroit. Air-conditioned urban skyscrapers seemed oblivious to the environment as well as the street, but sites were important in some suburban headquarters. The stacked, lozenge-shaped boxes of Paul Rudolph's Burroughs-Wellcome Pharmaceutical Company in North Carolina's Research Triangle (1970–72) echo the topography of the surrounding ridge, while the rhythmic play of light and views in the multifaceted interiors indeed suggests a flexible 'living organism'. Emilio Ambasz's Research Laboratories for the Schlumberger Oil Company near Austin, Texas (1982), used earth berms to integrate the structures into the land, distributing them through an arcadian landscape. Environmentally inflected Modernism was even more resonant in California and the Pacific North-west. One example is the Weyerhaeuser Headquarters

Paul Rudolph, Burroughs/Wellcome Headquarters, Research Triangle Park, North Carolina, 1970–72.

(1969–71), designed by SOM's San Francisco office, with sod roofs and stepped layers nestled in a rural valley in Washington State.

The strong pro-business mood of the late 1970s generated complaints about limitations on capital formation. The 'big bang' of deregulation and a new tax bill in 1978 converted the welfare state into a corporate-welfare state. President Jimmy Carter embraced 'public–private partnerships', hoping that private enterprise could solve public problems if given proper incentives. Desperate to keep large corporations, municipal governments kowtowed to demands for lucrative investment opportunities. Lax lending requirements and generous tax benefits spurred new commercial real estate, despite the glut of office space in every large city and the dire need for housing.

'Prestige' projects with opulent lobbies and crowns were especially popular. At once prescient and perverse, Philip Johnson turned from bold geometries to historicism. He was shown clutching a model of New York's ATT Building (1979–83), with its notorious Chippendale crown, on a 1979 cover of *Time*. Postmodernism, begun as a critique, had become a facetious game of quotations and pastiche by 'architectural monarchists', an expression of 'social and political neo-conservatism'.[22] The vital issue was much larger than nonchalant historicist games, but too many architects seemed oblivious to anything but stylistic controversies and developers' enticements, ignoring the devastation of the late 1970's crisis in American cities.

New technologies analysed certain kinds of problems. The 'Systems Approach', invoked repeatedly, used game-theory models to compare various building systems while 'fast-track' construction borrowed 'pre-programming' from the aerospace industry. These technocratic methods made it difficult for architects to modify schemes. A few architecture offices took up computer-assisted design (CAD), ranging from Beverly Willis's small firm in San Francisco to SOM's several corporate offices. The University of California at Berkeley installed its Urban Simulation Laboratories, while Carnegie-Mellon and MIT's Architecture Machine Group (precursor to today's Media Lab) experimented with design technologies that envisioned new kinds of creativity based on algorithms.[23]

State-sponsored workplaces put enormous demands on architects with bureaucratic red tape, budgetary strictures and shifting concepts of public welfare. Richard Meier's Bronx Developmental Center is a poignant case in point. The New York State Department of Mental Hygiene commissioned a total-care residential service for 750 mentally and physically disabled children in 1970. The site was forlorn, a dismal industrial tract surrounded by highways and railroad tracks. By the time

of the building's completion in 1977, the location and the design caused
an uproar. Patient advocates and many psychiatrists attacked Meier's
cloistered plan as an 'obsolete' concept and the shiny aluminium panels
as 'inhumane', while colleagues praised his elegant composition and his
sincere efforts to accommodate the children.[24] The controversy highlights both the faddishness of 'flexible' late 1960s modules and the
significance of cultural shifts outside architecture. Psychiatric treatment
had undergone an about-face during the 1970s: the early model of large-
scale respites from the world had swung 180 degrees to one of community
mental health integrated into neighbourhoods. Committed to the first
set of premises and frustrated by a cumbersome process, Meier had not
adapted to the shift, nor could his building. The complex was soon
abandoned and partially demolished.

Home Again, Home Again

The words *housing*, *home* and *shelter* resonated everywhere in the late
1960s and '70s. The women's movement contested conventional notions
of home and family. Betty Friedan's *The Feminine Mystique* (1963)
attacked suburbia as a 'comfortable concentration camp'. The 'typical
household' went from 70 per cent of the population in the 1950s to 15 per
cent by 1980. More than half the country's married women worked outside the home by 1970, including those with young children. The divorce
rate doubled and the birth rate declined. The exhilaration of women's
liberation had its dark side in the feminization of poverty with the massive increase in female-headed households. All these demographic and

cultural upheavals affected the realities of domestic architecture, although the changes were far from profound.

Developers, officials and architects saw new markets in the shift. Unmarried couples, single parents and single people of all ages wanted the comforts of home together with services like childcare and leisure activities. Nearly 23 million new dwelling units were built between 1963 and 1973, more than in any previous decade. Multi-family housing accounted for over half the new production until 1976, spurred in part by condominium ownership, made legal in all states in 1968. While some planned communities sought diverse residents, most were special-purpose enclaves for young single people (many refused children) or retirement villages for the elderly. Economics favoured relatively smooth and unornamented façades with strong, geometrical roofs, usually sharply angled shed roofs or barrel vaults. Four terms reverberated through the discussions – 'user needs', 'community', 'site' and 'identity' – all of which straddled modern innovations and familiar prototypes.

Robert Venturi's Guild House (1960–63) in Philadelphia announced the new sensibility. Sponsored by the Friends Neighborhood Guild, the building provided 91 apartments for elderly men and women who wanted to remain in a rundown area undergoing urban renewal. Venturi respected that desire for continuity with a neighbourhood and the con-cept of home. The six-storey structure engaged the street with slightly over-scaled, but unabashedly 'conventional' materials: brick walls, dou-ble-hung windows and the first self-conscious use of chain-link fencing. A large Roman arch at the top marked the residents' social area, even as it alluded to Palladio and Louis Kahn for the cognoscenti. The glazed-brick entry featured a sign in gilded block letters, a Pop Art allusion to a

Venturi & Rauch with Cope and Lippincott, Guild House, Philadelphia, 1960–63.

marquee or billboard. The gold-anodized 'TV antenna' on the roof was a sculpture, a signifier, for which the architects contributed most of the cost. More important but rarely discussed, the light-filled rooms and hallways were pleasant places and easy to comprehend. While Venturi is credited with the design, he was strongly influenced by Denise Scott Brown, who became his wife and design partner in 1967. Simultaneously provocative and proverbial, dissonant and calming, the pair asked that we see buildings from multiple perspectives.

Subsidized housing (including Guild House) remained well below 5 per cent of the American total, compared with more than half in Britain or on the Continent. President Johnson created HUD in 1965, a Cabinet-level agency for housing and urban development with a heroic new building by Marcel Breuer. HUD announced two principal goals: to coordinate all below-market-rate (BMR) construction and to stimulate the private home-building industry. Bent on decentralizing, grants favoured Sunbelt cities like Dallas and Phoenix. Prefabrication systems seemed a sure way to boost production while reducing costs. After all, one third of new single-family dwellings were now mobile homes, which Paul Rudolph heralded as 'the 20th-century brick' that could be stacked sky-high.[25] George Romney, Richard Nixon's HUD Secretary, launched

John Sharratt for the Emergency Tenants Association, Villa Victoria, Boston, Massachusetts, 1969–82.

Operation Breakthrough in 1969, providing generous subsidies for 22 consortiums of product engineers and management teams. But Romney's experience at GM was no longer viable, even for the auto industry. The prototypes were expensive, visually un-appealing and riddled with graft. Such efforts to promote industrialized systems only fuelled suspicions about visibly modern architecture.

Both the right and the left considered public housing truly emblematic of profound problems in Modernism and government.[26] Even the prestigious Douglas Commission on Urban Problems lamented the supposed negative effect of 'Le Corbusier's sky-scrapers-in-a-park' in 1968.[27] Public housing underwent significant changes as Congress provided higher cost/unit subsidies for elderly projects, resulting in well-designed towers such as San Francisco's Woodside Gardens (1968). New family housing favoured small infill garden apartments on 'scattered' or 'vest-pocket' sites. But the notorious super-blocks far out-numbered either of these initiatives, and conditions worsened as economic restructuring increased unemployment levels for urban black males and strained family bonds. As the crisis deepened, HUD gauged rents to incomes and gave preference to those with no other options. Local authorities subsequently went broke and froze maintenance budgets at already inadequate levels. The modernist project was reduced to 'the projects': unemployed African-American single mothers on welfare warehoused in dreary, dangerous towers and slabs.

Public housing, less than 2 per cent of the nation's total housing stock, became a looming presence in the national imagination. Resentments and apocalyptic fears festered as Americans grew increasingly apprehensive about the future of their cities. The urban designer Oscar Newman's *Defensible Space* (1972) used 'scientific' graphs to argue that high-rise towers inevitably cause crime. The 'Pruitt-Igoe Myth' falsely contended that architects had once lavished awards on this now infamous project. Its demolition became an easy target for pundits like Charles Jencks, who proclaimed that 'Modern Architecture died in St Louis, Missouri on July 15, 1972 at 3.32 p.m.'[28] President Nixon declared a moratorium on federal housing subsidies in 1973, using specious associations like this without mentioning conservative opposition or widespread agency scandals.

Innovative non-profit organizations partially offset the devolution of responsibility from the federal government. A desire for modesty favoured 'urban vernaculars'. New York State's Mitchell-Lama Housing Program sponsored rental housing like Davis/Brody's Riverbend in Harlem (1964–7), a skilful levitation of row-house units complete with individual 'stoops' as entries, varied massing, playgrounds and walkways that are visible, pleasant and safe – a type the firm adapted elsewhere to good effect. The Urban Development Corporation (UDC) built 23 handsome projects from 1968 to 1975. Good site planning characterized both low-rise enclaves and high-rise agglomerations, including thirteen diverse interventions at Twin Parks in the Bronx. Kenneth Frampton of IAUS collaborated with Ted Lieberman of UDC on Marcus Garvey Park Village in Brooklyn, a minimalist medium-density scheme influenced by Newman's *Defensible Space* and displayed at MOMA in 1973.

Similar initiatives elsewhere also favoured low-rise, medium-density modern housing with vernacular inflections, especially when tenants participated in deliberations. The Boston architect John Sharratt's Villa Victoria was built in six phases over thirteen years (1969–82) with funding from multiple non-profit organizations. The 750 units were a 'patch-work quilt' of new and restored row houses and apartment towers linked by an animated plaza, a priority for the Puerto Rican residents in the Emergency Tenants Association.[29] Chloethiel Woodard Smith's racially integrated projects in Washington, DC, and St Louis combined historic preservation, conventional wood-frame dwellings and ample public services interconnected through landscaped pathways, although several critics disdained her conspicuously familiar references as overly 'cute', too much like the neighbourhoods they replaced.[30]

California explored wide-ranging alternatives. A resurgence of interest in rural-housing reform led Sanford Hirshen to build or expand nineteen migrant farm workers' communities from 1965 to 1975, experimenting with inventive techniques such as folded-plate structures in treated paper. Most new housing was intentionally more familiar. Now critical of earlier urban-renewal projects, San Francisco built scores of block-sized variations on wood-frame, shed-roofed clusters with shared outdoor spaces in the Western Addition. Rehabilitated Victorian-era housing was interspersed among the new projects. But here as elsewhere, the supply of subsidized dwellings lagged far behind the ever-growing need.

Market-rate housing often followed the best design strategies of subsidized enclaves. Some apartment towers took dramatic shapes like

Sanford Hirshen with Sim van der Ryn, housing for migrant farmworkers, Indio, California, 1965.

cylinders and interlocking geometries and colonnades, especially popular in the Sunbelt. A new generation of agile modernists burst on the scene in Miami with the vibrant colours and playful shapes of Arquitectonica. The Atlantis (1978–82) was featured in the opening sequence of the television series *Miami Vice*, inaugurating a new form of branding. New York's Battery Park City Authority commissioned multiple teams of private developers and notable architects for more than 6,000 'high-end' apartment units. Cooper/Eckstut's 1979 master plan for the 37 hectares of downtown property broke conventions by making public space a priority, even along the waterfront. The architecture was stifled by guidelines that imposed an artificial diversity and 'contextual' references to Manhattan's pre-World War Two past. Since Battery Park

City was publicly owned and operated by the UDC, millions of dollars in surplus profits were set aside for low-income housing in other parts of the city, monies that disappeared into Mayor Rudy Giuliani's budget. Good intentions easily go awry without vigilance.

Architect-developer teams tried to counter sprawl with 'clusters' of attached 'town-homes' that updated the garden apartments of the 1920s with imaginative site plans. The privately owned town of Reston, Virginia, suggested an auspicious prototype for compact development of large-scale 'urbanized suburbs'. Federal New Towns included The Woodlands outside Houston; Irvine, California; and two New-Towns-in-Town, Cedar-Riverside in Minneapolis and Roosevelt Island alongside Manhattan. Architects evoked irregular 'vernacular' settlements, the fine-grain patterns of European 'carpet housing', or brash obliques and diagonals. In principle, cluster housing protected local ecologies, although many such landscapes consisted of lawns, artificial lakes and golf courses.

Environmentalist sympathies affected large-scale elite enclaves, three of which stand out. Sea Ranch on the rugged northern California coast epitomized the modern arcadian ideal of simple luxury in a wilderness preserve. Moore Lyndon Turnbull Whitaker (MLTW) completed the first condominium group in 1965, nestled in an unprepossessing corner of the 2,000-hectare meadow. They adapted the unadorned redwood sheathing of local barns and sheds with varied roof lines that followed the windswept crests of cypress trees and rocky promontories. The distinctive amalgam of sensuousness and rigour extended to the interior spaces, and to countless replications on much smaller sites all over the country.

Antoine Predock explored similar principles for La Luz (1967–73), a dense group of 100 luxury condominium units north of Albuquerque, New Mexico, whose owners protect the surrounding 200 hectares of bosque and mesa in a land trust. Solar heating and cooling were combined with a time-tested local material, sun-dried adobe covered with mud-coloured stucco, keeping the interiors a pleasant temperature year round while ensuring acoustical privacy at close quarter. While Predock's massing inevitably evokes the region's pueblo architecture, the plain, unadorned surfaces are sculptural. The site plan creates what he calls 'abstract landscapes', a modern sensibility at once local and universal.[31]

The town of Seaside also fits into this category of modern site planning, even though modern architects typically revile Duany/ Plater-Zyberk (DPZ) and their picture-perfect, 32-hectare Florida town with its neo-traditional dwellings and rigid design code. The core principle of DPZ's master plan (1979–80) was familiar typologies related to the street,

Antoine Predock,
La Luz, Albuquerque,
New Mexico, 1967–73.

La Luz, site plan.

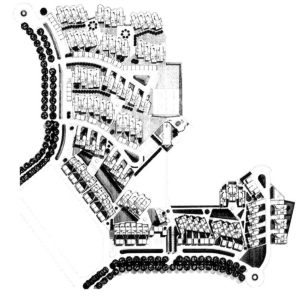

but progressive commitments to environmental protection, public transit and public open space were equally important. Hoping to provide an image of diverse experimentation, they invited modernists like Steven Holl, who built a Hybrid Building. Even if the overall impression remains monolingual, Andrés Duany's messianic calls for expert design and his declarations of war against the status quo had a distinctly modern ring that helped launch a crusade.

Discussion about modern single-family houses has usually ignored this larger context, although luxury dwellings are homes and market commodities as well as architectural statements. Complex geometries and dynamic sections literally broke out of the box, a striking contrast to the economical simple volumes of market-rate housing. As the prosperity and cultural freedoms of the 1960s stimulated architectural experiments, inflation saw house values double. Rising income inequalities in the narcissistic 'Me Decade' of the 1970s brought increased costs and cachet to designer houses.

The archetypal design of the era for architects, even those who hated it, was Robert Venturi's home for his mother, Vanna Venturi, in Chestnut Hill, Pennsylvania, completed in 1964 and soon famous as the Mother's House. The design juxtaposed layers of walls, spaces and historical references. A study in architectonic paradox – Venturi called it 'complex and simple', 'open and closed', 'big and little' – the house manifested its designer's intelligence and practicality. He made awkwardness a virtue, like the Italian Mannerists who purposefully sought to disrupt perfection. The façade, seemingly symmetrical, challenged first impressions with elements that were subtly off-centre, disjointed and literally split. This 'almost symbolic image of a house' emphasized 'almost' with studied ambiguities and pleasures.[32] The plan skewed the placement of walls and stairs, generating a complex, almost crowded interior that invited imaginative musing. Venturi's abstract concepts enhanced his appreciation of everyday realities.

Richard Meier's Smith House, near Darien, Connecticut (1965–7), used elementary geometries in a more abstract manner. The wood cladding was painted white, a sculptural object in a magnificent landscape. Expansive glass on the main façade overlooked a rocky coast. Stairs and balconies created overlapping cubist spaces, inside and out. Peter Eisenman's numbered series of 'post-humanist' houses used elaborate mathematical codes to determine the overlaid planes, but surely he enjoyed and to some extent calculated disruptive gestures like a column through the dining table or the bed in House VI. A book by his client Suzanne Frank described the 'annoyances', 'inconvenient elements' and 'compromises' she and her husband confronted. In 1974 the

Venturi & Short,
Vanna Venturi House,
Chestnut Hill,
Pennsylvania,
1959–64, main
façade.

Vanna Venturi House,
living room.

Vanna Venturi House,
ground-floor plan.

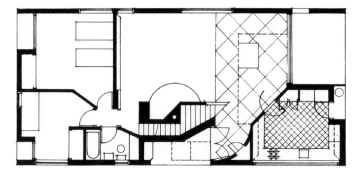

Richard Meier,
Smith House, Darien,
Connecticut, 1965–7,
living room.

Italian critic Manfredo Tafuri mocked the American avant-garde's indulgent pleasures for capitalism's new elite as 'architecture in the boudoir'.[33]

Some houses, highly acclaimed at the time, are less well known today. Mary Otis Stevens and Thomas McNulty caused a stir with their 1965 house in Lincoln, Massachusetts. *Life* praised the sensuous poured-concrete curves as 'sculpture to live in'. The young husband-and-wife architects were principally concerned with environmental factors and an open, non-hierarchical family life. The plan allowed them to do away with doors, while encouraging a palpable sense of movement and 'hesitations' – their word for places to reflect or inter-act.[34] The design /build firm Jersey Devil connected aesthetic experimentation with a strong environmentalist purpose, fusing sophisticated technology with hands-on construction. A nomadic collective, they lived on site throughout each project, deeply committed to the particularities of place and process, juxtaposing steel and computers

Mary Otis Stevens
and Thomas McNulty,
Stevens-McNulty
House, Lincoln,
Massachusetts, 1965.

with found objects and natural materials. As architect-contractors they defied the profession's gentlemanly traditions as much as John Portman had done.

Frank Gehry's series of inventive urban dwellings began with the 1977–8 adaptations to his own home in Santa Monica, California. Neighbours protested, but architects acclaimed the lyrical collages of raw construction materials like chain-link fencing and rough timber. Brash gestures were interwoven with poetic references to the original house (a 1920s builder's bungalow), the legacy of twentieth-century art and architecture, and Gehry's own family memories. While intentionally modest and slightly aggressive, this house would become an iconic object when he rose to celebrity status in the 1990s.

Residential architecture of the 1970s challenged conventions while enhancing design and domestic lives. Most Americans saw only three extremes: expensive custom-designed houses, distressed public-housing towers and large-scale multi-unit developments. These were the images

220

Jersey Devil, Hill
House, La Honda,
California, 1977–9.

Frank Gehry, Gehry
House, Santa Monica,
California, 1977-8,
kitchen.

of 'Modernism' when the mid-decade recession and urban-development policies wreaked havoc on moderate-income housing. A conservative backlash viewed all of these changes as 'anti-family'. Even positive trends took on dark connotations. Local governments granted special zoning privileges to large, relatively expensive Planned Unit Developments (PUDS) with dense configurations of condominiums and ample open space. Television specials about 'the housing crisis' portrayed this as the necessary if less-than-desirable solution for those who could not afford 'real' homes in the suburbs. Identified with economic and social disruptions, even purposefully moderate and ecological modern architecture came to be seen as an assault on the American way of life.

Marketing an Open Society

The exuberant public spaces of the late 1960s and '70s promised new kinds of freedom, some celebrating collective expression, others geared to particular groups. Presidents Johnson and Nixon invested in modern public architecture for education and the arts. States and municipalities did the same, often partnered with private businesses and cultural institutions. As Americans confronted a rise in urban violence, two seemingly opposite spatial paradigms defined a new degree of control over 'free' environments and activities. The interior 'street' brought the public realm indoors. Simultaneously, echoing office buildings of the era, exterior plazas of 'open rooms' were designed for surveillance and control as much as pleasure.

Progressive or 'open' schools embraced an energetic aesthetic of irregular clusters, diagonal rotations and animated layers. Spatial liberties aligned with pedagogical reforms like team-teaching and non-graded groups. Columbus, Indiana, a town of 40,000 inhabitants, inaugurated a programme for innovative schools funded by a philanthropic local businessman, J. Irwin Miller. The utopian mission extended to other building types as well, making Columbus a virtual museum of modern American architecture. One of the best examples was Mt Healthy Elementary School by Hardy Holzman Pfeiffer (1970–72). The public façades mixed references to familiar late nineteenth-century motifs such as industrial windows and red-brick schoolhouses, although these walls were thin and playful, like other cardboard motifs of the 1970s. The interior came alive, a kinetic sculpture with exposed high-tech elements in vivid colours along a circulation spine with niches, changes in level and moveable partitions along a diagonal 'street'. Learning could be fun and unstructured, at least for young children. Urban intermediate and high schools, on the other hand, often resembled another prime architectural motif of the era, the fortress or prison.

Hardy Holtzman
Pfeiffer, Mt Healthy
Elementary School,
Columbus, Ohio,
1970–72, interior.

Mt Healthy
Elementary School,
floor plan.

As baby-boomers reached college age, federal programmes expanded opportunities for higher education. College enrolment soared to over 6 million students in the mid-1960s, four times the post-war figure. Seeking to mask the increased scale, architects stressed illusions of spontaneity, 'planned chaos' and community with contrived simulations of those goals. Student centres proliferated, while large 'multiversity' campuses were subdivided into smaller clusters. The architecture tended to be imperious, even in small schools and historically black colleges like Tuskegee. SOM's Walter Netsch began the move by applying his 'Field Theory' to the new University of Illinois campus at Chicago Circle, completed in 1965. Elevated concrete 'expressways' for pedestrian traffic surrounded a huge rooftop 'agora' above the Brutalist-inspired classroom buildings.

New York and Massachusetts hired major architects to design outsized, often overbearing campuses. California commissioned three new universities. San Diego and Irvine were huge concrete behemoths, but Santa Cruz was known for its open-minded teaching and informality, with each college isolated from the others in lush natural landscapes. Charles Moore/MLTW's Kresge College (1965–74) was a 'non-institutional' alternative designed with student and faculty participation. A pedestrian 'street' formed the spine of an intimate village, its picturesque irregularity responding to trees and terrain. If Kresge was easily dismissed as a romantic stage set, the firm's Pembroke Dormitories at Brown University in Providence, Rhode Island (1970–75), won

SOM/Walter Netsch,
University of Illinois,
Chicago Circle
campus, Chicago,
Illinois, 1962–5,
central 'agora'
and classroom
buildings.

Donlyn Lyndon/MLTW,
Pembroke College,
Brown University,
Providence, Rhode
Island, 1968–70,
courtyard.

resounding praise. Spatial and budgetary restrictions had inspired an urbane design built around a multi-tiered internal court. The dense complex engaged the neighbouring streets, even in the choice of glazed coloured brick, a material simultaneously prosaic and scintillating.

Government architecture displaced the solemn New Monumentality of post-war modernists on several fronts. When President Johnson's Great Society programme funded projects in poor neighbourhoods, 'community

Hodgetts and Fung with Robert Mangurian/Studio Works, Southside Community Center, Columbus, Ohio, 1980, view of courtyard.

control' encouraged local residents' involvement in decision-making and design. Indeed, Johnson himself endorsed 'maximum feasible participation', sometimes as a substitute for new buildings and services. Established architects' offices donated their services *pro bono*; small firms like Friday Architects of Philadelphia and the all-women Open Design Office in New York specialized in community centres. These 'storefront' facilities combined renovations with new infill buildings to repair tears in the existing fabric of streets. Drawing on the neutral sets of modern stagecraft, these architects delighted in the possibilities of recycled and cheap materials. But the larger political picture shows the omnipresent shadow of the Vietnam War. Aesthetics had to be affordable in Johnson's War on Poverty, in part because the cost of that conflict radically depleted funds for housing and other reforms. If liberal policy-makers sought to win 'hearts and minds' in the ghettos, they also trained 'counter-insurgency' police and increased the number of armouries and prisons, soon achieving the world's highest rate of incarceration.

Expanding federal, state and municipal governments commissioned larger buildings. Complex massing supposedly encouraged democracy by revealing the inner workings of power and bureaucracy. The young firm of Kallmann, McKinnell and Knowles won the national competition for Boston's City Hall (1962–8), the centrepiece of an extensive new government centre. This was 'Action Architecture', in Gerhard Kallmann's words, a syncretic mixture of ad hoc events and organized movement.

A radial plaza conjured up the 'outdoor rooms' of Siena and Italian hill towns, then penetrated into the building through ramps and steps that implied accessible officials. In fact, the space was rigidly composed yet disorientating, especially the huge atrium lobby. The Brutalist concrete suggested a fortified barricade and the weight of authority. No one could match the protean scale of Governor Nelson Rockefeller's Empire State Plaza in New York, also known as the Albany Mall (1969–78), with ten high-rise buildings atop a six-storey platform and an eerie subterranean concourse. Grandiose 'public' gestures became so ostentatious that an inevitable reaction set in, evident in 'contextual' or colourful new post-modernist buildings and renovations of historic structures.

Government buildings were mostly a matter of boosterism and bureaucracy by the 1970s, since private corporations and real-estate developers now figured prominently in local decision-making. They convinced officials of two basic principles: first, that urban constituencies were investors and consumers, not citizens; second, that people thought of cities in terms of imagery and entertainment, not services. Neo-liberals argued that municipal funds were supposed to keep cities 'competitive' and 'attractive' with 'people-magnets' which would draw wealthy tourists and residents. The 'centre' trumped the mere building. Modern architecture predominated with new urban shopping centres, performing-arts centres, convention centres and arts centres. Sparked by Portman's Hyatt Hotels, the emerging 'hospitality industry' built lavish hotels alongside the new cultural emporia. Franchise motels and restaurants followed mediocre formulas, still plastic but lacking the idiosyncratic camp of earlier 'Googie' architecture. By the time Venturi and Scott Brown published *Learning from Las Vegas* in 1972, the neon world of the Strip was changing. Recent laws allowed corporations to be licensed as casino owners, resulting in huge high-rise towers behind lavish special-effects spectacles.

Fascination with local history sought to offset the glitz. Even race and ethnicity were recast as claims about cultural 'identity' morphed inequalities into particularities that might attract tourists eager

Harry Weese, Metropolitan Correctional Center, Chicago, 1975.

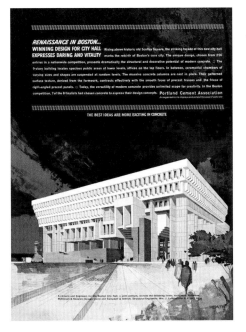

Kallmann, McKinnell
& Knowles, Boston
City Hall and Plaza,
1960–67, Portland
Cement company
advertisement.

for novelty. Japanese-American merchants joined with the San Francisco Redevelopment Center under Rai Okomoto in 1968 to create Nihonmachi, a cultural and economic centre for the area called Japantown, a themed complex of shops surrounding a landscaped plaza and Minoru Yamasaki's new Peace Pagoda. Los Angeles sponsored a similar fusion a decade later at Korean Village. Italian-Americans in New Orleans hired Charles Moore's Urban Innovations Group to design the Piazza d'Italia (1975), a 'destination' that ultimately failed, largely because the surrounding hotel, stores and offices never materialized.

A few cities rejected commercialized themed environments in favour of settings that fused old and new, building and landscape, commonalities and differences. Lawrence Halprin used dynamic concrete geometries for sculpture fountains in Portland, San Francisco and Seattle. These structures invited spontaneous participation, but they were confrontational too, often built over freeways or resembling the ruins of freeway extensions that had been stopped by citizen protests.

One of the most visited national-park sites in the country is the Martin Luther King Jr Center adjacent to Dr King's church on Sweet Auburn Avenue, the center of black Atlanta in its glory days. Plans for the MLK Center were fraught with tension after the rise of Black Power and the violent ghetto riots of the late 1960s. These were compounded by conflicts between federal agencies, the King family, the neighbourhood and the city government, all jockeying for cultural capital and economic benefits. The New York firm Bond Ryder James eventually won the commission in 1976 and completed it in 1981. The materials are humble: concrete columns with local wood and brick. The sequence of spaces repeats familiar patterns as if the complex had evolved over time. This is an eloquent, understated Modernism, a fitting expression of King's aspirations for justice.

For the most part, municipal and regional governments partnered with private sponsors for extravagant blockbuster facilities. As Charles Moore said in 1965, fascinated but also saddened by the shift: 'You Have To Pay for the Public Life.'[35] Aquariums were a big draw. Superstar athletes on big-league teams spurred huge sports stadiums, 'the civic icon

Bond Ryder James & Associates, Martin Luther King, Jr Center for Non-Violent Social Change, Atlanta, Georgia, 1976–81.

of the late-20th century', one architect told the *Wall Street Journal*, 'the equivalent of a cathedral'.[36] Early examples of engineering prowess include Houston's 1965 Astrodome with its retractable roof, an electronic scoreboard and surface parking for 30,000 cars. The Louisiana Superdome and Pontiac Silverdome (both 1975) soon upped the ante. 'Build It and They Will Come' was the mantra. Higher taxes and special bonds were necessary, but prestige and economic benefits were supposedly guaranteed. In fact, most new stadia showed a net loss.

Performing-arts centres provided cultural capital for a new urban elite that dreaded the thought of being provincial. These places did not just house culture; they transformed it with mass middle-class audiences for blockbuster performances. Grandiose scale and opulence certainly defined the first example, New York City's Lincoln Center, begun under Robert Moses in 1955, its initial phase completed in 1966. With Harrison & Abramowitz only nominal leaders, Philip Johnson took charge of the master plan, orchestrating the architecture to resemble Michelangelo's Campidoglio complex in Rome with repeating colonnades and uniform roof heights and entries. The extravagant size and gaudy ornamentation stressed the audience's performance as much as that of the artists. (The acoustics in the Philharmonic suffered from its grandiose scale until it was rebuilt in 1976.) But the Moses approach to urban renewal was the major problem. Lincoln Center was raised above the streets on a plinth, conspicuously aloof from the city streets, oblivious to the informal vitality and diversity that are essential to artistic creativity.

Hundreds of cities from coast to coast and deep in the heartland invested in performance centres. The Kennedy Center in Washington, DC, (1958–64) and the Los Angeles Music Center (1958–67) emulated New York's model of safe, sanitized grandiosity. Others opted for bold Brutalist geometries, while a few chose vibrant, small-scale modern architecture. John Johansen's Mummers Theatre in Oklahoma City (1964–70), now the Stage Center, has brightly coloured concrete boxes suspended vertiginously, linked by ramped circulation tubes, looking somewhat like a giant Tinkertoy construction. Johansen called his approach 'Kinetics', a very 1960s celebration of joy, change and human energy. His sketch for the

John Johansen, Mummers Theater, Oklahoma City, Oklahoma, 1964–70, aerial view (today the Stage Center).

Mummers Theater, sketch of section.

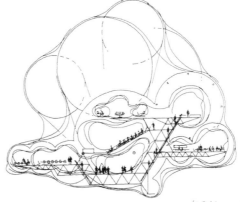

building captures the anticipated animation of a bubble diagram. Like the avant-garde theatre productions performed here, the building embodied self-conscious improvisation and experimentalism geared to smaller audiences. The intentionally haphazard assembly rejects any visible rules of composition. Some critics were outraged by the structure's fragmentation, yet awkwardness can be a virtue in buildings that encourage artists and audiences to explore unconventional forms of expression.

The visual arts spilled over into museum practice and architecture. Artists turned to 'alternative spaces' they defined themselves, some of which became major institutions in their own right. The largest and most potent is the Chinati Foundation in Marfa, Texas, where Donald Judd began to renovate a series of small, spare wood-frame houses and enormous industrial sheds in 1972, later interspersing these with his own concrete and aluminium boxes to create an elegant enfilade. The appropriate setting revealed the theatricality inherent in minimal art, what the critic Michael Fried called its 'objecthood', by emphasizing subtle variations in light and spatial context.[37] Artists likewise preferred Frank Gehry's Temporary Contemporary in Los Angeles of 1983, a funky industrial warehouse only slightly modified (now the Geffen Contemporary) to the polished museum by Arata Isozaki that opened in 1986.

The 'museum industry' borrowed public-entertainment tactics with amenities such as shops and restaurants and occasionally great architecture.[38] The category expanded to include every possible kind of collection. Kevin Roche's Oakland Museum (1961–8) grouped three separate troves of history and natural history in discreet, almost invisible structures beneath landscaped public terraces. But art museums were top of the line. I. M. Pei's huge East Wing expansion of the National Gallery of Art in Washington (1974–8) asserted authority with commanding geometrical shapes and blank façades. Richard Meier became master of the genre with the High Museum in Atlanta (1980–83). Gracefully expanding the interlocking white planes and curves characteristic of his houses, he created exhilarating spatial experiences as diagonal ramps accentuated the complex play of light, shadows and movement adjacent to contemplative spaces for viewing art.

The work of Louis Kahn defies easy classification. His Kimbell Museum in Fort Worth, Texas (1966–72) is inspiring but still, in Kahn's words, a 'friendly home', since both the architect and the museum's director, Richard Brown, wanted an institution that would convey dignity and joy without intimidation. Kahn achieved this with a graceful complex of six parallel concrete vaults that shelter an entrance court, enclosed galleries, garden courts and a stepped reflecting pool. Reaching back to 'simple beginnings', the curvature of the vaults was based on cycloid geometry, an ancient Mediterranean shape. The vaulting allows gallery spaces to be free

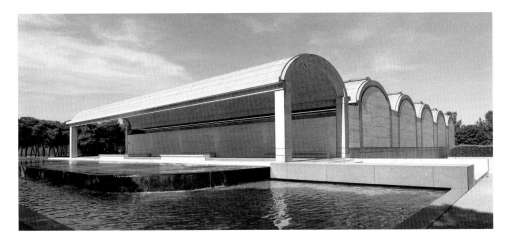

Louis Kahn, Kimbell
Museum, Fort Worth,
Texas, 1966–72.

Kimbell Museum,
upper floor plan.

1 garden entry
2 portico
3 gallery
4 kitchen
5 stairs from lower level lobby
6 bookstore
7 auditorium
8 library (mezzanine above)
9 light court

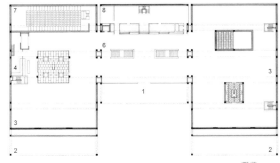

Kimbell Museum,
galleries.

of fixed walls while abundant natural light intensifies the elemental power of the structure and the open spaces. Daylight spills through openings at the centre of each vault onto upturned aluminium reflectors, infusing the travertine interior walls with the 'luminosity of silver' against the 'liquid stone' of the concrete.[39] Kahn's ability to imbue Modernism with emotional intensity, functional necessities and ordinary life provides a connector between diverse, seemingly antagonistic architectural groups.

Ronald Reagan's inauguration as President in 1980 proclaimed 'The Second American Revolution'. His administration advocated private economic gain and 'traditional' values, scuttling any residual social ideals.[40] Reagan even removed the solar panels that President Carter had installed on the White House roof. Tom Wolfe's simplistic, immensely popular 1981 book captured the mood. *From Bauhaus to Our House* lampooned modern architecture as an 'invasion' of European 'princes' committed to workers' housing and subservient Americans intimidated by a 'colonial complex'. Whites and Grays alike 'enunciated suitably obscure theories' to revile anything that looked '*too American,* too parochial, and too bourgeois'. Intellectuals on the left described the same situation with a twist. The geographer David Harvey argued that the fiscal crisis of the mid-1970s had driven a frenzied search for enticing display to suggest an open, pluralistic society. Postmodernism and late Modernism were caught in the same system, beholden to wealthy investors rather than European architects. For Harvey, modern architecture had 'shamelessly sold itself to the highest bidder without a shred of critical resistance'.[41]

Shock value was part of the calculated appeal in the polyphonous 'play' of contemporary architecture. Philip Johnson cheerfully proclaimed: 'I am a whore' to a privileged group of colleagues in 1982. 'I do not believe in principles', he added for effect, 'in case you haven't noticed'.[42] Narcissistic nonchalance became a sign of creative independence. Important architects were talked about on first-name terms – Philip, Peter and Bob – since everyone knew who they were (or scurried to find out). The media and big commissions made architects marketable, assuring major commissions for the select few. If this attitude liberated American design processes and forms, it also unmoored architects from an earlier sense of responsibility.[43]

No epoch can be reduced to an essence or a facile dichotomy. Cultural clichés about 'the architecture of Reaganism' and facile paeans to 'heterogeneity' are too one-dimensional, eliding anything that fails to fit the label. The early 1980s expanded opportunities for women, Asian, Latino and African-American architects. Some of the best-known works were exquisite small buildings, often constructed on restricted budgets. Fay Jones's Thorncrown Chapel in Eureka Springs, Arkansas (1979–80), sits atop a

Fay Jones,
Thorncrown Chapel,
Eureka Springs,
Arkansas, 1979–80.

stone base in a wooded glade. Gothic Revival allusions to vaulting as a forest connect the structure to medieval Christianity, yet the elemental qualities suggest a deistic worship of nature. So, too, with Maya Lin's Vietnam Veterans' Memorial in Washington, DC (1982), in which a young female undergraduate conveyed the power of abstract sculptural form and inspired connection to the earth. Metaphors resonated deeply, evoking the land and tectonics, human memories and aspirations. Eschewing superficial user-friendly iconography as well as hermetic hubris, this modern architecture reverberated within the discipline and far beyond it.

chapter seven

Disjunctures and Alternatives, 1985 to the Present

The 'new economy' became pre-eminent in the mid-1980s, affecting almost every aspect of architecture from programmes and façades to the very nature of the discipline. Delirious spending unleashed a bloated increase in the scale of consumer objects including buildings. Affluent individuals commissioned extravagant houses while global capital helped finance an interconnected world of mega-projects. Entrepreneurial cities invested in name-brand architecture as 'catalysts', hoping to stimulate a flow of outside investors, wealthy residents and tourists, including near-by suburbanites.[1] Haphazard development in the suburbs shifted towards large master-planned enclaves and gated residential communities, also known as 'common interest developments', predominantly neo-traditional enclaves under the aegis of leviathan home-building corporations that rarely hired professional architects. The media began to track a handful of 'boutique' or 'signature' architects, beginning with Frank Gehry after he traded the colliding elements in cheap materials of his earlier buildings for sinuous curves in expensive metals. Through these years, if only occasionally in the spotlight, hundreds of resilient modern architects around the country, most in relatively small practices, generated imaginative designs for workplaces, public buildings and moderate-income housing.

Networks were essential, given the pace of change and complexity of knowledge in every field. The NEA created the Mayors Institute on City Design in 1986, bringing mayors and key administrators from more than 200 cities together with designers and academics to discuss local initiatives from infrastructure to public housing. The structure of architectural practice underwent major shifts in the 1990s as large corporate firms merged, spawned regional offices and greatly increased non-design staff in public relations, construction management and other business skills. Once reluctant to show conspicuous commercial ambitions, architects were touting their savvy about real-estate, publicity and communications strategies, some to engage 'the market', others to press beyond its narrow conventions.

Frank Gehry, Frederick R. Weisman Art Museum at the University of Minnesota, Minneapolis, 1990–93, postcard.

William Massie, Big Sky House (Owens House), near White Sulpher Springs, Montana, 1999–2001, illustrated in *Metropolitan Home* magazine (November 2003).

Digital fabrication versioning for Big Sky House.

Computers were soon omnipresent, catapulting architecture far beyond the previous generation of CAD and computer-aided manufacture (CAM). Gehry appropriated technologies from the automotive, naval and aerospace industries, making fluid shapes feasible to build, if economical only in relative terms. Young architects then adapted 3-D modelling programmes from movie special effects and animation to create sinuous surfaces. Greg Lynn called his shapes 'blobitecture' and issued messianic assertions of a liberating new Zeitgeist.[2] Every technology has its drawbacks, of course. Speed encouraged dramatic imagery over more deliberative considerations; programmes become design

236

determinants rather than tools. Computers forced many architects to cut time, costs and the quality of materials, thus reducing design standards. Some cleverly turned the tables, simplifying schemes, then going directly into production in order to customize moderate-cost buildings adapted to their sites. William Massie told *Business Week* that he used computer technology to go back to 'the true beginning – when modernist homes were reasonably priced'.[3]

The Internet made research a buzzword, providing a base for design analysis, programs, specifications – and promotional imagery. Reams of data were compiled into vivid maps and 'datascapes', sometimes translated directly into morphology. Gensler and OMA created offshoot research units to study topics like workplace performance and branding strategies. Adopting a business model that delivered up-to-date generic products, more firms specialized in particular kinds of buildings, using detailed knowledge to reduce costs and maximize profits. Intrepid designers adopted scientific or management models of innovation, 'looking for loopholes' within existent systems. Small offices collaborated and augmented the range of in-house knowledge, as with New York's Sharples Holden Pasquarelli (SHOP), whose principals combined design skills with training in fields like financial management, allowing them to tackle large and small projects in ways that accentuate 'performance rather than form'.[4]

Building skins took on an ethereal lightness of being with advances that combined thinness, translucency, permeability and environmental adaptations. Architects were often directly engaged in the development of 'ultramaterials' that met performance criteria never before imagined.[5] Structural fibreglass and polymers, foamed aluminium, moiré and mesh metals, subtle patterned glass and seemingly weightless concrete directly influenced forms and perceptions. Modernism's early focus on transparency gave way to more subtle experiments in optical and cognitive reflection, a process brilliantly deployed by the artist James Carpenter and architects like Smith-Miller + Hawkinson. In a world obsessed with illusory images, the attention to precise textures and details in the Corning Museum of Glass (1995–7) in Corning, New York, renewed a passion for substance. Equally eloquent advocates took up inexpensive recycled debris. Fernau & Hartman explored the distinctive patinas and historical resonance of reused timber with several remarkable houses in northern California and beyond. Rick Joy juxtaposed rammed earth and rusted steel in simple cubic forms, a combination chosen for sustainability as well as sensuality. Others used recycled metal and plastic with aplomb, while several architects developed a fetish for shipping containers, an ingenious but scarcely empathetic solution to the housing crisis.

Smith-Miller +
Hawkinson, Corning
Museum of Glass,
Corning, New York,
1995–7, entry.

Beset by deep-rooted American anxieties about bilingualism, architects have had to negotiate between competing verbal and visual languages while surreptitiously borrowing from each other. Neo-avant-garde discourse continues to call for aggressive transgressions and defamiliarization. Philip Johnson, still a king-maker at 82, and co-curator Mark Wigley created a trendy new label with MOMA's *Deconstructivist Architecture* show (1988), fusing the skewed shapes of Russian Constructivism with the language games of Jacques Derrida's Deconstruction.[6] Apart from Gehry, the architects on display had little or no built work, but their drawings and models had extraordinary power, especially the pulsing energy of Zaha Hadid, the torqued geometries of Bernard Tschumi and the catastrophic scenarios of Daniel Libeskind. The catalogue praised these works as subversive assaults on the status quo, 'releasing' the 'instability' and 'impurity' that the Modern Movement had sought to repress. These references to revolutionary change suggested a spread from a fashion magazine more than a political manifesto. Indeed, in less than a decade the avant-garde moved on to Deleuzian folds, then allusions to mathematics with fractals and chaos theory, followed by biomorphic curves and genetic mutations. Analogies seem to metamorphose just as critics begin to probe them.

238

Another group rejected alienation by evoking the local, the everyday and the vernacular.[7] The Vernacular Architecture Forum, founded in 1980, promoted scholarship about 'ordinary' American buildings and cultural landscapes, past and present, not just rural but urban and suburban, too. *Vernacular*, originally a linguistic term for parochial dialects about everyday matters (a contrast to the Latin of scholars and the Church), now meant designs attuned to local landscapes and construction traditions.[8] Some aficionados espoused a romantic primitivism, a pathway to supposedly 'authentic' building practices and stable communities in perfect harmony with their surroundings. Others claimed that identity-based designs distilled and honoured the equally spurious 'authentic' nature of ethnic or racial groups.[9] Such essentialist aspirations served diverse purposes. In Miami, for example, Overtown Mall (1994) substituted formal expressions of African roots for the displaced African-Americans' rights of urban citizenship, while the Caribbean Marketplace (1997) in Little Haiti tried to promote local entrepreneurs, albeit unsuccessfully.

Staunch modernists often lump all such allusions together and dismiss the lot as unthinking imitations of inert traditions, repudiations of modern progress and dangerous right-wing populism. That caricature should not go unchallenged. True, romantic nationalists have long embraced vernaculars as ties to a *Heimat*, or homeland, but this does not signal a necessary correlation. Both critics and advocates of vernacular architecture are also mistaken about an unselfconscious, 'timeless' quality since traditions are continually evolving, often through the agency of individuals. In fact, architectural culture is a rarefied example of this very phenomenon. Resonant modern forms have emerged in response to specific site conditions and cultural milieux. In both the past and the present, this has been the work of skilled artisans and professional architects. The discussion needs to move beyond essentialist polemics about one's own or other cultures, asking instead how *all* designers can gain meaningful knowledge about the continuities and conflicts that affect people and places.

As environmental concerns grew stronger, they generated two distinct idioms. Distress about irreparable damage to landscapes and increased homogeneity throughout the world renewed a yearning for connection to 'place'. A new term, 'critical regionalism', questioned superficial postmodern efforts to assuage such longings. Liane Lefaivre and Alexander Tzonis coined the phrase in 1981 in reference to post-World War Two Greek architecture. For them, critical regionalism meant a 'self-reflective', locally inflected modern idiom that reveals the ecological and historical particularities of a specific site while simultaneously seeking to improve conditions. Kenneth Frampton brought the term into widespread use with a 1983 article, 'Toward a Critical Regionalism', a polemic that fused profound despair about human and ecological destructiveness under late capitalism with a deep commitment to the legacy of the Modern Movement. Citing Paul Ricoeur's challenge regarding 'how to become modern and to return to sources', Frampton's dialectical critique addressed dehumanization in the modern world while refusing facile evocations of harmony.[10] He gave little attention to cultural specifics, whether human or environmental, because of an unrelenting suspicion of any 'scenographic' reference as potentially kitsch. Instead, he urged architects to show 'resistance' with highly abstract, indirect references to tectonic traditions, local light and topographies.[11]

In contrast, ecologically minded architects used highly technical language to speak about effects, not just intentions, although they were equally concerned with moral issues. William McDonough first voiced concerns about the toxicity of materials and working conditions in major commercial facilities in the mid-1980s, a condition soon known as 'sick building syndrome'. The Environmental Protection Agency demanded extensive environmental-impact statements for large-scale projects. A 1985 court ruling ended a decade of grandiose plans for New York's Westway – an underground highway on Manhattan's West Side with 80 hectares of parks and commercial development on new landfill – largely because such evidence had been suppressed. Pliny Fisk and Gail Vittori founded the Center for Maximum Potential Building Systems near Laredo, Texas, in 1987, to study the local impact of high- and low-tech construction materials in different parts of the world. A fundamental question now arose: was any construction justifiable when buildings consume half the world's energy? The somewhat elusive term 'sustainable development' signalled a new ambition: 'zero-impact' buildings that generate more energy than they consume.

Chicago, Seattle and Los Angeles sponsored environmental initiatives. Green roofs, greenways and reclaimed brownfield sites became more common. The 1992 Public Art Master Plan for Phoenix, Arizona, coordinated interventions for the metropolis and its environs, directing development while protecting fragile landscapes. William Morrish and the late Catherine Brown generated more than 40 collaborative teams of architects, artists, engineers and landscape architects for projects ranging from highway underpasses and downtown cultural institutions to a solid-waste treatment plant on the periphery. A 1997 conference established the concept of Landscape Urbanism, which emphasizes long-term processes, a larger scale of connected interventions and collaboration across disciplines. Major architects soon entered competitions for leftover or abandoned *terrains vagues* in and around cities – Fresh Kills on

Sterling McMurrin, architect, with Linnea Glatt and Michael Singer, artists, and Black & Veatch, engineers, 27th Avenue Solid Waste Treatment Facility, Phoenix, Arizona, 1993.

Staten Island (the country's largest landfill), Seattle's Olympic Sculpture Park, New York's High Line – stimulating debate about linkages between ecological and artistic practices.

Yet investment in public infrastructure remains piecemeal at best, a point made brutally clear with the 2005 disaster of Hurricane Katrina and other recent catastrophes. Lax federal regulations allow the most egregious industrial polluters to proceed virtually unchecked. Economic growth still trumps all other considerations, factored in terms of corporate profits with little concern for ecologies, including the social and economic sustainability of local communities. Most environmentalist efforts are individual structures built for dedicated clients. Recognizing a potential in competition, the AIA and construction-industry leaders founded the US Green Building Council in 1993, then established voluntary goals called Leadership in Energy and Environmental Design (LEED) in 2000. These performance-based assessments encourage ongoing innovation from architects and developers, who can receive certification. Many companies, municipalities and federal agencies have already instituted LEED guidelines. American modern architecture has turned green – reminding us once again that architects are responsible only for 10 per cent of what gets built.

Re-engineering Workspaces

The tumultuous economic shifts of the 1980s and '90s saw workplaces change along two different trajectories. One route pursued a lean, cost-effective model with plain façades, large floor plates and generic environments, typically called 'exit-strategy' architecture because it is easy to reconfigure if an owner sells off a building. 'Value engineering' supposedly prioritized various concerns, but often degenerated into cost-cutting and fast-track design processes. The results were prosaic, but this approach forced designers and managers to think in terms of adaptive systems rather than expensive packaging. A parallel pathway drew businesses eager to attract 'creative' employees and wealthy clients. The Corporate Design Foundation, established in 1985, encouraged forward-looking CEOs to 're-engineer' architecture as well as management. Consultants emphasized that design could help build cohesion, collaboration and innovation among employees while strengthening company visibility in the marketplace. Preferences gradually shifted from shiny postmodern veneers towards a more idiosyncratic and dynamic, even rough-edged industrial aesthetic.

The two tracks, generic and customized, began to overlap as imaginative architects drew on inexpensive, standardized, flexible building typologies. *Business Week* and *Architectural Record* inaugurated the annual BW/AR awards programme in 1997, hailing aesthetic quality and employee satisfaction in the best new workplaces. Awards have gone to museums (the Corning Museum of Glass), scientific laboratories, manufacturing facilities, office buildings and non-profit facilities such as the Smith Group's 2001 Merrill Education Center for the Chesapeake Bay Foundation in Annapolis, Maryland, which also received the first platinum LEED rating for its graceful façade of galvanized siding made from recycled cars and cans.

Location proved relevant in every field. New office buildings were increasingly concentrated in 'edge cities', outlying metropolitan areas where land was relatively inexpensive, regulations few, and architecture mostly tedious.[12] When the first stage of IBM's Solana campus opened in 1989, not far from Dallas-Fort Worth Airport, a *Progressive Architecture* cover story lauded the 'bold experiment'. The Mexican architect Ricardo Legorreta was principal designer for the 365-hectare site (another 400 hectares were held in a land trust), with Mitchell/Giurgula and Barton Myers for sub-sections. Legorreta created a corporate realm of *réel maravilloso*, or Magic Realism. The enchanted setting begins at the highway interchange, where motorists encounter a gigantic magenta pylon and two red walls that mark the entry court. The landscape architects Peter Walker

Legorreta
Arquitectos with
Peter Walker/Martha
Schwartz, Solana IBM
Westland, near Dallas,
Texas, 1988–90.

and Martha Schwartz created environments that are at once indigenous and surreal. Even the parking garages are flanked by spacious 'outdoor rooms'. White limestone edges unify the diverse, brightly hued pieces.

The sensibilities of Luis Barragán, Legorreta's teacher, pervade the IBM complex, such that adjacent communities protested the colours for looking too conspicuously Mexican, which disturbed the cultural hierarchy of Anglo-Texans. Of course, Solana is not really multicultural, not even a village – despite the Village Center – but a site in the multinational economy. As one critic observed, the scenography, tight security and lack of street life make this a place of 'aching loneliness, reminding the visitor more of de Chirico than of Barragán'.[13] Good design prevailed, but it could not trump the global economic downturn that beset edge cities in the early 1990s. IBM was forced to downsize its workforce and sub-let large parts of the complex.

The 1985 Mast Advertising and Publishing Headquarters in suburban Kansas City by BNIM (then called PBNI) was one of the first American office buildings to emphasize energy conservation, natural light and cross-ventilation, together with a narrow footprint and terraced landscaping to preserve a former farm on the site. It also signalled the rising influence of media, advertising, communication and arts-related businesses, which came to be called 'new media'. This shift affected the personal-computer industry, previously bound to a self-consciously undistinguished 'garage' aesthetic. Studios Architecture, a San Francisco interiors firm, used colourful theatrical effects to produce a lively asymmetrical facility for Apple Computers in 1986, followed by a jaunty new headquarters for Silicon Graphics in 1994.

If Silicon Valley and its offshoots were concentrated in suburban locales, communities of innovation will always thrive in cities, leading developers to envision concentrated 'incubators' in this fast-growing field. The flashiest and best-known new media offices were in the Los Angeles area, where Franklin Israel and Frank Gehry redefined the nature of custom design to favour improvisation and montage, simultaneously practical and fanciful, stable and fleeting. Eric Owen Moss and the developer Frederick Smith joined forces to generate a series of eye-catching spectacles in the former industrial district of Culver City. Moss's architectural cadenzas begin with old warehouse structures, then twist and distort them in fearless amalgamations that celebrate cleverness, sometimes obtrusively so. More established businesses also wanted computer-based interactive environments that generated new kinds of architectural commissions. Asymptote's Virtual New York Stock Exchange (1999) is a real-time setting where 3-D settings visualize the convoluted flow of data in multiple financial sectors.

Social interaction and personal comforts became crucial assets in the new media. Flexible open spaces downplayed hierarchies and encouraged informal collaboration. The inevitable disorder of productive intensity no longer had to be concealed. Internal spines with power nodes provided state-of-the-art technologies, easily updated or repaired, allowing employees to hook up or disengage connecting stations as they wished. Even large businesses took down interior walls, which intensified the need for orientation and differentiation. Virtual work forces were a brief fad until managers realized that human contact spurs creative energy. Jaunty coffee bars and lunch-rooms proliferated, as did recreation areas, both indoor and outdoor, even on sets for TV sit-coms. The new workplace may be based on intangibles, but spaces for 'serious play' have become a necessity. They also provide a mask for higher-order Taylorism, encouraging total commitment around the clock from mid-level knowledge workers whose real wages have declined as their jobs have become increasingly precarious.[14]

Collaborative research efforts like biotechnology and neuroscience turned scientific laboratories into big business in the 1980s. High-quality modern architecture became an amenity for private companies and university labs that vied for the best scientists and lucrative federal grants. Signature architects were a premium, usually restricted to façades and social areas, while specialized firms oversaw the highly technical interiors. Given estimates that 80 per cent of scientific breakthroughs come through casual interaction, informal meeting places and circulation pathways became crucial elements.[15] Architects debated the nature of representation and effect. Were Venturi and Scott Brown too cautious with their woodsy, light-filled settings? Did Gehry try too hard to capture quirky, colliding unpredictability? Scientists consistently asked for flexibility, recognizing that even a bright, ecologically sound appearance can downplay difficulties in gauging what is truly safe and effective.[16] Hospital design began to change as well, with increased competition for prominent doctors, munificent donors and short-term patients with generous insurance coverage. While technological prowess defined surgeries and diagnostic services, 'the new residentialism' prevailed elsewhere. Hospital lobbies and corridors emulated shopping malls, directly evoking the consumer-based disparities in the nation's healthcare.

Commissions for infrastructure generated some of the most inventive architecture of the era.[17] The machine-based aesthetic of the early Modern Movement softened considerably, accepting the irregularities of

Interactive interior spaces at *Mode* magazine from the television show 'Ugly Betty', 2007.

nature, the coexistence of historic buildings, even a discrete ornamentalism. Definitions of function expanded to encompass public awareness or increased protection from toxic waste and noise pollution within and around these facilities. Buildings were visibly embedded in their natural and human landscapes, whether powerhouses in Appalachia, water-filtration plants in the West or sludge-dewatering plants in New York, all reminiscent of New Deal installations. Holt Hinshaw Jones's Chiller-Cogeneration Plant for the University of California at Los Angeles (1994) quickly became an icon, not just a high-tech trope but the real thing. Wes Jones was an articulate advocate, calling the plant a 'boss object' that revealed the 'provisionality of American reality'.[18] Andrea Leers's and Jane Weinzapfel's Modular VII Chiller Plant (2001) provides a more lyrical message as a gateway to the University of Pennsylvania, winning a *BW/AR* award. Nestled in a field of green, its smooth elliptical façade of specially perforated sheet-metal is variously transparent, translucent or invisible behind the cloud of mist it generates.

Holt Hinshaw Jones, architects, with Ralph M. Parsons, Inc., engineer, Chiller-Cogeneration Plant, UCLA, Los Angeles, 1992–4.

Transportation facilities again became significant architecture, first high-powered international services, then regional public transit. Helmut Jahn's United Airlines terminal at the company's Chicago hub (1987) swells skyward at ground level, filling the space with light, while an underground passageway between the two concourses surprises passengers with backlit glass walls and a neon sculpture overhead, pulsating in tandem with computer-generated music. The roofs at Denver's new airport by Fentress Bradburn Architects (1989–95) are Teflon-coated fibreglass membranes, capable of withstanding snow and wind deflections while allowing for easy expansion. Even parking facilities became positive fixtures in the landscape, equipped with mesh screens to shade cars and, eventually, solar-panel umbrellas to generate energy while minimizing heat build-up. Architects soon helped encourage more ecological avenues of human movement. Light-rail transit stations in Los Angeles and Minneapolis promote public transportation, as do new ferry terminals in New York, integrated with the immediate human and environmental surroundings, to emphasize variations within a larger system.

Considerable American manufacturing was outsourced abroad while health and safety conditions declined in many us plants, yet some industries used architecture to chart a more progressive path to profits. Small workshops balanced precision with respect most easily. Carlos Jimenez's Houston Fine Arts Press (1986) paid homage to the precision of craft-based skills with subtle references to vernacular prototypes from early in the century: loft-like spaces, saw-tooth roofs with north-facing clerestories, cheap industrial materials like corrugated metal and expansive glass window-walls. Julie Snow's several factories in the upper Midwest improved efficiency while promoting the employee's role in management. Her Short Run Production Company in Richmond, Wisconsin (1990), united light manufacturing and administration within a single cubic volume. A glass wall resolved acoustical problems, while the entry plaza continued the structural trusses of the interior to frame views of the prairie landscape. Frank Gehry followed similar principles with his Manufacturing and Distribution Facility for Herman Miller in the Sierra foothills of Rocklin, California (1989), highlighting sensual materials and workers' participation with an asymmetrical grouping of small sheds around a rocky berm.

Some larger companies are now seizing the initiative. Boeing reorganized its huge aircraft factories in Seattle to emphasize amenities for small working groups. William McDonough and Julie Bargman of D.I.R.T. Studio have undertaken the largest industrial-ecology project in the world for Detroit's Ford Motor Company, a $2 billion scheme to reclaim the heavily polluted 600-hectare River Rouge site that Ford has occupied for almost a century for an updated, modern factory. Cities and regions are making similar efforts. Portland, Oregon initiated plans for a '21st Century Urban Production District' that combined preservation with new light industries. The new Pittsburgh Technology Center is being developed on the site of former steel mills on the Monongahela River.

Commercial skyscraper design remained caught in a frenzied drive for height and flamboyance. Chicago saw an embarrassing number of garish and derivative buildings that mimicked Art Deco or classical motifs. Multinational firms like SOM, KPF and Cesar Pelli followed the money to Asia, which now dominated the competition for the tallest building in the world. Since transnational influence always follows multiple vectors, a handful of Americans took up the environmental technologies that had defined European and Asian skyscrapers for several decades. Fox & Fowle's Four Times Square (1999) in New York (now the Condé Nast Tower) provided the initial prototype, largely at the behest of the developer, the Durst Corporation. Renzo Piano then collaborated with Fox & Fowle to win the competition for the *New York Times* Building (2000–07), an ethereal design whose triple-skin walls modulate sun, heat and fresh air. Americans seemed ready for new high-rise design typologies.

The aftermath of the 9/11 attacks on New York's World Trade Center set the agenda back in disturbing ways. The redevelopment of Ground Zero since 2001 has been a deplorable enterprise, cloaked in secrecy, beset by greed and political ambitions that overwhelmed all other considerations. Rebuilding focused principally on the developer recouping all 185,000 square metres of prime office space from the Twin Towers, while Governor George Pataki insisted on undue speed, convinced this would make him a presidential contender. Unrelenting publicity about the Freedom Tower substituted celebrity gossip for serious deliberations about meaning and quality. The process manipulated public emotions, but ignored alternative development possibilities. Daniel Libeskind's overbearing design prevailed in a limited competition, despite its references to falling glass shards, in part because of patriotic flourishes. When the developer insisted on adding SOM's David Childs as a design partner, the series of changes reduced the twisted shape of the glass façades to a prosaic corporate design. Obsessive concerns about security then generated a twenty-storey concrete bulwark at the tower's base. As politicians fan American paranoia by militarizing modern architecture, heavy-handed surveillance and restricted access are undermining the principles of democratic freedoms.

Architects Daniel Libeskind and David Childs of SOM, Governor George Pataki, Speaker of the State Assembly Sheldon Silver, and developer Larry A. Silverstein look at the redesigned architectural model for the Freedom Tower at Ground Zero during a press conference at Cipriani Wall Street on 29 June 2005.

Housing First and Last

If Americans typically define their freedom in terms of their homes, the end of the twentieth century looked unsettling. The predilection for unique 'statements' precluded any consensus about iconic dwellings for the 1980s and '90s. Increased size was the only constant, evident in suburban 'McMansions' and luxury urban condos. Well-meaning paeans to restraint such as *The Not So Big House* (1998) signalled frustrated misgivings about the prevailing trend.[19] Costs rocketed everywhere, and soon 35 per cent of US households were paying more than a third of their monthly incomes for housing, often overcrowded and inadequate, an almost untenable expense for many families.[20] An exaggerated focus on home-ownership – which reached an all-time high of 67.7 per cent in 2000 – saw mortgage-lending practices increase financial risks for almost every class of Americans, soon posing a threat for the national economy. Cities tilted towards extremes of prosperity and poverty. Homelessness increased to affect more than 2.5 million Americans in 2007. When critics warned of a housing crisis similar to that after World War Two, Congress voted to repeal the goal stated in the Preamble to the 1949 Housing Act – 'a decent home and suitable living environment for every American family' – calling it unfeasible. The Bush administration disbanded most governmental programmes, claiming that private charities and faith-based groups provide the key to American reform.

Architects were sincerely distressed by these problems, but they felt thwarted on all sides. Less than 5 per cent of new home-buyers have any direct communication with a professional designer. (Fees for custom residences run up to fifteen times the cost of stock plans for the same-area house.)[21] Conceptual frameworks did change, however, as modernist assaults on domesticity disappeared with increased attention to the environment and the experience of dwelling. The rich legacy of twentieth-century housing experiments offered a counterpoint to nostalgic evocations of nineteenth-century stability.[22] Mid-century Modernism became especially popular: 'organic' mavericks such as Frank Lloyd Wright, Bruce Goff and John Lautner; the rational explorations of Mies, the Case Study Houses and pre-fab designs; inexpensive popular-culture mainstays like garden apartments, dingbats, ranch houses and modern suburbs.

Three basic themes or predilections stand out. The first is a renewed interest in the human body that extends far beyond amenities for health and fitness. The idea of equality now encompassed a recognition of physiological differences. The Americans with Disabilities Act of 1990 challenged architects to design for equitable access, redefining the term 'universal housing' to mean careful attention to fluid movement, simple procedures, flexible uses and tolerance for errors. Feminists reclaimed the domestic realm as a site to negotiate the everyday practices of modernity, reasserting the pleasures of home while taking account of domestic labour and the need for connections to the world beyond the dwelling.[23] Expanded notions of the family made some provisions for single people, single parents, the elderly and multi-generational house-holds. Rob Wellington Quigley's appealing 202 Island Inn for elderly men in San Diego (1992) changed perceptions of single-room-occu-pancy (SRO) hotels. San Diego became a hotbed of such experimentation, including a collaborative 'demonstration block', a patchwork of diverse living arrangements, incomes and buildings under the aegis of Ted Smith, and an ongoing sequence of improvements in Latino border towns by Estudio Teddy Cruz.

Second, a joyous materiality abounded in houses by the best-known architects of the era: the incadescent surfaces of Steven Holl, the reso-nant delight of Mark Mack, the austere beauty of Antoine Predock, the dynamic swoops of Frank Gehry. Anne Fougeron reinvigorated the modernist palette with load-bearing channel glass. Architects juxta-posed industrial products with natural wood and stone, often harvested nearby, and warm metals like copper. Recycled wood, metal, plastic and other materials enriched the play of tangible and emotional qualities. James Cutler's respect for concrete and his reverence for wood, whether

Rob Wellington
Quigley, 202 Island
Inn, San Diego,
California, 1992.

James Cutler (now
Cutler Anderson
Architects), Wright
Guest House,
The Highlands,
Washington, 1987.

Jones Studio, APS
Environmental
Showcase Home,
Phoenix, Arizona,
1994.

reused or new-cut, synthesized environmentalist sensibilities with the spiritual approach to materials of his teacher, Louis Kahn. Minimalism now engaged with materials in terms of their origins as well as ecological, phenomenological and psychological effects.

Third, environmental concerns now came to the fore. After decades of being dismissed as self-righteous, with 'no edge, no buzz, no style', sustainability finally gained cachet in the late 1990s.[24] Energy conservation, renewable resources and minimal disruption to the landscape became design incentives rather than restrictions. (Of course, the supposed autonomy of isolated, digitally mediated, sustainable dwellings subverts many basic principles of ecology.) Regional Modernism thrived in demanding climates like the upper Midwest, the North-west coast and the South-west. The 'Arizona School' of Will Bruder, Rick Joy, Wendell Burnette, Marwan Al-Sayed and others fused modern technologies with multiple legacies. Wright's Taliesin, Paolo Soleri's Arcosanti, Native American pueblos, and the adobe revival of the 1920s had all emphasized solar orientation, shading, cross-ventilation and recycled materials.

Architects also began to explore suburbia, a region they had long spurned. The Jones Studio's Environmental Showcase Home for Arizona Public Service (APS) in a Phoenix suburb (1994) was recognized as the top environmental project in North America. A demonstration and education project during its first three years, the design introduced and publicized a wide range of strategies for sustainability.

The popular media emphasized these themes in renewing an active promotion of modern houses. When *Dwell* magazine hit the stands in 2000, a hip young audience eager for simple, stylish design discovered ingenious work by architects much like themselves. *Dwell* juxtaposes contemporary design by 'Nice Modernists' with mid-century precedents, updating themes such as customized pre-fab houses, collaborations with producers, low-income housing and unusual 'Off the Grid' projects. 'The best modern architecture', contends editor Sam Grawe, 'responds through design, research, programming, and technology to the many demands of the modern world.'[25]

Another media phenomenon emerged almost simultaneously in 2001. The Houses at Sagaponac provided an idyllic beachfront escape in the

Hamptons for *über*-wealthy New Yorkers. The developer Harry (Coco) Brown marketed this prestigious community as an alternative to the extravagant and nostalgic luxury homes nearby. His latter-day *Weissenhofsiedlung* is a 25-hectare site with 37 houses by an international all-star team of modern architects selected by Richard Meier, with names that range from Steven Holl to Sam Mockbee and Hodgetts + Fung. Sagaponac may demonstrate the impressive diversity of modern idioms, but only eight houses have been completed. The claim of 'livable and affordable' models – initially $2 million, now $7 million and up – presumes great wealth as a norm.[26] Yet the site plan is banal given the focus on individual buildings. In the end this is just another subdivision, geared to narcissistic fantasies about autonomy without any larger vision.

New Urbanism is a distant relation of contemporary modern architecture, not its antithesis. The success of Duany/Plater-Zyberk's Florida resort town of Seaside (1982) launched the movement, which also drew on 1970s typological design studies by French and Italian neo-rationalists. Proponents soon adopted CAD technologies in their efforts to achieve greater density, social and environmental sustainability – and a database of historical typologies, The Congress for New Urbanism (CNU) began in 1993, a conscious play on the staunchly modernist CIAM. An official Lexicon recoded modernist words like *project, block* and *master-plan*, giving them neo-traditional intonations. Andrés Duany and Elizabeth Plater-Zyberk contend that historicist motifs are merely expedient, a way to build support for their alternative models of land use, although most of their cohorts demonize all forms of Modernism as inherently inhumane. In principle, New Urbanist architects want sustainable, mixed-income developments in cities and suburbs, but good intentions do not in themselves make for progress. Most developers adopt only the platitudinous imagery, foregoing any progressive aspirations.

Some advocates concede a dissonance between the ambitious New Urbanist agenda and the rigidly prescribed codes of a retro-styled architecture. Peter Calthorpe concentrates on a regional scale with retrofits for existing cities, suburbs, abandoned malls and industrial brownfield sites such as the former airport at Stapleton, Colorado – an approach sometimes called Smart Growth. Housing activists like Joan Goody, Daniel Solomon, Michael Pyatok and Jacquelin Robertson endorse the basic principles of New Urbanism while resisting its inflexible design rules, drawing instead on their personal observations and those of residents who evaluate programmatic and formal alternatives. A few private developers have hired modern architects to enliven façades in New Urbanist subdivisions like Prospect, Colorado, signalling positive attitudes about diversity and change. Given a shared critique of standard

Studio Completiva
for developer Kiki
Smith, Prospect
Townhomes,
Longmont, Colorado,
2000.

development practices, other modernists would do well to take up some of New Urbanism's goals and strategies, rather than dismissing everything about it.[27]

Economic and environmental pressures fuelled markets for multi-unit housing where innovations cross-fertilized, generating stronger hybrids. Cities from Atlanta to Portland encouraged Smart Growth with higher-density housing, including upper-level additions to existing structures. A variety of green features were introduced. Terraces and roof gardens shared glimpses of nature with passers-by. Glass became a new residential vernacular material. New York saw a bevy of luxury buildings by famous architects promising 'iconic' status with sleek curves, undulating façades and pristine modern boxes, not least a posthumous Urban Glass House by Philip Johnson (2002–06). The fad for converting urban warehouses into loft spaces accelerated across the US and around the world. Developers flooded the market with shoddy, overpriced loft-style buildings throughout the early 1990s, often manipulating legislation designed to provide or protect live/work spaces for artists. A counter-move to raise standards then took hold, epitomized by Stanley Saitowitz's 200-unit Yerba Buena Lofts in San Francisco, completed in 2001. This block relates intimately to its surroundings, a warehouse district south of Market Street where concrete and glass seem entirely appropriate, especially with the rhythmic composition of setbacks.

Stanley Saitowitz
Architects, Yerba
Buena Lofts, San
Francisco. 1999–2001,
street façade.

The surge in luxury dwellings reduced the supply of moderate-cost buildings and inflated prices in all sectors, spurring a nationwide call for 'affordable housing'. *Progressive Architecture* devoted a special issue to the subject in 1988 and then sponsored a competition, one of many

around the country. Non-profit organizations funded local American projects alongside international relief efforts.[28] The Housing Act of 1990 focused on special groups such as the elderly, the disabled and people with AIDS. Several cities set up programmes to protect and expand the stock of moderate-priced dwellings, but could not keep up with the need. The stylistic bent was conspicuously historicist, as if familiarity could alleviate neighbours' tendency to cry 'NIMBY' (Not in My Backyard), driven by fears about their own financial and social instability. But style is not the main issue. Modernism entails all sorts of alternatives to conventional practices, not just formal idioms but programmes, site plans, even clientele. The MacArthur Foundation committed $100 million to housing programmes, mostly to planners and community organizations, while architects struggled to break out of a tendency to see invention solely in terms of formal pyrotechnics or unprecedented technologies.

Some individuals and firms seized the initiative with singular testimonies to resourceful, exuberant design. Sam Mockbee brought the first group of Auburn University architecture students to an impoverished African-American settlement in Hale County, Alabama, in 1994, founding Rural Studio. His method begins with a close analysis of each family's specific problems and potentials, then seeks an inspiring poetry in the resolution. The houses cost a maximum of $20,000, revealing surprising beauty in cheap, recycled materials like car windscreens and straw bales, together with unexpected imaginaries. Rural Studio still thrives despite Mockbee's early death in 2001. An inspiring and singular accomplishment, it sometimes serves as a collective conscience or sanctified ideal. Due respect for Mockbee and his legacy would also encourage other designers who are creating their own small miracles in myriad circumstances.

The architects of contemporary modern housing are mostly radical incrementalists. Aesthetic verve helps bring small, but significant changes in the existing order. Michael Bell initiated Sixteen Houses in Houston in 1996, collaborating with various experts, including community activists in the impoverished African-American Fifth Ward. He asked sixteen architects to design prototypes compliant with federal home-ownership voucher standards, then put the work on display at a local museum. The extensive publicity raised funds to build new homes and provide job training, fending off displacement in one embattled neighbourhood.

Several firms use expensive commissions to underwrite ongoing projects in the public sector. Koning Eizenberg of Santa Monica, California, explores conjoined terrains of modernity, fusing professional

Rural Studio/Sam
Mockbee, Harris
(Butterfly) House,
Mason's Bend,
Alabama, 1997.

rigour with delightful surprises, local vernacular forms with a strong
industrial aesthetic. Their assemblages, while adamantly modern, connect
with people almost viscerally, simultaneously familiar and unpredictable.
The designs emphasize the crucial role of site plans, as with the zigzag
courtyards of Harold Way, which maximize internal and external views
while encouraging serendipitous pleasures. Such architects infuse low-
budget projects with the verve of urban vitality and the 'simple joy of
living', principles too easily forgotten.[29]

A rather surprising ally is a new breed of developer that emerged in
the 1990s. Some are committed to modern design or to green architecture. Inclusionary zoning entices others with tax benefits for adding
below-market-rate units. Architect-developers have negotiated success-
es that might otherwise have remained stillborn. Community design
centres reclaimed their activist role, while new non-profit groups used
innovative architectural tactics to address problems and rally support.
Rosanne Haggerty's Common Ground Community, founded in 1991
and now the nation's largest provider of supportive housing, tackles
homelessness for specific populations. Potential residents vet the proposals, adding their knowledge to that of other experts. Recent projects
include the award-winning Schermerhorn House in downtown
Brooklyn (2007) for Actors' Equity, designed by the Polshek
Partnership, and a renovated flophouse on the Bowery in Manhattan.
The Chicago Community Development Corporation, founded in 1988,
has acquired more than 2,000 subsidized units, protecting the tenants

Pugh + Scarpa for
Livable Places,
Colorado Court,
Santa Monica,
California, 2005–6.

while modernizing the buildings with bravura and adding market-rate
expansions. Stanley Tigerman and Helmut Jahn have recently completed sro shelters with social services, green roofs, gardens, wind turbines
and solar panels. Livable Places in Los Angeles focuses on green affordable housing on difficult sites. Their first project is Colorado Court
by Pugh + Scarpa, an sro hotel in Santa Monica. It combines familiar
climatic adaptations like breezeways and awnings with state-of-the art
photovoltaic panels in dazzling cobalt blue on the façade. These
groups may exercise relatively little power in comparison with major
developers, but they are having a palpable effect on architecture, neighbourhoods and human lives.

Koning Eizenberg
Architects, Harold
Way, Santa Monica,
California, 2000–03.

Reclaiming the Public Sphere

Good housing entails far more than dwelling units, especially for those who cannot purchase the support services and safe, congenial social spaces everyone needs. Since the mid-1980s architects like Koning Eizenberg have built gymnasiums, elderly and childcare centres, and other community services, an approach that harks back to New Deal projects. Michael Pyatok emphasizes the need for micro-businesses as part of low-income dwellings. He allocates spaces inside and around the units where residents can set up places for hairdressing, cooking, appliance repairs or other jobs. This shift in the typical residential programme is a modern innovation that challenges traditional ideas about the separation between work and home.

When David Burney, chief of design for the New York City Public Housing Authority (NYCHA), discovered that almost half of NYCHA residents were children or teenagers, he commissioned 104 new or renovated community centres, most keyed to gyms and computer facilities. Each one is ingenious and extremely popular. The Melrose Community Center in the Bronx (2001) is especially striking, with an elliptical gymnasium clad in gleaming aluminium panels and a rectangular building for classrooms that features abundant glass. Disproving fears about vandalism, visibility is an asset in these facilities. Architects, administrators and young people all get to perform in full view of their peers.[30]

Government has struggled to sustain a significant role in a culture that now equates democracy with the freedom to buy what you want. Helmut Jahn's virtuoso State of Illinois Center (1985) – today the James R. Thompson Center – inaugurated a strong populist attitude, eschewing the dignified monumentality that had long characterized such institutions. The gigantic glass-and-steel cone is truncated and rakishly off-kilter, its façade covered with flashy pinstripes rising from a gaudy colonnaded base. Offices for 3,000 employees look out over an equally brash rotunda suggestive of a Hyatt hotel, with two floors of commercial rentals at the base to maximize the flow of people. Even critics admired the vitality – but this is not the same as respect. Americans have become increasingly distrustful of the modern state with its inflated bureaucracies, conspicuous corruption, wasteful profligacy and increased surveillance. They often judge governmental architecture along similar lines, wary of financial and rhetorical excess. Congressmen sometimes emulate this suspicious rectitude, hoping to appeal to taxpayers.

The situation changed when Edward A. Feiner became chief architect of the Government Service Administration (GSA) in 1996. Disturbed by

Agrest/Gandelsonas
with Wank Adams
Slavin Associates,
Melrose Community
Center, Bronx, New
York, for the New
York Public Housing
Authority, 2001.

'K-Mart versions of mid-century Modern', he created the Design
Excellence Program, commissioning significant architects, both young
and well-established, then pressing them to generate compelling reinter-
pretations of American ideals and iconography for modern times.[31]
Those values include sustainability. All GSA projects after 2002 must rate
at least silver on the LEED scale. The major investment was $5 billion for
federal courthouses across the country, including the Sandra Day
O'Connor Courthouse in Phoenix by Richard Meier & Partners, completed in 2000, a magnificent glass structure that integrates shading
devices and a resourceful evaporative system.[32] Feiner also commissioned the nation's first federal courthouse by an African-American (by
Ralph Jackson, in Columbia, South Carolina) and the first federal building by a woman (Carol Ross Barney's Oklahoma City Federal Campus,
a phoenix rising from the ruins of the building a right-wing extremist
had bombed in 1995).

The San Francisco Federal Building by Thom Mayne/Morphosis,
commissioned in 1999 and completed in 2005, won kudos for its lithe
façade. The 'living skin' of perforated metal has operable windows
and undulating ceilings to help channel fresh air, providing natural
ventilation for 50 per cent of the office tower. The city's planning depart-

Murphy/Jahn, James R. Thompson Center, Chicago, 1981–5, atrium.

ment would surely have rejected the design as lacking sensitivity to its context, but zoning regulations do not apply to federal buildings. Mayne fought to make the plaza and an eleventh-floor 'skygarden' accessible to everyone, downplaying the necessary security provisions as much as possible. He treated the plaza's bollards like random sculptural seats, defusing the siege mentality that pervades so much governmental architecture. Definitions of freedom continue to evolve.

Smaller civic buildings are equally significant, albeit often stifled by pressures to idealize a mythic past or impose budgetary constraints in the present. The Bainbridge Island City Hall near Seattle, by the Miller/Hull Partnership, reveals unexpected possibilities in seemingly restrictive conditions. Wood and sturdy industrial materials allude to the island's history as a major lumber town, while varied roof lines extend the public realm towards an inviting plaza to create an urban focus for today's diverse residents. The project was completed in 2000, the same year that Mark Robbins, Director of Design Arts for the NEA, established the New Public Works initiative to sponsor competitions for creative civic buildings in other small towns, seeking to democratize debate about architecture and the rights of citizenship.

That said, the 'experience economy' has dramatically altered the nature of the collective realm.[33] Consumerism extends almost every-

Miller/Hull Partnership, Bainbridge Island City Hall, Bainbridge Island, Washington, 2000.

Jon Jerde, Horton
Plaza, San Diego,
1984–5.

Jon Jerde, Horton Plaza, San Diego, 1984–5.

where, not just to shopping malls and big-box retail but to historic sites, universities, sports venues, museums and other forms of urban entertainment. Jon Jerde emerged as the most agile manipulator of hyper-commodified urban culture with Horton Plaza, a four-block mixed-use redevelopment project in downtown San Diego alongside a restored Victorian enclave called the Gas Light District. Completed in 1985, it immediately became a tourist 'destination'. Jerde's office thrived with a formula he called 'experiential design', based on multi-level movement through dynamic diagonal compositions of trendy fragments, historical and contemporary, with surprises carefully calculated to multiply incentives to shop. Market-driven 'postmodern urbanism' emphasizes set pieces, supposedly vibrant affirmations of a locale, but in fact disconnected from the immediate surroundings and larger city. The carefully programmed sites and events of urban 'revitalization' now draw multimedia and information-technology sponsors, a trend that has generated ever more enticing and expensive spaces of consumption.

Modern civic life occurs in all kinds of settings that bring citizens together. As tourism transformed cities into museums, museums became extravaganzas. Peter Eisenman won his first large-scale commission with the Wexner Center for the Arts at Ohio State University in Columbus (1983–9). The composition's myriad grids, with their references to the city's Jeffersonian grid; the original campus plan; Terragni's Casa del Fascio; drawings by Sol Lewitt; FAA flight maps above the site; geological fault lines below it; and other sources created an intriguing caged overlay on the exterior and rather jarring galleries inside. Eisenman views design as a formal game in which he invents and controls elaborate rules. When the disorienting interior spaces frustrated artists, curators and viewers alike, he contended that such distress was a

Eisenman Robertson Architects, Wexner Center for the Arts, Ohio State University, Columbus, 1983–9.

purgative tonic; when leaks and major environmental-control problems necessitated a three-year closure for a complete makeover, he suggested that these failings were signs of great architecture. In any case, the cerebral challenges stirred interest along with controversy. Eisenman's career took off, along with a spate of new publications and events to promote his ideas and visibility.

Other kinds of museums flourished as well, typically seeking to inspire rather than disorient. The soaring glass structure of the Polshek Partnership's National Investors' Hall of Fame in Akron, Ohio (1988–95) celebrated this city's legacy as an incubator of innovations, reminding us that American experiments have often occurred outside the mainstream. Polshek's Rose Center for Earth and Space at New York's American Museum of Natural History (1994–2000) combined Modernism with Enlightenment-era ideals of clarity and transparency in a immensely appealing public institution.

The surge in new museums and performing-arts centres since the late 1980s spurred architectural experimentation in trendy hotels, boutiques and restaurants. But the leap in scale and expense required municipal funds to supplement donations from local power elites who have always overseen American high culture. Higher costs required bigger crowds, who were drawn to blockbuster repertoires. The cultural complexes soon became theme parks for the arts with tight security, prestige condominiums and other developer formulas for mixed use.

The stunning success of Frank Gehry's Guggenheim Museum in Bilbao, Spain, completed in 1997, saw cities everywhere try to replicate 'the Bilbao effect', generating their own architectural icons in the hope of similar tourist pilgrimages. Content mattered less than the spectacle of the building and the buzz. If Gehry himself took on a score of commissions, large and small, others also shared the glory. The swell of new high-profile museums is especially marked in Midwestern cities: Zaha Hadid's Rosenthal Center at Cincinnati's Contemporary Arts Center (2003); SANAA's Glass Pavilion at the Toledo Museum of Art (2006); Daniel Libeskind's Hamilton Building at the Denver Art Museum (2006); Herzog & de Meuron's Walker Art Center in Minneapolis (2007); and Steven Holl's resplendent addition to the Nelson-Atkins Museum in Kansas City (2007). American modern architecture at the start of a new millennium is openly global while proudly displaying its own diverse talents.

Of course, exciting artistic 'events' tend to happen outside institutionalized settings, so enterprising museum administrators organized these as well. Some are temporary venues, others rehabilitated buildings like Dia:Beacon, or MOMA Queens and the nearby P.S.1, intended as interim facilities but far more dynamic than the new MOMA by Yoshio

Diller + Scofidio,
Blur Building, media
pavilion for Swiss
EXPO 2002,
Lake Neuchâtel,
Switzerland, 2002.

Taniguchi, completed in 2006 (which doubled the area of the earlier museum).

Elizabeth Diller and Ricardo Scofidio specialized in museum installations that revealed, subverted and revelled in the seductive allure of display. As architects they created mutable environments that were transformed in response to participants or to unpredictable conditions. The Blur Building for the Swiss EXPO 2002 exhibition, used hybrid technological systems to recycle water from Lake Neuchâtel, creating a fluctuating cloud of mist. The structure and its visitors literally disappeared in an apparition that was simultaneously visible and invisible, precisely orchestrated and unpredictable in response to wind and other factors. Diller + Scofidio have now moved into more established architectural terrains with the new Museum of Contemporary Art in Boston (2006) and a redesign for New York's Lincoln Center (2006–09). Such projects still feed into an intensified consumption of images, ideas and places. Yet they give pause, pressing everyone to reflect, however briefly, on the systems within which we all perform.

Smaller museums provide a more nuanced alternative to grandiose cultural extravaganzas. The Renzo Piano Building Workshop designed several discreet masterpieces in the US. The first, the Menil Collection in Houston, completed in 1987, used simple facades and slightly asymmetrical siting to mitigate its formality, enhancing the residential fabric of small frame houses nearby. An innovative roof and ceiling provide diffused natural light, filtering the strong Texas sun, while the interior 'treasure chamber' displays exquisite artworks in the context of ongoing curatorial work. The American Folk Art Museum by Tod Williams and Billie Tsien (2001) is an elegantly restrained presence in midtown Manhattan. The main façade, set back from the street, consists of overlapping folded planes in a white bronze alloy more commonly used for ship propellers, a fitting paean to the ingenious creativity and material delights of handicraft aesthetics. Yet can any piece of architecture really live up to the Arup World Architecture Award of 2002, which ranked this the 'Best Building in the World'?

Significant architecture helps us confront contentious topics. Huff + Gooden, an African-American firm based in Charleston, South Carolina, have designed a small museum for the Virginia Key Beach Park (2005–8) that underscores the ambiguities of racial pride and segregation. The site was a 'coloured' beach in the 1950s, when any municipal services were a civil-rights victory. Historic photos laminated onto the glazing show the overlapping realities of that past. The structure and the larger landscape by Walter Hood continue the theme of multiplicities and changes over time. The building is perched on stilts to avoid potential floodwater and reveal trails that interweave human memories with environmental legacies. This new sensibility in American modern architecture encourages visitors to contemplate multiple dimensions of the past and the future, buildings and their surroundings.

Frank Gehry's Walt Disney Concert Hall in Los Angeles (1989–2003) inaugurated a radical rethinking of the experience of art and music. Skilled designers realize that freedom encounters constraints in the challenge of creating good acoustical design, especially for venues that must shift dramatically in size and to accommodate the kinds of instruments being played. They are also aware of psycho-acoustics, the recognition that a hall's visual characteristics might affect how audiences experience music. Most challenging of all, they confront the need to assert excitement while somehow resisting the inescapable power of global marketing. If architecture is a tool of global economic interests, can it also help human beings discover moments of respite?

The relationship between modesty and marketing affects even higher education in today's culture. The continuing construction boom at colleges and universities features striking new gymnasiums, dormitories, cultural facilities and student centres. Donors are pleased with the visibility, while view-books for potential students promote the appeal of campus life. The University of Cincinnati may be the best known for its signature buildings, part of a conscious effort to 'rebrand' the institution.[34] Stars seem worth the high fees if they bring the buzz of a big name and a powerful visual presence to the campus. New buildings embrace practicality and temporality as virtues, sometimes literally so.

Tod Williams + Billie Tsien, American Folk Art Museum, New York City, 1999–2001.

The response to Hodgetts + Fung's Towell (the Temporary Powell) Library at UCLA (1992), a vivacious conjunction of serendipitous fragments and off-the-shelf industrial materials, was so positive that the temporary structure has been preserved. The McCormick Tribune Campus Center at IIT by Rem Koolhaas/OMA (2003), which embraces the elevated train line, is likewise immensely popular.

A bevy of appealing small libraries appeared in the 1980s and '90s, refuting projections that the Internet would make them obsolete. Many juxtaposed surprisingly diverse materials on their façades, evoking the lively patchwork of contemporary cultural life. The Seattle Public Library by Rem Koolhaas/OMA (2004) carries this textural and experiential attitude throughout the building. Will Bruder's Phoenix Central Library (1988–94) achieved an intense hyper-reality appropriate to the fastest-growing metropolitan region in the nation. Two fully glazed walls orient visitors to the distant desert landscape, while views of the activities inside engage drivers on fast-paced Central Avenue. These façades are transformed in response to the intense Arizona sunlight, the southern wall with computer-controlled slats and louvres, the northern one with angled Teflon 'sails'. The entrance juxtaposes sinuous stone walls with inexpensive pre-cast concrete, which Bruder considers a 'late-20th century vernacular material in the southwest'.[35] Off-the-shelf components throughout the interiors provide economy with a deft 'ready-made' artistry. The Crystal Canyon at the centre rises the full height of the building, its multi-faceted layers showing the workings of the structure, including transparent elevator shafts that make every floor enticingly visible. This is resonant public architecture, highlighting the beauties of quotidian realities as well as those of a harsh yet enthralling locale.

Other public buildings achieve a serenity that is hard to come by in modern cities. Steven Holl's remarkable Chapel of St Ignatius at Seattle

Hodgetts + Fung,
Towell (Temporary
Powell) Library, UCLA,
Los Angeles, 1992.

University (1994–7) drew from the sacred liturgy that unites a diverse student body in an urban setting. Scarce economic resources led him to emphasize natural light and the tactile surfaces of inexpensive materials. Visitors proceed through a sequence of seven 'bottles of light', folds in the ceiling illuminated by coloured reflectors and complementary glass prisms. The luminosity bathes the walls and the polished concrete floor in opaline splendour, simultaneously tangible and mystical. Even the construction process became a ritual with the 23 tilt-up concrete panels lifted into place, the holes from the crane left exposed, then capped with special bronze covers. This building is an emotional and educational experience, a fusing of industrial and hand-crafted materiality that intensifies spiritual awareness for everyone who encounters it.

Education remains a key modern value in American life, even though school boards are being hit hard by tax cuts and social problems like falling test scores, rising violence and student lethargy. Recent pedagogical theories emphasize different ways of learning and the importance of

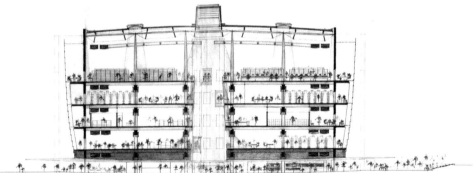

Will Bruder
Architects, Phoenix
Central Library,
Phoenix, Arizona,
1988–94, view
from Central Avenue.

Phoenix Central
Library, section.

small groups, especially in large, anonymous schools. Thom Mayne of Morphosis seized these issues in a creative manner with the Diamond Ranch High School in exurban Pomona, California (1993–9), all the while staying within a constrained budget. Mayne was the surprise winner of a competition for this difficult, 30-hectare site, largely because he chose to preserve and work with the steep hills while other contenders proposed flattening them. The most dynamic element is an angular 'main street' that unifies all the buildings and a student body of 2,000.

previous page
Steven Holl,
St Ignatius Chapel,
Seattle University,
Seattle, Washington,
1994–7, interior.

Thom Mayne/
Morphosis, Diamond
Ranch High School,
Pomona, California,
1993–9, view of
internal 'street'.

Diamond Ranch High
School, view from
playing fields.

Large, irregular openings offer surprising views, while niches cut into the buildings provide opportunities for students and teachers to congregate, interact and watch each other. Three terraces correspond to 'campuses' with smaller clusters of 300 students. A monumental stairway embedded in the hillside doubles as an amphitheatre. The plan takes advantage of a natural bowl, integrating the playing fields into the surrounding terrain.

Inventive small projects are often appealing because of the spirited interaction as buildings, sites and people adapt to ongoing changes. Architects have always taken up difficult challenges with ingenuity. The imaginative public responses also offer welcome alternatives to a world too often defined by glitz and excess. Today's obsession with celebrity architects and lavish mega-projects instead promotes the values of real-estate developers and passive consumer-spectators. The prevailing focus has direct and indirect implications. Public money for grandiose museums or stadiums diminishes funds for public education. Modern luxury apartment-buildings may be striking, but the trend is depleting the stock of affordable housing in most cities. No matter how progressive the design of individual buildings, environmental and infrastructure problems require large-scale collective reforms. The incentive to address such issues has declined in recent decades. The fact is that everyone – the architectural profession, governments, schools, the media and the public – must take account of these larger contexts.

The history of American modern architecture offers a useful perspective at the start of the twenty-first century. Reflecting on the achievements and mistakes of the past provides a framework for judgement and imagination about the future. We have seen that innovations can easily become narcissistic indulgences unless the advances build on precedents and engage the tumultuous give-and-take of modern life. In architecture, as in all things, life is the best criterion for judgement and the ultimate source of inspiration.

Epilogue

This book has explored a matrix of external pressures and internal shifts in the history of modern American architecture. Both major buildings and some lesser-known surprises show definite configurations without cohering into formulas or essences. To think historically is to see myriad changes and alternative possibilities as well as broad patterns. This does not entail nostalgia for an illusory past or limitations on present-day freedoms. The relative clarity of earlier circumstances makes it easier to discern such possibilities in the murky confusion of our own time, encouraging diversions from the usual paths of passive acceptance or antagonistic opposition. That current of thought runs throughout the lineage of American modern architecture, which has always opposed mindless historicism but not thoughtful lessons from the past.

Despite rhetoric about totally new circumstances, a familiar refrain for over a century, today's options are still conditioned in part by culture and history. The themes and typologies of this book remain potent. Hybrid cross-fertilization generates new forms and ideas, some exhilarating, others unsettling, whether intentionally so or not. Commercial values are certainly more powerful and omnipresent than ever. Architects can respond by actively encouraging greater public access and enabling alternative values rather than merely capitulating to market forces. Industrial production continues to emphasize diversity and choice, which promotes unique opportunities but also heightens consumerism. New media have expanded access to ideas, information and opinions, often blurring critical distinctions between these categories.

Green architecture and site planning have at last become decisive themes. No one can allege a choice about whether to engage with environmental issues, since we now recognize that all buildings have repercussions. Seizing hold of these circumstances, architects and developers are now generating energy-efficient designs that are visually compelling. Infrastructure services have again become a critical challenge. As with other issues, architecture cannot solve environmental problems, but it inevitably worsens or improves conditions. The same is true of social and economic issues.

The greatest legacy of American modern architecture may be its variety – the mixture of audacity and subtlety, high art and popular culture, dominant trends and startling originality. This does not mean all options are equally good or feasible. There are significant variations in quality together with diverse standards and vantages from which to appraise. Artistic virtuosity may be a goal, though perhaps one that is over-emphasized. Surely the diffusion of social justice and aesthetic quality are equally valid if rarely discussed values to consider. Environmental design may provide a lingua franca that transcends the divisions of formal languages, budgets and locales. Since the criteria for appraising 'good' architecture are never fixed, the challenge is to look as broadly as possible while exercising judgement.

Modern architecture is still under attack on many fronts, which sometimes encourages ongoing defensiveness. Many critics wrongly blame it for causing larger social problems that range from urban unrest to banal environments. Today's modernists no longer claim the power to transform the world, but they cannot abdicate all responsibility. Architects' distinctive expertise is essential to public conversations about housing, work conditions and public life. Built environments do affect how people live and how they feel about the world. Repercussions extend beyond specific clients, although paeans to 'the public' tend to obscure different preferences and unequal power.

Fortunately there are new opportunities to discuss both the past and the future of modern architecture in the US and around the world. The recent surge of museums has seen exhibits shift from celebrity spectacles to thoughtful deliberations about issues like prefabrication, ecologies, infrastructure and amenities. Venues for deliberation continue to expand along with enticing ideas. The aftermath of disasters like 9/11 and Hurricane Katrina has brought a new seriousness. Architecture became a way to imagine multiple prospects and ground debates about competing meanings, goals and effects. These creative possibilities extend throughout the discipline and far beyond its boundaries.

Modern architecture continues to evolve through continuities with the past and distinctive contemporary innovations. Modernists are collaborating with historic preservationists, aware of shared commitments in a world increasingly subservient to real estate interests. Health, safety and maintenance have again come to the fore, alongside beauty and well-being. Caught in the inescapable web of global marketing, architecture can also help human beings discover moments of respite and explore alternative possibilities.

The twenty-first century will see new buildings that inspire and anger us, separately and collectively. New talents will emerge. Some will be daring, their work brilliant and coruscating; others will seek to refine ideas and extend quality beyond the exceedingly narrow population that now employs architects' services. The most ingenious individuals will continue to embrace the actual conditions of American life while pressing for improvement. The future needs a range of approaches and ambitions.

Seen from this perspective, history reaches far beyond names, dates, stylistic labels and decoding games. It becomes a necessary frame or foundation for even the most audacious choices and deliberations made in the present. Whatever the field of inquiry, historical awareness liberates rather than limits creative processes. After all, the US Patent Office requires a statement about 'Prior Art' for any new invention. An understanding of patterns from the past is a prerequisite for envisaging viable alternatives in psychoanalysis, the law, and all the sciences. This should be the case for modern architecture and the communities we build. In that spirit I hope this book encourages readers to look anew at the world around them, past and present, fascinating and disturbing, and thereby to imagine new possibilities.

References

Abbreviations

AA *American Architect*
AF *Architectural Forum*
AR *Architectural Record*
GR *Grey Room*
HB *House Beautiful*
JAE *Journal of Architectural Education*
JAIA *Journal of the American Institute of Architects*
JSAH *Journal of the Society of Architectural Historians*
PA *Progressive Architecture*
PP *Pencil Points* [became *Progressive Architecture* in 1944]

Introduction

1 Sheldon Cheney, *The New World Architecture* (New York, 1930), p. 18. Also see Thomas Bender, *The Unfinished City: New York and the Metropolitan Idea* (New York, 2002).

2 See Jean-Louis Cohen, *Scenes of the World to Come: European Architecture and the American Challenge* (Paris, 1995); Jeffrey Cody, *Exporting American Architecture, 1870–2000* (London and New York, 2003).

3 William James, 'What Pragmatism Means', from *Pragmatism* (1907); reprinted in John J. McDermott, ed., *The Writings of William James* (Chicago, 1977), p. 376. Also see James T. Kloppenberg, 'Pragmatism: An Old Name for Some New Ways of Thinking?', *Journal of American History*, LXXXIII (June 1996), pp. 100–138; Joan Ockman, ed., *The Pragmatist Imagination: Thinking about 'Things in the Making'* (New York, 2000); Thomas Fisher, 'Architecture and Pragmatism', in *In the Scheme of Things* (Minneapolis, 2000), pp. 123–32; Mark Linder, 'Architectural Theory is no Discipline', in John Whiteman, Jeffrey Kipnis and Richard Burdett, eds, *Strategies in Architectural Thinking* (Chicago and Cambridge, MA, 1992), pp. 167–79; John Rajchman, *Constructions* (Cambridge, MA, 1998).

4 Gwendolyn Wright, 'Learning from Cultural History', *JSAH*, XLIV (December 2005), pp. 436–40. Also see Bruno Reichlin, 'Controlling the Design Process: A Modernist Obsession?', *Daidalos*, LXXI (1999), pp. 6–21; Sarah Williams Goldhagen, 'Something to Talk About: Modernism, Discourse, Style', *JSAH*, LXIV (Summer 2005), pp. 144–67.

5 Bruno Latour, *Reassembling the Social: An Introduction to Actor-Network-Theory* (Oxford and New York, 2005). Also see Latour's photographic essay with Emilie Hermant, *Paris: ville invisible* (Paris, 1998).

6 See Tom Porter, *Archispeak* (London and New York, 2004); Adrian Forty, *Words and Buildings: A Vocabulary of Modern Architecture* (London, 2000); Raymond Williams, *Keywords: A Vocabulary of Culture and Society* (New York and London, 1983); Tony

Bennett, Lawrence Grossberg and Meaghan Morris, eds, *New Keywords* (Oxford and Malden, MA, 2005).

7 Jürgen Habermas, 'Modernity: An Incomplete Project' (1980), in Hal Foster, ed., *The Anti-Aesthetic: Essays on Postmodern Culture* (New York, 1998), pp. 1–15; T. J. Clark, *Farewell to an Idea: Episodes from a History of Modernism* (New Haven, 1999), pp. 2–3.

8 See Néstor García Canclini, *Hybrid Cultures: Strategies for Entering and Leaving Modernity*, trans. C. L. Chiappari and S. L. López (Minneapolis, 1995); Gwendolyn Wright, 'On Modern Vernaculars', in Chris Wilson and Paul Groth, eds, *Everyday America: Cultural Landscape Studies after J. B. Jackson* (Berkeley, CA, 2003), pp. 163–77.

9 Elizabeth Grosz, *Architecture from the Outside: Essays on Virtual and Real Space* (Cambridge, MA, 2001), p. 92.

chapter one: Modern Consolidation, 1865–1893

1 Charles and Mary Ritter Beard, *Rise of American Civilization* (New York, 1929).

2 E. A. Atkinson, 'The Relative Strength and Weakness of Nations', Address read before the American Association for the Advancement of Science in 1886; reprinted in Henry Nash Smith, ed., *Popular Culture and Industrialism, 1865–1890* (New York, 1967), p. xiii.

3 John Root, 'A Great Architectural Problem', *Inland Architect and News Record* (June 1890); reprinted in Donald Hoffmann, ed., *Meanings of Architecture: Buildings, and Writings of John Root* (New York, 1967), p. 141.

4 Louis Sullivan, *The Autobiography of an Idea* [1924] (New York, 1956), p. 247.

5 William Conant, 'Will New York Be the Final World Metropolis?', *Century*, XXVI (1883); Montgomery Schuyler, 'Brooklyn Bridge as a Monument', *Harper's Weekly*, XVII (26 May 1883); reprinted in William H. Jordy and Ralph Coe, eds, *American Architecture and Other Writings by Montgomery Schuyler* (Cambridge, MA, 1961), p. 173.

6 Sullivan, *Autobiography*, p. 285. Burnham and Root designed more than 200 buildings in 18 years, McKim, Mead and White more than 940 in 30 years. See Kristen Schaffer, *Daniel Hudson Burnham: Visionary Architect and Planner* (New York, 2003).

7 The term 'process space' was first used in John Brinckerhoff Jackson, *American Space: The Centennial Years: 1865–1876* (New York, 1972), pp. 85–6.

8 Alfred Chandler, *The Visible Hand: The Managerial Revolution in American Business* (Cambridge, MA, 1977), cited in John Micklethwait and Adrian Wooldridge, *The Company: A Short History of a Revolutionary Idea* (New York, 2003), p. 60.

9 Matthew Smith, *Sunshine and Shadow in New York* (Hartford, CT, 1868), pp. 706, 26.

10 Steve Fraser, *Every Man a Speculator: A History of Wall Street in American Life* (New York, 2005), p. 93.

11 Rosemarie H. Bletter, 'The Invention of the Skyscraper: Notes on Its Diverse Histories', *Assemblage*, II (February 1987), pp. 110–17.

12 'A Great Commercial Edifice', *New York Sun*, (4 November 1869), cited in Sarah Bradford Landau and Carl W. Condit, *Rise of the New York Skyscraper, 1865–1913* (New Haven, 1996), p. 71.

13 Gerald Larson and Roula Gerantiotis, 'Toward a Better Understanding of the Evolution of the Iron Skeleton Frame in Chicago', *JSAH*, XLVI (March 1987), pp. 39–48.

14 Colin Rowe, 'Chicago Frame' (1956), reprinted in *The Mathematics of the Ideal Villa and Other Essays* (Cambridge, MA, 1976), pp. 100–101.

15 Montgomery Schuyler, 'Modern Architecture', *AR*, IV (July–September 1894), reprinted in Jordy and Coe, *American Architecture*, p. 78.

16 Siegfried Giedion, *Space, Time and Architecture: The Growth of a New Tradition*

(Cambridge, MA, 1941), pp. 368–95, 846. Phillip Johnson's MOMA catalogue, *Early Modern Architecture in Chicago, 1870–1910* (New York, 1940), affirmed the idea of Chicago as prophecy or 'protomodernism', as did Henry-Russell Hitchcock, *Modern Architecture: Romanticism and Reintegration* [1929] (New York, 1993). For an insightful analysis, see Robert Bruegmann, 'Myth of the Chicago School', in Charles Waldheim and Katerina Rüedi Ray, eds, *Chicago Architecture: Histories, Revisions, Alternatives* (Chicago, 2005), pp. 15–29.

17 Peter Brooks, letter to *Chicago Economist* (8 June 1889), p. 477; Montgomery Schuyler, 'D. H. Burnham and Co.', AR, V (February 1896), p. 56; cited in Donald Hoffman, *The Architecture of John Wellborn Root* (Chicago, 1973), pp. 155, 157, 161.

18 By 1890 women held 60 per cent of all typing and stenography jobs in the US; by 1900, 77 per cent; by 1920, 90 per cent.

19 *Architect* (8 December 1894), p. 895; Manfredo Tafuri and Francesco Dal Co, *Modern Architecture* [1976] (New York, 1977), p. 67; William H. Jordy, *Progressive and Academic Ideals at the Turn of the Twentieth Century* (New York, 1972), p. 61; Giedion, *Space, Time and Architecture*, p. 388; as cited in Joanna Merwood, 'The Mechanization of Cladding: The Reliance Building and Narratives of Modern Architecture', GR, 04 (Summer 2004), pp. 55, 60.

20 Louis H. Sullivan, 'The Tall Office Building Artistically Considered', *Lippincott's* (March 1896), reprinted in *Kindergarten Chats and Other Writings* (1918; reprinted New York, 1979), p. 202.

21 Louis Sullivan, letter to Claude Bragdon, 1903, and 'The Tall Office Building', cited in William H. Jordy, 'The Tall Buildings', in Wim de Wit, ed., *Louis Sullivan: The Function of Ornament* (New York, 1986), pp. 78, 203.

22 Sullivan, 'The Tall Office Building' and 'Characteristics and Tendencies of American Architecture' (1885); reprinted in *Kindergarten Chats*, pp. 205, 208, 178.

23 Russell Sturgis, 'The Warehouse and the Factory in Architecture', AR, XV (January 1904), p. 14; Mariana Griswold van Rensselaer, 'Recent Architecture in America, III: Commercial Buildings', *Century Magazine*, XXVII (August 1884), p. 512; C. W. Westfall, 'Buildings Serving Commerce', in John Zukowsky, *Chicago Architecture, 1872–1922* (Munich, 1987), pp. 77–89.

24 Frederick Law Olmsted, 'Future of New York', *New York Daily Tribune* (28 December 1879); cited in Thomas Bender, *The Unfinished City: New York and the Metropolitan Ideal* (New York, 2002), p. 21; *Industrial Chicago* (Chicago, 1891), vol. I, p. 72.

25 On Riverside, see Walter Creese, *The Crowning of the American Landscape: Eight Great Spaces and Their Buildings* (Princeton, 1985), pp. 219–40.

26 See Stuart Blumin, *The Emergence of the Middle Class: Social Experience in the American City, 1760–1900* (Cambridge, MA, 1989); Gwendolyn Wright, *Moralism and the Model Home* (Chicago, 1981); Joseph Biggott, *From Cottage to Bungalow: Houses and the Working Class in Metropolitan Chicago, 1879–1929* (Chicago, 2001).

27 Catharine E. Beecher and Harriet Beecher Stowe, *The American Woman's Home* [1869] (New Brunswick, 2002), pp. 22, 24.

28 Clarence Cook, *The House Beautiful* (New York, 1878), p. 19.

29 'Crazy-Quilt Architecture', *Scientific American*, LIII (25 July 1885); cited in Arthur Schlesinger, *Rise of the City, 1878–1898* (New York, 1933), p. 280.

30 Paul Sédille, 'American Architecture from a French Standpoint', *American Architect and Building News*, XX (11 September 1886), pp. 122–4; cited in Jean-Louis Cohen, *Scenes of the World to Come: European Architecture and the American Challenge, 1893–1960* (Paris, 1995), p. 20.

31 Vincent Scully, *The Shingle Style and the Stick Style* [1955] (New Haven, 1971).

32 'A Revolution in Living', *New York Times* (3 June 1878).

33 Charlotte Perkins Gilman, 'The Passing of the Home in Great American Cities', *Cosmopolitan*, XXXVIII (December 1904), p. 138. Also see Gilman, *Women and Economics* [1898] (New York, 1966); John Pickering Putnam, *Architecture Under Nationalism* (Boston, MA, 1890); Elizabeth Collins Cromley, *Alone Together: A History of New York's Early Apartments* (Ithaca, NY, 1990).

34 See Michael B. Katz, *In the Shadow of the Poorhouse: A Social History of Welfare in America* (New York, 1996); Paul Groth, *Living Downtown: The History of Residential Hotels in the United States* (Berkeley, CA, 1994); Richard Plunz, *A History of Housing in New York* (New York, 1990).

35 Edward Bellamy, *Looking Backward, 2000–1887* [1888] (New York, 1960), p. 207.

36 Walter Benjamin, *Charles Baudelaire: A Lyric Poet in the Era of High Capitalism* (London, 1976), originally an essay (1928); cited in M. Christine Boyer, *Manhattan Manners: Architecture and Style, 1850–1900* (New York, 1985), p. 91. Also see Neil Harris, 'Shopping – Chicago Style', in Zukowsky, *Chicago Architecture*, pp. 137–55; Elaine S. Abelson, *When Ladies Go a'Thieving: Middle-Class Shoplifters in the Victorian Department Store* (New York, 1982); William Leach, *Land of Desire: Merchants, Power and the Rise of a New American Culture* (New York, 1993).

37 Theodore Dreiser, *Sister Carrie* [1900] (New York, 1961), p. 299.

38 *New York Times*, (26 June 1889); Mariana van Rensselaer, 'Madison Square Garden', *Century*, XLIV (March 1894); cited in Robert A. M. Stern, Thomas Mellins and David Fishman, *New York 1880: Architecture and Urbanism in the Gilded Age* (New York, 1999), pp. 698, 705.

39 Joseph Siry, *The Chicago Auditorium Building* (Chicago, 2002), p. 174. Also see Dankmar Adler, 'The Chicago Auditorium', *AR*, I (April–June 1892), pp. 416–34.

40 Sullivan, *Autobiography of an Idea*, p. 325.

41 Montgomery Schuyler, 'Last Words about the World's Fair', *AR*, III (January–March 1894); reprinted in Jordy and Coe, *American Architecture*, pp. 290–91. Also see Neil Harris, Wim de Wit, James Gilbert and Robert Rydell, *Grand Illusion: Chicago's World's Fair of 1893* (Chicago, 1993); James Gilbert, *Perfect Cities: Chicago's Utopias of 1893* (Chicago, 1991); Peter Bacon Hales, *Silver Cities: The Photography of American Urbanization, 1839–1915* (Philadelphia, 1998).

chapter two: **Progressive Architectures, 1893–1918**

1 William Herbert [Herbert Croly], *Houses for Town or Country* (New York, 1903), p. 5; *idem*, 'The Contemporary Suburban Residence', *AR*, XI (January 1902), p. 2; Herbert, 'The New World and the New Art', *AR*, XII (June 1902), p. 53; Herbert, 'Civic Improvements', *AR*, XXI (May 1907), pp. 347–453.

2 Herbert Croly, *The Promise of American Life* (New York, 1909), p. 446. In 1913 Croly became founding editor of *New Republic*. The next year he published *Progressive Democracy*. See David Levy, *Herbert Croly of the New Republic: The Life and Thought of an American Progressive* (Princeton, 1985); Suzanne Stephens, 'Architectural Criticism in a Historical Context: The Case of Herbert Croly', in Elisabeth Blair MacDougall, ed., *The Architectural Historian in America* (Washington, DC, 1990), pp. 275–87.

3 On progressivism, see James Kloppenberg, *Uncertain Victory: Social Democracy and Progressivism in European and American Thought, 1870–1920* (New York and Oxford, 1986); Robert Crunden, *Ministers of Reform: The Progressives' Achievement in American Civilization, 1889–1920* (New York, 1982).

4 William James, 'Bergson and his Critique of Intellectualism', in *A Pluralistic Universe* (New York and London, 1909).

5 William James, 'The Dilemma of Determinism', in *The Will to Believe* [1897] (Cambridge, MA, 1979), pp. 114–40; James, *Essays in Radical Empiricism* [1912] (Cambridge, MA, 1976), p. 22.

6 See Robert B. Westbrook, *John Dewey and American Democracy* (Ithaca, NY, 1991); Richard Shusterman, *Pragmatist Aesthetics* (Oxford and Cambridge, MA, 1992).

7 Frederic C. Howe, *The City: The Hope of Democracy* (1905; reprinted Seattle, 1967), p. 7.

8 Marston Hartley, 'The Importance of Being DADA' in *Adventures in the Arts* (New York, 1921); cited in Francis Naumann, *Making Mischief: Dada Invades New York* (New York, 1996), p. 17.

9 See Alan Trachtenberg's essay in *America and Lewis Hine: Photographs 1904–1940* (Millerton, NY, 1977). Hine's *Men at Work* [1932] (New York, 1977) depicts the heroism of skyscraper construction.

10. Randolph Bourne, 'Trans-National America' (1916) and 'The Architect' (1916); reprinted in Olaf Hansen, ed., *Randolph Bourne: The Radical Will, Selected Writings, 1911–1918* (Berkeley, CA, 1977), pp. 248–64, 279–81. On Bourne and other public intellectuals' responses to the city, see Thomas Bender, *New York Intellect: A History of Intellectual Life in New York City, from 1750 to the Beginnings of Our Own Time* (New York, 1987).

11 Randolph Bourne, 'Pageantry and Social Art' (n.d.), first published in *The Radical Will*, p. 515.

12 Reyner Banham, *A Concrete Atlantis: US Industrial Building and European Modern Architecture* (Cambridge, MA, 1986), pp. 11, 68, 72.

13 Erich Mendelsohn, *Amerika* [1926] (New York, 1993), p. 45.

14 Cited in David Hounshell, *From the American System to Mass Production: The Development of Manufacturing Technology in the United States* (Baltimore, 1984), p. 229; Thomas P. Hughes, *American Genesis: A Century of Invention and Technological Enthusiasm* (New York, 1989), pp. 204–5.

15 Frank Lloyd Wright, 'In the Cause of Architecture', *AR*, XXIII (March 1908), p. 166; Wright, 'The New Larkin Administration Building', *The Larkin Idea* (November 1906); cited in Jack Quinan, *Frank Lloyd Wright's Larkin Building: Myth and Fact* (Cambridge, MA, 1987), p. 140.

16 Louis Sullivan, 'The Modern Phase of Architecture', *Inland Architect and News Record* (June 1899); cited in Lauren Weingarden, *Louis H. Sullivan: The Banks* (Cambridge, MA, 1987), p. 18.

17 Mary Gay Humphries, 'House Decoration and Furnishing', in Lyman Abbott, ed., *The House and Home* (New York, 1896), vol. 1, p. 157.

18 'Houses and Habits', *Harper's Bazaar*, 45 (February 1911), p. 57.

19 James Scott, *Domination and the Arts of Resistance* (New Haven, 1990); Robin D. G. Kelley, *Race Rebels: Culture, Politics and the Black Working Class* (New York, 1996), p. 77.

20 Joanne E. Meyerowitz, *Women Adrift: Independent Wage-Earners in Chicago, 1880–1930* (Chicago, 1988), pp. 5–7. Also see Ellen Fitzpatrick, *Endless Crusade: Women Social Scientists and Progressive Reform* (New York, 1990); Robyn Muncy, *Creating a Female Dominion in American Reform, 1890–1935* (New York, 1991); Dolores Hayden, *The Grand Domestic Revolution: A History of Feminist Designs for American Homes, Neighborhoods and Cities* (Cambridge, MA, 1981).

21 Helen Campbell, 'Household Art and the Microbe', *HB*, VI (October 1895), pp. 18–21; Campbell, *Household Economics* (New York, 1897); Isabel Bevier, *The House: Its Plan, Décor and Care* (Chicago, 1904; title varies in later edns).

22 Charlotte Perkins Gilman, *The Home: Its Work and Influence* [1903] (Urbana, 1972), pp. 52,

67. Also see Poly Wynn Allen, *Building Domestic Liberty: Charlotte Perkins Gilman's Architectural Feminism* (Amherst, 1988).

23 See Jean-Louis Cohen, *Scenes of the World to Come: European Architecture and The American Challenge, 1893–1960* (Paris, 1995), p. 77, for an illustration from Bruno Taut's *Die neue Wohnung* (Berlin, 1924).

24 Adolf Loos, 'Plumbers' (1898); reprinted in James O. Newman and John H. Smith, eds and trans., *Spoken into the Void: Collected Essays, 1897–1900* (Cambridge, MA, 1982), pp. 45–9. These passions still ran strong 25 years later when D. H. Lawrence described 'some insisting on the plumbing, and some on saving the world: these being the two great American specialties' (*Studies in Classic American Literature* [1923; New York, 1964], pp. vii–viii).

25 Marion Talbot, *Proceedings of the Fourth Annual Conference on Home Economics* (Lake Placid, NY, 1902), p. 22; cited in Sarah Stage and Virginia Vincenti, eds, *Rethinking Home Economics* (Ithaca, NY, 1997), p. 28.

26 The *Journal* published two other models by Wright, one later that year, the other in 1907.

27 Frank Lloyd Wright, *Modern Architecture: Being the Kahn Lectures for 1930* (Princeton, 1931), pp. 73–5.

28 Cited in Samuel Howe, 'Do Architects Read?', *AR*, XXXII (December 1912), p. 569. In addition to monographs, see Richard Longstreth, *On the Edge of the World: Four Architects in San Francisco at the Turn of the Century* (Cambridge, MA, 1983); Robert Winter, ed., *Toward a Simpler Way of Life: The Arts and Crafts Architects of California* (Berkeley, CA, 1997).

29 Irving Gill, 'The Home of the Future: The New Architecture of the West: Small Homes for a Great Country', *The Craftsman* (May 1916); reprinted in Thomas S. Hines, *Irving Gill and the Architecture of Reform* (New York, 2000), p. 126.

30 Katherine Cole Stevenson and H. Ward Jandl, *Houses by Mail: A Guide to Houses from Sears, Roebuck and Company* (Washington, DC, 1996), p. 19; David D. Reiff, *Houses from Books* (University Park, PA, 2000).

31 Laura Chase, 'Eden in the Orange Groves: Bungalows and Courtyard Houses in Los Angeles', *Landscape*, XXV (1981), pp. 29–36; J. Curtis and L. Ford, 'Bungalow Courts in San Diego', *Journal of San Diego History*, XXXIV (1988), pp. 78–92.

32 Eric Sandweiss, *St Louis: The Evolution of an American Urban Landscape* (Philadelphia, 2001), pp. 199–204; Christopher Silver, 'Neighborhood Planning in Historical Perspective', *Journal of the American Planning Association*, LI (Spring 1985), p. 174.

33 Also see Abigail Van Slyck, *Free to All: Carnegie Libraries and American Culture, 1890–1920* (Chicago, 1995).

34 Jane Addams, 'A Function of the Social Settlement', *Annals of the American Academy of Political and Social Science* (May 1899); cited in Christopher Lasch, ed., *The Social Thought of Jane Addams* (New York, 1965), p. 187.

35 Frank Lloyd Wright, 'The Art and Craft of the Machine', *Annual of the Fourteenth Annual Exhibit of the Chicago Architectural Club* (1901); reprinted in Bruce Brooks Pfeiffer, ed., *Frank Lloyd Wright: Collected Writings* (New York, 1992), vol. I, pp. 66, 69.

36 Rem Koolhaas, *Delirious New York: A Retroactive Manifesto for Manhattan* (New York, 1978), pp. 21–65.

37 Frederic Thompson, 'Amusing the Million', *Everyman's Magazine* (September 1908); cited in John F. Kasson, *Amusing the Million: Coney Island at the Turn of the Century* (New York, 1978), p. 63.

38 Simon M. Paten, *The New Basis of Civilization* (New York, 1907); cited in Daniel M. Fox, *The Discovery of Abundance: Simon N. Patten and the Transformation of Social Theory* (Ithaca, NY, 1967), pp. 102–3.

1   Sheldon Cheney, *The New World Architecture* (New York, 1930), p. viii; Robert Updegraff, *The New American Tempo and the Stream of Life* (Chicago, 1929).

2   William Carlos Williams, 'The Wanderer: A Rococo Study: Paterson – The Strike' (1914); reprinted in A. Walton Litz and Christopher MacGowan, eds, *The Collected Poems of William Carlos Williams* (New York, 1987), p. 31.

3   Statements by Ralph Walker and George Howe in 'Modernist and Traditionalist', *AF*, LIII (July 1930), pp. 49–50.

4   Henry McBride, 'Modern Art', *Dial* (April 1919), pp. 353–5; cited in Maria Morris Hambourg and Christopher Phillips, *The New Vision: Photography between the World Wars* (New York, 1989), p. 46.

5   Irving K. Pond, 'From Foreign Shores', *JAIA*, XI (December 1923), p. 475; XII (March 1924), p. 122; cited in Mardges Bacon, *Le Corbusier in America* (Cambridge, MA, 2001), p. 14.

6   Cheney, *New World Architecture*, p. 80; Edwin Avery Park, *New Backgrounds for a New Age* (New York, 1928), pp. 143, 147; Harvey Wiley Corbett, 'Architecture', in *Encyclopaedia Britannica* (New York, 1926), vol. I, p. 199.

7   Edith Elmer Wood and Frederick Ackerman, *The Housing Famine: How To End It* (New York, 1920); Ackerman, diary note for 1934 cited in Michael H. Lang, 'Town Planning and Radicalism in the Progressive Era: The Legacy of F. L. Ackerman', *Planning Perspectives*, XVI (2001), p. 147.

8   Frederick Ackerman, 'Art and Americanization', *Western Architect*, XXIX (March 1920), pp. 23–4; Cheney, *New World Architecture*, p. 120.

9   Le Corbusier, *Towards a New Architecture*, trans. Frederick Etchells [1923] (New York, 1927), p. 33.

10 Robert Park and Ernest Burgess, *The City* (Chicago, 1925). Perry's 1929 scheme appropriated the text and term from William Drummund's 1913 proposal for the Chicago City Club.

11 Frederick Ackerman, Foreword to Charles G. Ramsey and Harold R. Sleeper, *Architectural Graphic Standards* (New York, 1932). Ramsey and Sleeper worked in Ackerman's office. See Paul Emmons, 'Diagrammatic Practices: The Office of Frederick L. Ackerman and *Architectural Graphic Standards*', *JSAH*, LXIV (March 2005), pp. 4–21.

12 For example, see Daniel Bell. *Work and its Discontents* (Boston, MA, 1956), p. 8.

13 Michael A. Mikkelson, 'A Word about the New Format', *AR*, LXIII (January 1928), pp. 1–2; 'Two Problems of Architecture', *AR*, LXV (January 1929), p. 65; Robert L. Davison, 'Prison Architecture', *Annals of the American Academy of Political and Social Science* (1931); cited in Hyungmai Pai, *The Portfolio and the Diagram: Architecture, Discourse, and Modernity in America* (Cambridge, MA, 2002), p. 151.

14 Henry-Russell Hitchcock, Jr, *Modern Architecture: Romanticism and Reintegration* [1929] (New York, 1993), pp. 205–6.

15 Henry-Russell Hitchcock and Philip Johnson, *The International Style* [1932] (New York, 1995), p. 19.

16 Ibid. Also see Terence Riley, *International Style: Exhibition 15 and the Museum of Modern Art* (New York, 1992)

17 Henry-Russell Hitchcock, 'The International Style Twenty Years After' (1951), appendix to reprint of *The International Style* (1995), pp. 241, 243, 252.

18 Knud Lönberg-Holm, 'Two Shows: A Comment on the Aesthetic Racket', *Shelter*, II (April 1932), p. 17.

19 Manfredo Tafuri, 'The Disenchanted Mountain: The Skyscraper and the City', in Giorgio Ciucci, et al., *The American City from the Civil War to the New Deal*, trans. Barbara

Luigia La Penta (Cambridge, MA, 1979); Katherine Solomonson, *The Chicago Tribune Tower Competition: Skyscraper Design and Cultural Change in the 1920s* (1993; Cambridge and New York, 2000), p. 293.

20 The first use of the term in English was in Bevis Hillier, *Art Deco* (London and New York, 1968).

21 Herbert Croly, 'New Dimensions in Architectural Effects', AR, LVII (January 1925), pp. 93–4; Ezra Pound, 'Patria Mia' (1913), in William Cookson, ed., *Ezra Pound, Selected Prose, 1909–1965* (New York, 1950), p. 107; cited in Wanda Corn, *The Great American Thing: Modern Art and National Identity, 1915–1935* (Berkeley, CA, 1999), p. 158.

22 Fiske Kimball, *American Architecture* (New York, 1928); Ely Jacques Kahn, 'The Office Building Problem in New York', AF, XLI (September 1924), p. 96; cited in Jewel Stern and John A. Stuart, *Ely Jacques Kahn, Architect: Beaux-Arts to Modernism in New York* (New York, 2006), p. 95.

23 Michael Lewis, 'Rhapsody in Chrome', *New York Times* (26 May 2005), p. F8. A 1997 survey of New York architects rated the Chrysler far and away their favourite building, while it ranked ninth on the AIA's 2006 survey of the American public.

24 Emily Thompson, *The Soundscape of Modernity, 1900–1933* (Cambridge, MA, 2003), pp. 225–8. San Antonio's 1928 Milam Building first provided air conditioning in rental spaces. The best account of PSFS is William Jordy, *American Buildings and their Architects: The Impact of European Modernism in the Mid-Twentieth Century* (Garden City, NY, 1976), pp. 87–164.

25 Edward Wolner, 'Design and Civic Identity in Cincinnati's Carew Tower Complex', *JSAH*, XCII (March 1992), pp. 35–47. The other garage was in Chicago's Jewelers Building (1926).

26 Lewis Mumford, 'The Sky Line: The American Tradition', *New Yorker* (11 March 1939), p. 37; 'Frozen Music or Solidified Static? Reflections on Radio City', *New Yorker* (20 June 1931), p. 28; 'The Sky Line', *New Yorker* (11 March 1935), p. 37.

27 Carrier Engineering Corporation, *The Story of Manufactured Weather* (New York, 1919).

28 Eric Sundstrom, *Work Places: The Psychology of the Physical Environment in Offices and Factories* (New York, 1986), pp. 44–7.

29 Henry-Russell Hitchcock, Jr, Review of *Wie Baut Amerika?*, AR, LXIII (June 1928), pp. 594–5.

30 Keller Easterling, *Organization Space: Landscapes, Highways and Houses in America* (Cambridge, MA, 1991), pp. 17, 77; RPAA texts in Carl Sussman, ed., *Planning the Fourth Migration* (Cambridge, MA, 1976).

31 Donald A. Johnson, *Planning the Great Metropolis: The 1929 Regional Plan* (London, 1996).

32 The word *realtor* was invented in 1916 to distinguish members of the National Association of Real Estate Boards from less ethical sellers. See Jeffrey Hornstein, *A Nation of Realtors: A Cultural History of the Twentieth-Century American Middle Class* (Durham, NC, 2005); Carolyn S. Loeb, *Entrepreneurial Vernacular: Developers' Subdivisions in the 1920s* (Baltimore, 2001); Robert Fogelson, *Bourgeois Nightmares: Suburbia, 1870–1930* (New Haven, 2005).

33 Henry Wright, 'The Home Ideal versus Reality', *American Federationist* (June 1926), pp. 65–9.

34 For astute early recognition of Southern California modernists, see Cheney, *New World Architecture*; Pauline Gibling [Schindler], 'Modern California Architects', *Creative Art*, X (1932), pp. 111–15; and the pioneering work of Esther McCoy.

35 Richard Neutra, *Amerika: Die Stilbildung des neuen Bauens in den Vereinigten Staaten* (Vienna, 1930), p. 76.

36   Frank Lloyd Wright, *An Autobiography* [1932] (New York, 1977), p. 258.

37   Rudolph Schindler, 'A Cooperation Dwelling', *T-Square*, II (February 1932), pp. 20–21;
     Pauline Schindler, letter (1918); cited in Robert Sweeney, 'Life at King's Road', in Elizabeth
     A. T. Smith and Michael Darling, eds, *The Architecture of R. M. Schindler* (Los Angeles,
     2000), p. 87. Also see Enric Miralles, 'Schindler-Chace House', *Quaderns*, CLXXXV
     (April–June 1990), pp. 4–11.

38   See Stefanos Polyzoides, 'Schindler, Lovell and the Newport Beach House', *Oppositions*,
     XVIII (Fall 1979), pp. 60–73; August Sarnitz, 'Proportion and Beauty:The Lovell Beach
     House', *JSAH*, XLV (December 1986), pp. 374–88; 'Unusual House is Built of Concrete and
     Glass', *Popular Mechanics*, XLVII (June 1927), p. 969.

39   Richard Neutra, *Life and Shape* (New York, 1962), p. 220.

40   Thomas S. Hines, *Richard Neutra and the Search for Modern Architecture* (New York,
     1982), p. 89.

41   Wright, *Autobiography,* p. 277. See Alice T. Friedman, *Women and the Making of the
     Modern House: A Social and Architectural History* (New York, 1998), pp. 32–61, on
     Barnsdall's Hollyhock House.

42   Lewis Mumford, *Sketches from Life: The Autobiography of Lewis Mumford* (New York,
     1982), p. 343.

43   Clarence Stein, *Toward New Towns for America* (Cambridge, MA, 1957).

44   R. Buckminster Fuller, 'Universal Requirements of a Dwelling Advantage' (1927), *Shelter*
     (1931); reprinted in James Meller, ed., *The Buckminster Fuller Reader* (London, 1970),
     p. 242.

45   Martin Pawley, *Buckminster Fuller* (New York, 1990), p. 30.

46   Randolph W. Sexton, *American Apartment Houses, Hotels, and Apartment Hotels of
     Today* (New York, 1929), p. 1.

47   Henry Wright, 'The Apartment House: A Review and A Forecast', *AR,* LXIX (March 1931),
     pp. 186–7.

48   A. Lawrence Kocher and Albert Frey, 'Real Estate Subdivisions for Low-Cost Housing',
     AR, LXIX (April 1931), pp. 324–7.

49   Knud Lönberg-Holm, 'The Gasoline Filling and Service Station', *AR,* LXVII (June 1930),
     pp. 562–84.

50   George Nichols, 'The Development of the Medical Center', *Architect*, X (July 1928), p. 451;
     Marrion Wilcox, 'New York's Great Medical Center', *AR,* LVIII (August 1925), pp. 101–15;
     cited in Aaron Betsky, *James Gamble Rogers and the Architecture of Pragmatism* (New
     York, 1994), pp. 214, 223. Also see Dr Henry Williams, 'A Hospital in the Clouds: The
     Story of New York's Skyscraper Medical Center', *World's Work*, LIII (February 1927),
     pp. 408–18.

51   Allan Brandt and David Sloane, 'Of Beds and Benches: Building the Modern American
     Hospital', in Peter Galison and Emily Thompson, eds, *The Architecture of Science*
     (Cambridge, MA, 1999), pp. 101–15.

52   Vachel Lindsay, *Art of the Moving Picture* (New York, 1916), pp. 273–9.

53   John Eberson, 'The Capital Theatre', *AF,* XLII (June 1925), p. 373.

54   Maggie Valentine, *The Show Starts on the Sidewalk: An Architectural History of the
     Movie Theatre Starring S. Charles Lee* (New Haven, 1994), p. 9. Also see David James,
     The Most Typical Avant Garde: History and Geography of Minor Cinemas in Los Angeles
     (Berkeley, CA, 2005); David Naylor, *American Picture Palaces* (New York, 1981); Lary
     May, 'Making the American Way: Moderne Theatres, Audiences and the Film Industry,
     1929–1945', *Prospects* (1987), pp. 89–124; Ben Schlanger, 'Motion-Picture Theaters',
     in Talbot Hamlin, ed., *Forms and Functions of Modern Architecture* (New York, 1952),
     vol. III, pp. 445–77.

55 Frederick Kiesler, *Contemporary Art Applied to the Store and its Display* (New York, 1930), p. 118. Kiesler's 'Design-Correlations' series appeared in *AR*, LXXXII, LXXXIV (April–July 1937; September 1939).

56 Janet Flanner, *The Cubical City* [1926] (Carbondale, IL, 1974).

chapter four: Architecture, the Public and the State, 1933–1945

1 T. V. Smith, 'The New Deal as a Cultural Phenomenon', in F.S.C. Northrup, ed., *Ideological Differences and World Order* (New Haven, 1949), pp. 214–15, 225.

2 Thurman Arnold, *The Symbols of Government* (New Haven, 1935), p. 241; Arnold, *The Folklore of Capitalism* (New Haven, 1937); cited in Michael Szalay, *New Deal Modernism: American Literature and the Invention of the Welfare State* (Durham, NC, 2000), p. 10.

3 An important book is Jean-Louis Cohen, ed., *Les Années 30s: l'architecture et les arts de l'espace entre industrie et nostalgie* (Paris, 1997), on overlaps and incongruities in France, Germany, Italy, the USSR and the United States. Also see Nicholas Bourriaud, *Relational Aesthetics* (Dijon, 2002).

4 Frederick Gutheim, 'Seven Years of Public Buildings', *Magazine of Art*, XXVII (July 1940), pp. 433, 443.

5 *Make It New: Essays by Ezra Pound* (London, 1934).

6 Joseph Hudnut, 'Architecture Discovers the Present', *American Scholar*, VII (Winter 1938), p. 106. See Jill Pearlman, *Inventing American Modernism: Joseph Hudnut, Walter Gropius, and the Bauhaus Legacy at Harvard* (Charlottesville, 2007).

7 MOMA Committee on Architecture and Industrial Art, 'Architecture in Government Housing', bound typescript, 1936. The curator was Ernestine Fanti.

8 See Telesis Environmental Research Group, *Space for Living* (San Francisco, 1940).

9 'Where is Modern?', *AF*, LXVIII (June 1938), p. 468.

10 Catherine Bauer, *Modern Housing* (Boston, MA, 1934), pp. 147–8, 157, 253–4; Bauer, 'The Dreary Deadlock of Public Housing', *AF*, CVI (May 1957), pp. 140–42, 219, 221.

11 Lewis Mumford, *The South in Architecture* [1941] (New York, 1967), pp. 51–2.

12 Mary Colter, *Manual for Drivers and Guides Descriptive of the Indian Watchtower at Desert View and its Relation, Architecturally, to the Prehistoric Ruins of the Southwest* (Grand Canyon National Park, 1933); cited in Arnold Berke, *Mary Colter: Architect of the Southwest* (New York, 2002), pp. 187–225.

13 See, for example, Garrett Eckbo, Daniel Kiley and James Rose, 'Landscape Design in the Urban Environment', *AR*, LXXXVII (May 1939); reprinted in Marc Treib, ed., *Modern Landscape Architecture* (Cambridge, MA, 1993), pp. 78–82.

14 Wolfgang Born, 'Geo-Architecture: An American Contribution to the Art of the Future', *Magazine of Art*, XVI (January 1944), pp. 202–7.

15 James Marston Fitch, *American Building: The Forces that Shape It* (Boston, MA, 1947), pp. 143–92.

16 *Public Works Administration: The First 3 Years* (Washington, DC, 1936), p. 1; *America Builds: The Record of the PWA* (Washington, DC, 1939), pp. 288–91; C. W. Short and R. Stanley-Brown, *Public Buildings: Architecture under the Public Works Administration, 1933–39* [1939] (New York, 1986).

17 'PWA Has Changed Face of US', *Life* (1 April 1940), p. 61.

18 'Alphabets and Architects', *AA*, CLXVIII (January 1936), p. 18. The Golden Gate Bridge ranked fifth in a 2007 poll of Americans' favourite architecture sponsored by the AIA (see www.aia150.org). A 1937 exhibition on modern landscape architecture at the San Francisco Museum of Art featured Margaret Keeley Brown's prescient but unbuilt

response to homelessness: a trailer camp for 300 families at the San Francisco approach to the new Bay Bridge with gardens and basic services (Grace Morley, ed., *Contemporary Landscape Architecture and its Sources*, San Francisco, 1937, p. 33).

19 Le Corbusier, *When the Cathedrals Were White: A Journey to the Country of Timid People* [1937] (New York, 1947), pp. 75–7; cited in Mardges Bacon, *Le Corbusier in America: Travels in the Land of the Timid* (Cambridge, MA, 2001), pp. 265, 269.

20 The two opposing interpretations of Moses are Robert Caro's critique of abusive power, *The Power Broker: Robert Moses and the Fall of New York* (New York, 1974), and the neo-liberal apology, Hilary Ballon and Kenneth T. Jackson, eds, *Robert Moses and the Modern City: The Transformation of New York* (New York, 2007).

21 Michael Denning, *The Cultural Front* (New York, 1997), pp. 118–23; Pat Kilham, *Charles and Ray Eames: Designers of the Twentieth Century* (Cambridge, MA, 1995).

22 Frederick Gutheim, 'TVA: A New Phase in Architecture', *Magazine of Art*, XXXIII (September 1940), p. 527; Arthur Morgan, 'The Human Problem of the Tennessee Valley Authority', *Landscape Architecture*, XXIV (April 1934), p. 12; Walter Creese, *TVA's Public Planning: The Vision, The Reality* (Knoxville, TN, 1990); Tim Culvahouse, ed., *The Tennessee Valley Authority: Design and Persuasion* (New York, 2007).

23 The MOMA exhibition on TVA was in 1941. The quote is from Elizabeth Mock, *Built in USA, 1932–1944* (New York, 1944), p. 111.

24 Stuart Chase, quoted in 'A Vision in Kilowatts', *Fortune* (April 1933); cited in Christine Macy and Sarah Bonnemaison, *Architecture and Nature: Creating the American Landscape* (London and New York, 2003), p. 138.

25 Marshall Wilson, 'Photographs in Norris Reservoir Area' (n.d.); cited in Phoebe Cutler, *The Public Landscape of the New Deal* (New Haven, 1985), p. 137. By 1942 up to 2,000,000 American and European tourists a year were visiting the dams.

26 Frank Lloyd Wright, 'The New Building for S. C. Johnson & Son, Inc.' (unpublished 1936 press release); 'Frank Lloyd Wright Designs the Office of the Future', *American Business* (May 1939), p. 41; 'Johnson's Wax', *Life* (8 May 1939); cited in Jonathan Lipman, *Frank Lloyd Wright and the Johnson Wax Buildings* (New York, 1986), pp. 182, 93.

27 Frank Lloyd Wright, 'Broadacre City: An Architect's Vision', *New York Times Magazine* (20 March 1932); Wright, 'Today . . . Tomorrow, American Tomorrow', *AA*, CXLI (May 1932), pp. 14–17, both cited in Donald Leslie Johnson, *Frank Lloyd Wright versus America: The 1930s* (Cambridge, MA, 1990), pp. 109–10.

28 See Neil Levine, *The Architecture of Frank Lloyd Wright* (Princeton, 1996); Franklin Toker, *Fallingwater Rising: Frank Lloyd Wright, E. J. Kaufmann, and America's Most Extraordinary House* (New York, 2003).

29 'Frank Lloyd Wright', special issue of *AF*, LXVIII (January 1938), p. 78.

30 Gertrude Fish, ed., *The Story of Housing* (New York, 1979), p. 203. Wealthy families like the Kaufmanns did not need FHA loans.

31 Howard Myers, 'Editorial: Modern Houses in America', *AF*, LXXI (July 1939), p. 34.

32 Ibid.; Katherine Morrow Ford, 'Modern is Regional', *House and Garden*, *AF*, LXXIX (March 1941), pp. 14–17; James Ford and Katherine Morrow Ford, *The Modern House in America* (New York, 1940), pp. 6–14.

33 Walter Gropius, *Scope of Total Architecture* (New York, 1962), p. 14.

34 'Modernism: The House That Works', *Fortune*, XII (October 1935), pp. 59–65, 94.

35 Sandy Isenstadt, *The Modern American House: Spaciousness and Middle-Class Identity* (New York and Cambridge, 2006).

36 Gail Radford, *Modern Housing for America: Policy Struggles in the New Deal Era* (Chicago, 1996), pp. 100–101. Bauer estimated that, since World War One, European governments had aided in the construction of at least 4.5 million new housing units,

providing shelter to around 16 per cent of the population, though only about half was affordable for the lowest-paid workers.

37 Joseph Hudnut, 'Housing and the Democratic Process', AR, XCIII (June 1943), p. 44.

38 Richard Pommer, 'The Architecture of Early Housing in the United States during the Early 1930s', JSAH, XXXVII (December 1978), pp. 235–64.

39 Federal Writers' Project, WPA Guide to New York City [1941] (New York, 1992), p. 392; Radford, Modern Housing, pp. 146–76; Richard Plunz, A History of Housing in New York City (New York, 1990), pp. 207–35; Roy Strickland and Joel Saunders, 'The Harlem River Houses', Harvard Architectural Review, II (Spring 1981), pp. 48-51.

40 R. L. Duffus, 'The Architect in a Modern World', AR, LXXIX (September 1936), p. 182.

41 Means tests required that tenant incomes be at least 20 per cent below what local realtors considered the bare minimum for market-rate rentals, which discouraged aspirations.

42 'Farm Security Architecture', AF, LXXIV (January 1941), p. 3; Talbot Hamlin, 'Farm Security Architecture,' PP, XXII (November 1941), pp. 709–20.

43 Albert Roth, Nouvelle architecture/Neue Architektur/New Architecture (Zurich, 1940); 'Genetrix', in Machine-Made America, special issue of AR, CXXI (May 1957), p. 356.

44 Ludwig Mies van der Rohe, 1960 speech accepting the AIA Gold Medal; cited in William H. Jordy, American Buildings and their Architects, vol. 4: The Impact of European Modernism in the Mid-Twentieth Century (Garden City, 1976), p. 221.

45 Mies van der Rohe, Introduction to Ludwig Hilberseimer, The New City: Principles of Planning (Chicago, 1944), p. xv.

46 Daniel Bluestone, 'Mecca Flat Blues', JSAH, LVII (December 1998), pp. 382–403; Sarah Whiting, 'Bas-Relief Urbanism: Chicago's Figured Field', in Phyllis Lambert, ed., Mies in America (New York, 2005), pp. 642–91.

47 Joel Davidson, 'Building for War, Preparing for Peace: World War II and the Military-Industrial Complex', in Donald Albrecht, ed., World War II and the American Dream: How Wartime Building Changed a Nation (Cambridge, MA, 1995), p. 197.

48 'A New Era in Plastics', Newsweek (17 May 1943), p. 42.

49 'The Seabees: The Navy's Fighting Builders', AF, LXXX (February 1944), pp. 48–58; 'Navy Architecture', AF, LXXXIII (December 1945), pp. 73–9; Julie Decker and Chris Chiei, Quonset Hut: Metal Living for a Modern Age (New York, 2005). Goff's Ruth Ford House in Aurora, Illinois (1947), took inventive Quonset-based designs even farther by adding wartime detritus like acrylic aircraft nose-cones.

50 1956 conversation cited in Philip B. Welch, ed., Goff on Goff: Conversations and Lectures (Norman, OK, 1996), pp. 23–9.

51 Peter Reed, 'Enlisting Modernism', in Albrecht, World War II, pp. 2–41; Hugh Casson, Homes for the Million: An Account of the Housing Achievement of the USA, 1940–1945 (Harmondsworth, 1946), pp. 5, 16–17.

52 Elaine Tyler May, 'Rosie the Riveter Gets Married', in Lewis A. Erenberg and Susan E. Hirsch, eds, The War in American Culture: Society and Consciousness during World War II Chicago, 1996), p. 130; Dolores Hayden, Redesigning the American Dream: The Future of Housing, Work and Family Life (New York, 1984), pp. 4–6.

53 Robert Friedel, 'Scarcity and Promise: Materials and American Domestic Culture during World War II', in Albrecht, World War II, p. 54.

54 Casson, Homes, p. 45.

55 Antonin Raymond, 'Working with USHA under the Lanham Act', special Defense Housing issue, PP, XXII (November 1941), p. 694.

56 'Wartime Housing', Bulletin of the Museum of Modern Art, IX (May 1942); special War Housing issue, AF, LXXVI (May 1942).

57 'Carver Court', AF, LXXXI (December 1944), pp. 109–16; Sarah Williams Goldhagen,

Louis Kahn's Situated Modernism (New Haven, 2001), pp. 18–33. Stonorov and Kahn also produced two popular pamphlets for the Revere Company Better Living series.

58 'Defense Houses by Skidmore, Owings & Merrill, Architects', *AF*, LXXIII (November 1940), pp. 444–9; Neil Levine, '"The Significance of Facts": Mies' Collages Up Close and Personal', *Assemblage*, XXXVII (December 1998), pp. 70–101. Hyun-Tae Jung's forthcoming dissertation (Columbia University) on the origins of SOM has been a valuable asset.

59 Citation from wall panel in *1945: Creativity and Crisis: Chicago Architecture and Design of the World War II Era*, Art Institute of Chicago exhibition, 2005.

60 Roland Wank, 'Nowhere to Go but Forward', *Magazine of Art*, XXXIV (January 1941), p. 8.

61 Henry R. Luce, 'The American Century', *Life* (17 February 1941), p. 63. Luce's writings from *Life* also appeared in an edited volume, *The American Century* (New York, 1941). He published *Time, Life, Fortune* and *Architectural Forum*. Olivier Zunz's *Why the American Century?* (Chicago, 1998) argues that the ideology of American exceptionalism pre-dates World War II, but was imposed on the world only after the war ended.

62 Charles Eames and John Entenza, 'House' and 'Prefabricated Housing', *Arts & Architecture*, XLIV (July 1944), pp. 24–52.

63 Mock, *Built in USA*, pp. 13, 14, 21–2. The project originated as Mock's section of a major MOMA exhibition in 1944; a new catalogue of 1947 entitled *Built in USA, 1932–1944* was translated into German the following year.

chapter five: The Triumph of Modernism, 1946–1964

1 Marcel Breuer, Conference proceedings for 'What is Happening to Modern Architecture?', *Bulletin of the Museum of Modern Art*, XV (Spring 1948), p. 15.

2 Henry-David Hitchcock and Arthur Drexler, *Built in USA: Post-war Architecture* (New York, 1952), pp. 12, 17.

3 Clement Greenberg, 'Modernist Painting' (1960); reprinted in *Clement Greenberg: The Collected Essays and Criticism* (Chicago, 1993), vol. IV, p. 85.

4 Henry-Russell Hitchcock, 'The Architecture of Bureaucracy and the Architecture of Genius', *Architectural Review*, CI (January 1947), pp. 3–6.

5 Vance Packard, *The Status Seekers* (New York, 1959), pp. 72–4.

6 Chester Hartman, 'The Housing of Relocated Families', in James Q. Wilson, ed., *Urban Renewal: The Record and the Controversy* (Cambridge, MA, 1966), p. 321; Douglas S. Massey and Nancy A. Denton, *American Apartheid: Segregation and the Making of the Underclass* (Cambridge, MA, 1993), pp. 69–75.

7 'The New City', *Fortune* (February 1960); cited in Michael Johns, *Moment of Grace: The American City in the 1950s* (Berkeley, CA, 2003), p. 30.

8 Frederick Gutheim, *Housing as Environment: A Report on the Research Conference 'The Role of Social Research in Housing Design'* (New York, 1953).

9 '19 Office Floors without Columns', *AF*, CII (May 1955), p. 116; Clarence Randall, Chairman of Inland Steel Company, quoted in 'Inland's Steel Showcase', *AF*, CVIII (April 1958), p. 89; both cited in Reinhold Martin, *The Organization Complex: Architecture, Media and Corporate Space* (Cambridge, MA, 2003), p. 104.

10 'The Architects from Skid's Row', *Fortune*, LVII (January 1958), p. 215.

11 Mies van der Rohe, Transcript of a 1955 interview with John Peters; cited in Phyllis Lambert, 'Mies Immersion', in Lambert, ed., *Mies in America* (New York, 2001), p. 193; Lambert, 'How a Building Gets Built', *Vassar Alumni Magazine* (February 1959), pp. 14–16; cited in Franz Schulze, *Mies van der Rohe: A Critical Biography* (Chicago, 1985), p. 272.

12 Lewis Mumford, 'The Sky Line: The Lesson of the Master', *New Yorker* (13 September

1958); Manfredo Tafuri and Francesco Dal Co, *Modern Architecture*, trans. Robert Erich Wolfe [1976] (New York, 1979), pp. 340–41.

13 'Architecture for the Future Constructs a Versailles of Industry', *Life* (21 May 1956); cited in Scott Knowles and Stuart Leslie, '"Industrial Versailles": Eero Saarinen's Corporate Campuses for GM, IBM and AT&T', *Isis*, XCII (March 2001), p. 5.

14 Peter Galison and Emily Thompson, eds, *The Architecture of Science* (Cambridge, MA, 1999); Peter Galison and Bruce Hevly, eds, *Big Science: The Growth of Large-Scale Research* (Stanford, 1992).

15 Gwendolyn Wright, 'The Virtual Architecture of Silicon Valley,' *JAE*, LIV (November 2000), pp. 88–94. John Harwood, 'The White Room: Eliot Noyes and the Logic of the Information Age Interior', *GR*, XII (Summer 2003) pp. 3–31.

16 'Hospital of Ideas', *AF*, XCVI (February 1952), pp. 116–23.

17 'New Shells', *Time* (15 August 1949), p. 60.

18 'Residential Design, 1951', *PA*, XXXII (March 1951), pp. 67–86; Sarah Amelar, 'The Long Journey Back: 50 Years of *Record* Houses', *AR,* CXCVI (April 2005), p. 132. Various annual awards were inaugurated, beginning with *PA*'s in 1948 and the AIA's in 1949.

19 'American Style House', *HB* (February 1951), pp. 80–83; Marion Gough, 'Defining the American Way of Life Executed in the New American Style', *HB*, XCIII (May 1951), pp. 167–75; T. H. Robsjohn Gibbings, 'Do You Know the Difference between Modern and Modernistic?', *HB*, LXXXVIII (October 1946), pp. 135, 236.

20 'Richard Neutra Is "Man of the Year"', *Time* (15 August 1949), p. 2.

21 Reyner Banham, 'Klarheit, Ehrlichkeit, Einfachkeit . . . and Wit Too!: The Case Study Houses in the World's Eyes', in Elizabeth A. T. Smith, ed., *Blueprints for Modern Living: History and Legacy of the Case Study Houses* (Cambridge, MA, 1989), pp. 183–96.

22 Marc A. Weiss, *The Rise of the Community Builders* (New York, 1987), p. 161; Jon C. Teaford, *The Twentieth-Century American City* (Baltimore, 1986), p. 100.

23 'New Shells', p. 58. William H. White accentuated the advantages of cities and problems of 'sprawl' in *The Exploding Metropolis* (Garden City, NY, 1958), a book he edited for *Fortune*. See Robert Bruegmann, *Sprawl: A Compact History* (Chicago, 2005). These 'first-tier suburbs' are now seen in a more positive light, in comparison with later developments.

24 William Dobriner, ed., *Class in Suburbia* (Englewood Cliffs, NJ, 1963); cited in Lizabeth Cohen, *A Consumers' Republic: The Politics of Mass Consumption in Postwar America* (New York, 2003), pp. 200–214.

25 Michael Sorkin, in *Hollin Hills: Community of Vision, A Semicentennial History, 1949–1999* (Alexandria, VA, 2000), p. 39.

26 Alice T. Friedman, *Women and the Making of the Modern House: A Social and Architectural History* (New York, 1998), pp. 126–59. Citation (p. 147) is from Hilary Lewis and John O'Connor, *Philip Johnson: The Architect in His Own Words* (New York, 1994), p. 49.

27 'Regionalism and Nationalism', *Texas Quarterly*, I (February 1958); reprinted in Vincent B. Canizaro, ed., *Architectural Regionalism: Collected Writings on Place, Identity, Modernity and Tradition* (New York, 2007), pp. 57–63, which also contains thoughtful statements by Neutra, Belluschi and other modernists.

28 *Plastics in Housing* (Cambridge, MA, 1955); Stephen Phillips, 'Plastics', in Beatriz Colomina, Annmarie Brennan and Jeannie Kim, eds, *Cold War Hothouses: Inventing Postwar Culture, from Cockpit to Playboy* (New York, 2004), pp. 91–123; Carl Koch, *At Home with Tomorrow* (New York, 1958), p. 49; Bryan Irwin, 'The Grandfather of Prefab', *PA*, LXXV (February 1994), pp. 62–5.

29 Esther McCoy, 'Sim Bruce Richards', *Nature in Architecture*, exh. cat., San Diego Natural History Museum (1984); cited in Alan Hess, *Organic Architecture: The Other Modernism* (Layton, UT, 2006), p. 76.

30   Beatriz Reciado, 'Pornotopia', in Colomina et al., *Cold War Hothouses*, p. 218.

31   Hitchcock and Drexler, *Built in USA*, p. 21.

32   Reyner Banham, *Los Angeles: The Architecture of Four Ecologies* (London and Baltimore, 1971). Also see John Chase, *Glitter Stucco and Dumpster Diving: Reflections on Building Production in the Vernacular City* (New York, 2000).

33   James Marston Fitch, in *San Francisco Chronicle* (11 December 1949); cited in Pierluigi Serraino, *NorCalMod: Icons of Northern California Modernism* (San Francisco, 2006), p. 20.

34   Elizabeth Wood, 'Realities of Urban Redevelopment', *Journal of Housing,* III (December 1945–January 1946), pp. 12–14.

35   Alistair Gordon, *Beach Houses: Andrew Geller* (New York, 2003), p. 95.

36   Wallace Harrison, cited in George Dudley, *The Workshop of Peace: Designing the United Nations* (New York, 2003).

37   Martin Pawley, *Buckminster Fuller* (New York, 1990), p. 183.

38   Jane C. Loeffler, *The Architecture of Diplomacy: Building America's Embassies* (New York, 1998), pp. 98–100.

39   Haskell coined the term in an unsigned affirmation, 'Googie Architecture', *House and Home*, I (February 1952), pp. 86–8. As Alan Hess explains in *Googie Redux: Ultramodern Roadside Architecture* (San Francisco, 2006), this exuberant 'style' emerged in the 1930s.

40   The 940 shopping centres in 1957 more than doubled by 1960, and doubled again by 1963. Like downtowns and suburbs, they were increasingly divided by class. See Cohen, *Consumers' Republic,* pp. 258, 292–309.

41   Morris Lapidus, 'The Architecture of Emotion', *JAIA*, XXXVI (November 1961), pp. 55–8; cited in Alice Friedmann, 'Merchandising Miami Beach: Morris Lapidus and the Architecture of Abundance', *Journal of Decorative and Propaganda Arts*, XXV (2005), p. 249.

42   Douglas Haskell, 'Eero Saarinen, 1919–1961', *AF,* XV (October 1961), p. 96; 'Airport City, USA', *Newsweek* (5 April 1965), p. 90; *Wall Street Journal (*26 April 1966); cited in Alastair Gordon, *Naked Airport: A Cultural History of the World's Most Revolutionary Structure* (New York, 2004), pp. 186, 215.

43   Katherine Kuh, 'What Should a Museum Be? Plus and Minus of the Building Boom', *Art in America*, XLIX (1961), pp. 41–5.

44   'Desegregation's Impact on Building', *AF*, CVII (November 1957), pp. 128–31, 233.

45   Paul Tillich, 'Contemporary Protestant Architecture' (1962); reprinted in Tillich, *On Art and Architecture* (New York, 1987), pp. 214–20.

46   Anne Loveland and Otis Wheeler, *From Meetinghouse to Megachurch* (Columbia, MI, 2003), p. 153.

47   Douglas Haskell, 'Architecture and Popular Taste', *AF*, CIX (August 1958), pp. 104–9; Haskell, 'Jazz in Architecture', *AF*, CXIII (September 1960), pp. 110–15; Thomas Creighton, 'The New Sensualism', *PA*, XL (October 1959), pp. 80–87; Creighton, 'Sixties, the State of Architecture', *PA*, XLII (March–May 1961).

chapter six: Challenging Orthodoxies, 1965–1984

1   See Todd Gitlin, *The Sixties: Years of Hope, Days of Rage* (New York, 1993).

2   Peter Eisenman, in 'Cardboard Architecture', *Casabella*, XXXVII (February 1973), said the term 'questions the nature of reality of the physical environment' (p. 24).

3   Robert Venturi, *Complexity and Contradiction in Architecture* (New York, 1966), p. 16.

4   Robert Venturi and Denise Scott Brown, 'A Significance for A&P Parking Lots or Learning from Las Vegas', *AF*, CXXVIII (March 1968); reprinted in Kate Nesbitt, ed., *Theorizing a New Agenda for Architecture* (New York, 1996), pp. 308–21; Moore cited in

John W. Cook and Heinrich Klotz, *Conversations with Architects* (New York, 1973), p. 235.

5   See Robert Melnick and Arnold Alanen, eds, *Preserving Cultural Landscapes in America* (Baltimore, 2000); *Future Anterior: Journal of Historic Preservation History, Theory and Criticism.*

6   Paul Davidoff, 'Advocacy and Pluralism in Planning', *Journal of the* APA (1965); reprinted in Richard T. LeGates *et al.*, eds, *The City Reader* (New York, 1996), pp. 421–34; Rex Curry, 'Community Design Centers', in Bryan Bell, ed., *Good Deeds, Good Design: Community Service through Architecture* (New York, 2004), pp. 61–70; *Designer/Builder*, based in Santa Fe, which describes contemporary advocacy.

7   Theodore Roszak, quoted in 'Advertisements for a Counter Culture', PA, LI (July 1970), p. 70.

8   The Cosanti Foundation reissued Soleri's *Arcology: The City in the Image of Man* on the occasion of its 30th anniversary in 2000.

9   Douglas Davis, 'New Architecture: Building for Man', *Newsweek* (19 April 1971), pp. 78–90.

10   Charles Moore described 'exclusive' groups, and a new more 'inclusive' one, in 'Statement of the Jurors', PA, XLVIII (January 1967); cited in Robert A. M. Stern, *New Directions in American Architecture* [1969] (New York, 1977), p. 117.

11   Vernon E. Jordan, 'The New Negativism', *Newsweek* (14 August 1978), p. 13.

12   Robert Stern's 'The Doubles of Post-Modern' in the first *Harvard Architecture Review* (Spring 1980) played up this schism, but reduced it to a literally superficial notion of 'schismatic' dichotomies.

13   Ada Louise Huxtable, 'The Troubled State of Modern Architecture', *New York Review of Books*, XXVII (1 May 1980).

14   Richard Edwards, *Contested Terrain: The Transformation of the Workplace* (New York, 1979), p. 3.

15   Michael Sorkin, *Exquisite Corpse: Writings on Buildings* (New York, 1991), p. 272.

16   C. Sibley and P. Beney, *Atlanta: A Brave and Beautiful City* (Atlanta, 1986); cited in Charles Rutheiser, *Imagineering Atlanta: The Politics of Place in the City of Dreams* (London and New York, 1996), p. 54.

17   Arthur Drexler, *Transformations in Modern Architecture* (New York, 1979), p. 72.

18   Ibid., p. 83; Pamela Heyne, *Today's Architectural Mirror* (New York, 1982).

19   Quoted in Joseph Giovannini, 'The Grand Reach of Corporate Architecture', *New York Times* (20 January 1985), sect. 3, p. 28.

20   Richard Ingersoll, 'Die Tunnels der Liebe', *Archithèse*, XX (January 1990), pp. 28–30.

21   Citations from James Glanz and Eric Lipton, *City in the Sky: The Rise and Fall of the World Trade Center* (New York, 2003), p. 116.

22   Ada Louise Huxtable, 'The Tall Building Artistically Reconsidered', *New Criterion*, I (November 1982), p. 17.

23   See Nicholas Negroponte, *The Architecture Machine* (Cambridge, 1970); Negroponte, *Soft Architecture Machines* (Cambridge, MA, 1975), p. 177.

24   Tod Marder, ed., *The Critical Edge: Controversy in Recent American Architecture* (Cambridge, MA, 1985), pp. 63–74.

25   Paul Rudolph, 'The Mobile Home is the 20th Century Brick', AR, CXLIII (April 1968), pp. 137–46.

26   Robert Goodman's *After the Planners* (New York, 1971) castigated even well-intended modern architecture as irrelevant at best and at worst oppressive, co-opted by corporate capitalism and the war machine.

27   *Building the American City: Report of the National Commission on Urban Problems* (Washington, DC, 1968), pp. 123–8.

28   Katharine Bristol, 'The Pruitt-Igoe Myth', JAE, XCIV (May 1991), pp. 163–71, reprinted in Keith L. Eggener, ed., *American Architectural History* (London and New York, 2004), pp.

352–64; Charles Jencks, *The Language of Postmodern Architecture* [1974] (New York, 1984), p. 9.

29 See John Sharratt, 'Urban Neighborhood Preservation and Development', *Process Architecture*, XIV (1980), pp. 28–32; Peter G. Rowe, *Modernity and Housing* (Cambridge, MA, 1993), pp. 244–52.

30 Stern, *New Directions*, p. 86.

31 Antoine Predock, 'Surrogate Landscapes', *Places*, V (1988), pp. 54–9.

32 Venturi; cited in Ellen Perry Berkeley, 'Complexities and Contradictions', *PA*, XLVI (May 1965), p. 168.

33 Manfredo Tafuri, 'L'Architecture dans le boudoir: The Language of Criticism and the Criticism of Language', *Oppositions*, III (1974); expanded in Tafuri's *The Sphere and the Labyrinth: Avant-Gardes and Architecture from Piranesi to the 1970s* (Cambridge, MA, 1987), and reprinted in K. Michael Hays, ed., *Architecture Theory since 1968* (Cambridge, MA, 1998), pp. 146–73.

34 'Sculpture for Living', *Life*, LIX (3 December 1965) pp. 124–9; cited in Liane Lefaivre, 'Living Outside the Box: Mary Otis Stevens and Thomas McNulty's Lincoln House', *Harvard Design Magazine*, XXIV (Spring–Summer 2006), pp. 72–8.

35 Charles Moore, 'You Have To Pay for the Public Life', *Perspecta* (1965); reprinted in Moore's collected essays of that title, ed. Kevin Keim (Cambridge, MA, 2001), pp. 111–41.

36 Hal Lancaster, 'Stadium Projects are Proliferating amid Debate over Benefit to Cities', *Wall Street Journal* (20 March 1987), p. 37; cited in Bernard J. Frieden and Lynne B. Sagalyn, *Downtown, Inc.: How America Rebuilds Cities* (Cambridge, MA, 1989), p. 277.

37 Michael Fried, 'Art and Objecthood', *Artforum*, V (June 1967), pp. 12–25; Phil Patton, 'Other Voices, Other Rooms: The Rise of the Alternative Space', *Art in America*, LXV (July–August 1977), pp. 80–87; Helen Searing, 'The Brillo Box in the Warehouse: Museums of Contemporary Art and Industrial Conversions', in *The Andy Warhol Museum* (Pittsburgh, 1994), pp. 39–66.

38 Guggenheim Director Thomas Krens, cited in Rosalind Krauss, 'The Cultural Logic of the Late Capitalist Museum', *October*, LIV (Fall 1990), pp. 3–17.

39 Latryl Ohendalski, 'Kimbell Museum to Be Friendly Home, Says Kahn', *Fort Worth Press* (4 May 1969); Louis I. Kahn, 'Space and Inspiration', 1967 lecture, *L'Architecture d'aujour-d'hui*, XL (February–March 1969), pp. 15–16, cited in Patricia Cummings Lord, *The Art Museums of Louis I. Kahn* (Durham and London, 1989), p. 115.

40 See Mary McLeod, 'Architecture and Politics in the Reagan Era: From Postmodernism to Deconstruction', *Assemblage*, VIII (February 1989); reprinted in Hays, *Architecture Theory*, pp. 678–702.

41 David Harvey, 'Looking Backward on Postmodernism', in Andreas Papadakis, ed., *Post-Modernism on Trial* (London, 1990), p. 12.

42 *The Charlottesville Tapes* (New York, 1985), pp. 19, 15 – transcripts of a 1982 conference at the University of Virginia School of Architecture that brought together 25 'starchitects' including Johnson, Peter Eisenman, Frank Gehry, Rem Koolhaas, Robert A. M. Stern and Stanley Tigerman.

43 See Reinhold Martin, 'Architecture's Image Problem: Have We Ever Been Postmodern?', *GR*, XXII (Winter 2005), pp. 6–29.

chapter seven: Disjunctives and Alternatives, 1985 to the Present

1 John Logan and Harvey Moloteh, *Urban Fortunes: The Political Economy of Place* (Berkeley, CA, 1987); Alan Altshuler, *Mega-Projects: The Changing Politics of Urban Public*

Investment (Washington, DC, and Cambridge, MA, 2003); Deyan Sudjic, *The Edifice Complex: How the Rich and Powerful Shape the World* (London, 2005).

2 Greg Lynn's manifestos, *Folds, Bodies and Blobs: Collected Essays* (Brussels, 1998) and *Animate Form* (New York, 1999), promoted blobs. Reed Kroloff refined the terminology, with later comments by William Safire ('On Language: Defenestration', *New York Times*, 1 December 2002).

3 'Daring Modernist Homes on the Cheap', *Business Week* (18 June 2002).

4 SHOP/Sharples Holden Pasquarelli, guest eds, *Versioning: Evolutionary Techniques in Architecture*, special issue of *A.D.*, LXXII (September–October 2002).

5 Key works include David Leatherbarrow and Mohsen Mostafavi, *Surface Architecture* (Cambridge, MA, 2002); Toshiko Mori, ed., *Immaterial/Ultramaterial* (New York, 2002).

6 Wigley acknowledged Aaron Betsky's telling phrase, which became the basis for Betsky's *Violated Perfection: Architecture and the Fragmentation of the Modern* (New York, 1990). Also see Bernard Tschumi, 'Disjunctions' (1987), in *Architecture and Disjunction* (Cambridge, MA, 1996).

7 See Steven Harris and Deborah Berke, eds, *Architecture of the Everyday* (New York, 1997); John Chase, Margaret Crawford and John Kaliski, eds, *Everyday Urbanism* (New York, 1999); the work of Venturi Scott Brown, especially *A View from the Campidoglio* (New York, 1984); and renewed interest in J. B. Jackson, whose influence is summarized in Chris Wilson and Paul Groth, eds, *Everyday America: Cultural Landscape Studies after J. B. Jackson* (Berkeley, CA, 2003).

8 Recent explorations seek to bridge the two realms, notably Vicky Richardson, *New Vernacular Architecture* (New York, 2001); Maiken Umbach and Bernd Hüppauf, eds, *Vernacular Modernism: Heimat, Globalization, the Built Environment* (Stanford, 2005).

9 This only accentuates the need to engage questions of identity in today's world. See Chris Abel, *Architecture and Identity* (London, 1997); Dolores Hayden, *The Power of Place: Urban Landscapes as Public Culture* (Cambridge, MA, 1995); Albert Borgmann, *Crossing the Postmodern Divide* (Chicago, 1993).

10 Paul Ricoeur, 'Universal Civilization and National Cultures' (1955); reprinted in *History and Truth* (Evanston, 1965), cited in Kenneth Frampton, 'Towards a Critical Regionalism', in Hal Foster, ed., *The Anti-Aesthetic* [1983] (New York, 1998), p. 18, and several later versions of this essay.

11 Among the best discussions of the issue are Vincent B. Canizaro, ed., *Architectural Regionalism: Collected Writings on Place, Identity, Modernity and Tradition* (New York, 2007), which includes Frampton's essay; Liane Lefaivre and Alexander Tzonis, *Critical Regionalism: Architecture and Identity in a Globalized World* (Munich and New York, 2003).

12 Joel Garreau's book, *Edge City: The New Frontier*, appeared in 1992 as the phenomenon was in decline.

13 Joel Warren Barna, *The See-Through Years: Creation and Destruction in Texas Architecture and Real Estate, 1981–1991* (Houston, 1992), p. 190.

14 See Robert H. Frank, *The Winner-Take-All Society* (New York, 1995); Arlie Hochschild, *The Time Bind: When Work Becomes Home, and Home Becomes Work* (New York, 1997); Ulrich Beck, *The Brave New World of Work* (Cambridge, 2000).

15 Stephen Zacks, 'The DNA of Science Labs', *Metropolis*, XXVI (February 2007), p. 79.

16 An article about Behnische's Genzyme Center receiving a 2006 BW/AR award noted that 58 per cent of the employees reported that they were more productive there than in the previous building: 'Genzyme Center', *AR,* CXCIV (November 2006), p. 102.

17 Sarah Williams Goldhagen rightly critiques the focus on bravura and deferred maintenance in 'American Collapse', *The New Republic* (27 August 2007), pp. 26–32.

18 Wes Jones, *Instrumental Forms* (New York, 1998), esp. pp. 70–73. On infrastructure, also

see Richard Datner, *Civil Architecture: The New Public Infrastructure* (New York, 1995);
Brian Hayes, *Infrastructure* (New York, 2005); David E. Miller, *Toward a New Regionalism:
Environmental Architecture in the Pacific Northwest* (Seattle, 2005).

19   Susan Susanka's popular book launched a little empire with *Inside the Not So Big House,
Outside It* and even *The Not So Big Life*.

20   Tony Favro, 'Affordable Housing Crisis Casts a Shadow over the American Dream',
City Mayors Society (9 March 2007), p. 1.

21   Data from www.ekekt.com, cited in *Praxis*, III, special *Housing Tactics* issue (2001), p. 15.

22   Stephanie Coontz, *The Way We Never Were: American Families and the Nostalgia Trap*
(New York, 1992), shows the historical flaws in these fantasies.

23   Clare Cooper Marcus and Wendy Sarkissian, *Housing As If People Mattered* (Berkeley,
CA, 1986); Karen A. Franck and Sherry Ahrentzen, eds, *New Households, New Housing*
(New York, 1989); Joan Forrester Sprague, *More Than Housing: Lifeboats for Women and
Children* (Boston, MA, 1991).

24   Susannah Hagan, 'Five Reasons to Adopt Environmental Design', *Harvard Design
Magazine*, XVIII (Spring–Summer 2003), p. 5.

25   Personal communication with Sam Grawe, 22 June 2007.

26   *American Dream: The Houses at Sagaponac* (New York, 2003).

27   John Dutton, *New American Urbanism* (Milan, 2000); Peter Calthorpe and William
Fulton, *The Regional City: Planning for the End of Sprawl* (Washington, DC, 2001).

28   For an overview of many such efforts, see Bryan Bell, ed., *Good Deeds, Good Design:
Community Service through Architecture* (New York, 2004). Habitat for Humanity has
built more than 100,000 houses in the US and a comparable number abroad. This faith-
based organization, founded in 1976 in Americus, Georgia, relies on sweat equity and
volunteer labour. While the goals and bonding experience are commendable, the stylistic idiom and environmental politics are not. Some local architects have negotiated a
more engaging contemporary style, for example, Olson Sundberg Kundig Allen's
ten-house enclave in Seattle (2004).

29   Koning Eizenberg Architects, *Architecture Isn't Just for Special Occasions* (New York,
2006), p. 32.

30   Jayne Merkel, 'Fine Tuning', in Lucy Bullivant, ed., *Home Front: New Developments in
Housing* (London, 2003), pp. 70–81.

31   Karen E. Steen, 'Hail to the Chief', *Metropolis* (January 2002), p. 44.

32   See Steven Flanders, ed., *Celebrating the Courthouse* (New York, 2005), esp. Nathan
Glazer's epilogue, 'Daniel Patrick Moynihan and Federal Architecture', about the New
York Senator's passion for reform.

33   B. Joseph Fine II, and James H. Gilmore, *The Experience Economy: Work Is Theatre and
Every Business a Stage* (Boston, MA, 1999), originally a 1998 article in *Harvard Business
Review*. Cited in Sandy Isenstadt, 'Recurring Surfaces: Architecture in the Experience
Economy', in Annmarie Brennan and Brendan Moran, eds, *Resurfacing Modernism:
Perspecta 32* (Cambridge, MA, 2001), pp. 108–19. Also see Ann Bergren, 'Jon Jerde and
the Architecture of Pleasure', *Assemblage*, XXXVII (1998), pp. 8–33.

34   Steve Litt, 'UC x 3', *Metropolis* (February 2005), p. 106.

35   'William Bruder: New Phoenix Central Library', *A+U*, CCCXXI (June 1997), pp. 60–73.

Select Bibliography

This selection does not include readily available monographs on individual architects, buildings or cities.

Abu-Lughod, Janet, *New York, Chicago, Los Angeles: America's Global Cities* (Minneapolis, 1999)

Albrecht, Donald, ed., *World War II and the American Dream: How Wartime Building Changed a Nation* (Washington, DC, and Cambridge, MA, 1995)

— and Chrysanthe B. Broikos, eds, *On the Job: Design and the American Office* (New York, 2000)

Alofsin, Anthony, *The Struggle for Modernism: Architecture, Landscape Architecture and City Planning at Harvard* (New York, 2002)

Archer, John, *Architecture and Suburbia* (Minneapolis, 2005)

Baird, George, *The Space of Appearance* (Cambridge, MA, 1995)

Banham, Reyner, *The Architecture of the Well-Tempered Environment* [1969] (Chicago, 1984)

—, *Los Angeles: The Architecture of Four Ecologies* (London and Baltimore, 1971)

—, *A Concrete Atlantis: US Industrial Building and European Modern Architecture* (Cambridge, MA, 1986)

—, *A Critic Writes: Essays by Reyner Banham*, ed. Mary Banham, Paul Barker, Sutherland Lyall and Cedric Price (Berkeley, CA, 1996)

Barna, Joel Warren, *The See-Through Years: Creation and Destruction in Texas Architecture and Real Estate, 1981–1991* (Houston, 1992)

Baumann, John, Roger Biles and Kristin Szylvian, eds, *From Tenements to the Taylor Homes: In Search of Urban Housing Policy in Twentieth-Century America* (University Park, PA, 2000)

Beauregard, Robert A., *Voices of Decline: The Postwar Fate of US Cities* [1991] (New York, 2003)

—, *When America Became Suburban* (Minneapolis, 2006)

Bell, Michael, and Sze Tsung Leong, eds, *Slow Space* (New York, 1998)

Bender, Thomas, *The Unfinished City: New York and the Metropolitan Idea* (New York, 2002)

Berkeley, Ellen Perry, and Matilda McQuaid, *Architecture: A Place for Women* (Washington, DC, 1989)

Blake, Peter, *No Place Like Utopia: Modern Architecture and the Company We Kept* (New York, 1993)

Bluestone, Daniel, *Constructing Chicago* (New Haven, 1991)

Boyer, M. Christine, *Manhattan Manners: Architecture and Style, 1850–1900* (New York, 1985)

—, *The City of Collective Memory* (Cambridge, MA, 1994)

Braham, William W., and Jonathan A. Hale, eds, *Rethinking Technology: A Reader in Architectural Theory* (New York and London, 2007)

Brennan, Annmarie, and Brendan Moran, eds, *Resurfacing Modernism: Perspecta 32* (Cambridge, MA, 2001)

Bridge, Gary, and Sophie Watson, eds, *A Companion to the City* (London and Boston, MA, 2000)

Bruegmann, Robert, ed., *Modernism at Mid-Century: The Architecture of The United States Air Force Academy* (Chicago, 1994)

Burchard, John, and Albert Bush-Brown, *The Architecture of America: A Social and Cultural History* (Boston, MA, 1961)

Burke, Peter, ed., *New Perspectives on Historical Writing* (University Park, PA, 1991)

Burns, Carol J., and Andrea Kahn, eds, *Site Matters: Design Concepts, Histories and Strategies* (London and New York, 2005)

Canclini, Néstor Garciá, *Consumers and Citizens: Globalization and Multicultural Conflicts,* trans. George Yúdice (Minneapolis, 2001)

Canizaro, Vincent, ed., *Architectural Regionalism: Collected Writings on Place, Identity, Modernity and Tradition* (New York, 2007)

Chase, John, *Glitter Stucco and Dumpster Diving: Reflections on Building Production in the Vernacular City* (New York, 2002)

—, Margaret Crawford and John Kaliski, eds, *Everyday Urbanism* (New York, 1999)

Clausen, Meredith L., *The Pan Am Building and the Shattering of the Modernist Dream* (Cambridge, MA, 2005)

Ciucci, Giorgio, Francesco Dal Co, Mario Marieri-Elia and Manfredo Tafuri, *The American City: From the Civil War to the New Deal,* trans. Barbara Luigia La Penta [1973] (Cambridge, MA, 1979)

Cody, Jeffrey, *Exporting American Architecture, 1870–2000* (London and New York, 2003)

Cohen, Jean-Louis, *Scenes of the World to Come: European Architecture and The American Challenge, 1893–1960* (Paris, 1995)

Cohen, Lizabeth, *A Consumers' Republic: The Politics of Mass Consumption in Postwar America* (New York, 2003)

Colomina, Beatriz, Annmarie Brennan and Melanie Kim, eds, *Cold War Hothouses: Inventing Postwar Culture, from Cockpit to Playboy* (New York, 2004)

Conn, Steven, and Max Page, eds, *Building the Nation: Americans Write About Their Architecture, Their Cities and Their Landscape* (Philadelphia, 2003)

Conzen, Michael, ed., *The Making of the American Landscape* (London and New York, 1994)

Craig, Lois, and Staff of the Federal Architecture Project, *The Federal Presence: Architecture, Politics and Symbols in United States Government Building* (Cambridge, MA, 1978)

Creese, Walter, *Crowning of the American Landscape: Eight Great Spaces and Their Buildings* (Princeton, 1986)

Crysler, C. Greig, *Writing Spaces: Discourses of Architecture, Urbanism and the Built Environment* (New York and London, 2003)

Cuff, Dana, *Architecture: The Story of Practice* (Cambridge, MA, 1991)

—, *The Provisional City: Los Angeles Stories of Architecture and Urbanism* (Cambridge, MA, 2000)

Cullingworth, Barry, *Planning in the USA: Policies, Issues and Processes* (New York, 1997)

Davis, Mike, *City of Quartz: Excavating the Future in Los Angeles* (London and New York, 1990)

Dutton, Thomas, and Lian Hurst Mann, eds, *Reconstructing Architecture: Critical Discourses and Social Practices* (Minneapolis, 1997)

Easterling, Keller, *Organization Space: Landscapes, Highways, and Houses in America* (Cambridge, MA, 1991)

Eggener, Keith, ed., *American Architectural History: A Contemporary Reader* (New York and London, 2006)

Ellin, Nan, *Postmodern Urbanism* (Oxford, 1996)

—, ed., *The Architecture of Fear* (New York, 1997)

Filler, Martin, *Makers of Modern Architecture: From Frank Lloyd Wright to Frank Gehry* (New York, 2007)

Findley, John, *Magic Lands: Western Cityscapes and American Culture after 1940* (Berkeley, CA, 1992)

Fishman, Robert, *Bourgeois Utopias: The Rise and Fall of Suburbs* (New York, 1987)

Fitch, James Marston, *American Building: The Environmental Forces That Shape It* [1948] (New York, 1999)

—, *James Marston Fitch: Selected Writings on Architecture, Preservation and the Built Environment*, ed. Martica Sawain (New York, 2007)

Fogelson, Robert, *Downtown: Its Rise and Fall, 1880–1950* (New Haven, 2001)

Foner, Eric, *Who Owns History?: Rethinking the Past in a Changing World* (New York, 2002)

Ford, Larry R., *Cities and Buildings* (Baltimore, 1994)

Frampton, Kenneth, *Modern Architecture: A Critical History* [1980] (London and New York, 2007)

—, *American Masterworks: The Twentieth-Century House* (New York, 1995)

Friedman, Alice T., *Women and the Making of the Modern House: A Social and Architectural History* (New York, 1998)

Galison, Peter, and Emily Thompson, eds, *The Architecture of Science* (Cambridge, MA, 1999)

Garvin, Alexander, *The American City* (New York, 1996)

Ghirardo, Diane, *Architecture after Modernism* (London and New York, 1996)

—, ed., *Out of Site: A Social Criticism of Architecture* (Seattle, 1991)

Giedion, Siegfried, *Mechanization Takes Command: A Contribution to Anonymous History* (New York, 1948)

Glazer, Nathan, *From a Cause to a Style: Modernist Architecture's Encounter with the American City* (Princeton, 2007)

Goldhagen, Sarah Williams, and Réan Legault, eds, *Anxious Modernisms: Experimentation in Postwar Architectural Culture* (Cambridge, MA, 2001)

Gordon, Alastair, *Naked Airport: A Cultural History of the World's Most Revolutionary Structure* (New York, 2004)

Gottdiener, Mark, *The Theming of America: American Dreams, Media Fantasies, and Themed Environments* (Cambridge, MA, 2001)

Gowans, Alan, *Styles and Types of North American Architecture: Social Functions and Cultural Expressions* (New York, 1992)

Graham, Stephen, and Simon Marvin, *Splintering Urbanism: Networked Infrastructures, Technological Mobilities and the Urban Condition* (London and New York, 2002)

Groth, Paul, *Living Downtown: The History of Residential Hotels in the United States* (Berkeley, CA, 1994)

Hamlin, Talbot, ed., *Forms and Functions of Modern Architecture*, 4 vols (New York, 1952)

Handlin, David P., *The American Home: Architecture and Society, 1815–1915* (Boston, MA, 1979)

—, *American Architecture* (London and New York, 2004)

Harpman, Louise, and Evan M. Supcoff, eds, *Settlement Patterns: Perspecta 30* (Cambridge, MA, 1999)

Harris, Neil, *Cultural Excursions: Marketing Appetites and Cultural Tastes in Modern America* (Chicago, 1990)

—, *Building Lives: Constructing Rites and Passages* (New Haven, 1999)

—, 'Architecture and the Corporation', in Carl Kaysen, ed., *The American Corporation Today* (New York, 1996), pp. 436–86

Harris, Steven, and Deborah Berke, eds, *Architecture of the Everyday* (New York, 1997)

Harvey, David, *The Condition of Postmodernity* (Oxford, 1990)

—, *Spaces of Hope* (Berkeley, CA, 2000)

Hayden, Dolores, *Redesigning the American Dream: Gender, Housing and Family Life* (New York, 2002)

—, *Building Suburbia: Green Fields and Urban Growth, 1820–2000* (New York, 2003)

Hays, K. Michael, ed., *Architecture Theory since 1968* (Cambridge, MA, 1998)

Hess, Alan, *Googie Redux: Ultramodern Roadside Architecture* (San Francisco, 2004)

—, *Organic Architecture: The Other Modernism* (Salt Lake City, 2006)

Heynen, Hilde, *Architecture and Modernity: A Critique* (Cambridge, MA, 1999)

Hise, Greg, *Magnetic Los Angeles: Planning the Twentieth-Century Metropolis* (Baltimore, 1997)

Hitchcock, Henry-Russell, Jr, *Modern Architecture: Romanticism and Reintegration* [1929] (New York, 1993)

—, and Philip Johnson, *The International Style: Architecture since 1922* [1932] (reprinted with 'The International Style Forty Years Later', New York, 1966)

Hughes, Thomas, and Agatha Hughes, eds, *Lewis Mumford, Public Intellectual* (New York, 1990)

Hurly, Andrew, *Diners, Bowling Alleys and Trailer Parks: Chasing the American Dream in Postwar Consumer Culture* (New York, 2001)

Huxtable, Ada Louise, *Will They Ever Finish Bruckner Boulevard?* [1970] (Berkeley, CA, 1989)

—, *Kicked a Building Lately?* [1976] (Berkeley, CA, 1988)

—, *The Tall Building Artistically Reconsidered* (New York, 1984)

—, *Unreal America: Architecture and Illusion* (New York, 1997)

Isenstadt, Sandy, *The Modern American House: Spaciousness and Middle-Class Identity* (Cambridge and New York, 2006)

Jackson, John Brinckerhoff, *Landscape in Sight: Looking at America*, ed. Helen Lefkowitz Horowitz (New Haven, 1997)

Jacobs, Jane, *The Death and Life of Great American Cities* (New York, 1961)

Jandl, H. Ward, *Yesterday's Houses of Tomorrow* (Washington, DC, 1991)

Jarzombek, Mark, *The Psychologizing of Modernity: Art, Architecture, History* (Cambridge and New York, 2000)

Jencks, Charles, *The Language of Postmodern Architecture* [1977] (New York, 1984)

Jordy, William H., *American Buildings and Their Architects*, vol. III, *Progressive and Academic Ideals at the Turn of the Twentieth Century*; vol. IV, *The Impact of European Modernism in the Mid-Twentieth Century* (Garden City, NY, 1972)

—, *'Symbolic Essence' and Other Writings on Modern Architecture and American Culture*, ed. Mardges Bacon (New Haven, 2005)

Koolhaas, Rem, *Delirious New York: A Retroactive Manifesto for Manhattan* [1978] (New York, 1994)

Larson, Magali Sarfatti, *The Rise of Professionalism* (Berkeley, CA, 1977)

—, *Behind the Postmodern Façade: Architectural Change in Late Twentieth Century America* (Berkeley, CA, 1993)

Leatherbarrow, David, *Uncommon Ground: Architecture, Technology, and Topography* (Cambridge, MA, 2000)

Liebs, Chester, *Main Street to Miracle Mile: American Roadside Architecture* (Boston, MA, 1985)

Longstreth, Richard, *City Center to Regional Mall: Architecture, the Automobile and Retailing in Los Angeles, 1920–1950* (Cambridge, MA, 1997)

—, *The Drive-in, the Supermarket and the Transformation of Commercial Space in Los Angeles, 1914–1941* (Cambridge, MA, 1999)

Lynch, Kevin, *The Image of the City* (Cambridge, MA, 1960)

MacDougall, Elisabeth Blair, ed., *The Architectural Historian in America* (Washington, DC, 1990)

Macrae-Gibson, Gavin, *The Secret Life of Buildings: An American Mythology for Modern Architecture* (Cambridge, MA, 1985)

Macy, Christine, and Sarah Bonnemaison, *Architecture and Nature: Creating the American Landscape* (London and New York, 2003)

Marder, Tod, ed., *The Critical Edge: Controversy in Recent American Architecture* (Cambridge, MA, 1985)

Margolies, John, *Home Away from Home: Motels in America* (Boston, MA, 1995)

Marot, Sébastien, *Sub-Urbanism and the Art of Memory* (London, 2003)

Martin, Reinhold, *The Organizational Complex: Architecture, Media and Corporate Space* (Cambridge, MA, 2003)

McCoy, Esther, *Five California Architects* (New York, 1960)

—, *The Second Generation* (Salt Lake City, 1984)

McLeod, Mary, 'Architecture and Politics in the Reagan Era: From Postmodernism to Deconstructivism', *Assemblage*, VIII (February 1989), pp. 23–59

Meikle, Jeffrey, *Twentieth-Century Limited: Industrial Design in America* (Philadelphia, 1979)

Miller, David, *Toward a New Regionalism: Environmental Architecture in the Pacific Northwest* (Seattle, 2005)

Mock, Elizabeth, *What is Modern Architecture?* (New York, 1942)

—, *Built in USA: Since 1932* (New York, 1945)

—, *Modern Gardens and the Landscape* (New York, 1964)

Moskowitz, Marina, *Standard of Living: The Measure of the Middle Class* (Baltimore, 2004)

Moudry, Roberta, ed., *The American Skyscraper: Cultural Histories* (New York, 2005)

Mumford, Eric, 'The "Tower in a Park" in America: Theory and Practice, 1920–1960', *Planning Perspectives*, X (1995), pp. 17–41

Mumford, Lewis, ed., *Roots of Contemporary American Architecture* (New York, 1959)

—, *The Lewis Mumford Reader*, ed. Donald L. Miller (New York, 1986)

Nesbitt, Kate, ed., *Theorizing a New Agenda for Architecture: An Anthology of Architectural Theory, 1965–1995* (New York, 1996)

Noble, David W., *Death of a Nation: American Culture and the End of Exceptionalism* (Minneapolis, 2002)

Nye, David, *American Technological Sublime* (Cambridge, MA, 1994)

Ockman, Joan, and Edward Eigen, eds, *Architecture Culture, 1943–1968: A Documentary Anthology* (New York, 1993)

Page, Max, *The Creative Destruction of Manhattan, 1900–1940* (Chicago, 1999)

—, and Randall Mason, eds, *Giving Preservation a History: Histories of Historic Preservation in the United States* (London and New York, 2004)

Pai, Hyungmin, *The Portfolio and the Diagram: Architecture, Discourse and Modernity in America* (Cambridge, MA, 2002)

Radford, Gail, *Modern Housing for America: Policy Struggles in the New Deal Era* (Chicago, 1996)

Ransom, Harry S., ed., *The People's Architects* (Chicago, 1964)

Rowe, Peter G., *Making a Middle Landscape* (Cambridge, MA, 1991)

—, *Modernity and Housing* (Cambridge, MA, 1993)

Scardino, Barrie, William F. Stern and Bruce C. Webb, eds, *Ephemeral City: Cite Looks at Houston* (Austin, 2003)

Scott, Felicity, *Architecture or Techno-utopia: Politics after Modernism* (Cambridge, MA, 2007)

Schwarzer, Mitchell, 'Modern Architectural Ideology in Cold War America', in Martha Pollak, ed., *The Education of the Architect* (Cambridge, MA, 1997), pp. 87–109

—, *Zoomscape: Architecture in Motion and Media* (New York, 2004)

Scully, Vincent, *American Architecture and Urbanism* (New York, 1969)

—, *Modern Architecture and Other Essays*, ed. Neil Levine (Princeton, 2003)

Serraino, Pierluigi, *Modernism Rediscovered: The Photography of Julius Shulman* (Cologne and New York, 2000)

—, *NorCalMod: Icons of Northern California Modernism* (San Francisco, 2006)

Sies, Mary Corbin, and Christopher Silver, eds, *Planning the Twentieth-Century American City* (Baltimore, 1996)

Smith, C. Ray, *Supermannerism: New Attitudes in Post-Modern Architecture* (New York, 1977)

Smith, Terry, *Making the Modern: Industry, Art and Design in America* (Chicago, 1993)

Somol, R. E., ed., *Autonomy and Ideology: Positioning an Avant-Garde in America* (New York, 1997)

Sorkin, Michael, *Exquisite Corpse: Writings on Buildings* (New York, 1991)

—, ed., *Variations on a Theme Park: Scenes from the New American City and the End of Public Space* (New York, 1992)

Stern, Robert A. M., *New Directions in American Architecture* [1967] (New York, 1977)

Taylor, William, ed., *Inventing Times Square: Culture and Commerce at the Crossroads of the World* (New York, 1996)

Torre, Susana, ed., *Women in American Architecture* (New York, 1977)

Treib, Marc, ed., *An Everyday Modernism: The Houses of William Wurster* (Berkeley, CA, 1995)

—, ed., *Modern Landscape Architecture* (Cambridge, MA, 1993)

Tzonis, Alexander, Liane Lefaivre and Richard Diamond, *Architecture in North America since 1960* (Boston, MA, 1995)

Upton, Dell, *Architecture in the United States* (New York and Oxford, 1998)

Vale, Lawrence, and Sam Bass Warner, *Imagining the City* (New Brunswick, NJ, 2001)

Van Leeuwen, Thomas A. P., *The Skyward Trend of Thought: The Metaphysics of the American Skyscraper* [1986] (Cambridge, MA, 1988)

Venturi, Robert, Denise Scott Brown and Stephen Izenour, *Learning from Las Vegas* (Cambridge, MA, 1977)

—, and Denise Scott Brown, *A View from the Campidoglio: Selected Essays, 1953–1984* (New York, 1984)

Vidler, Anthony, *The Architectural Uncanny: Essays in the Modern Unhomely* (Cambridge, MA, 1992)

Waldheim, Charles, *The Landscape Urbanism Reader* (New York, 2006)

—, and Katerina Rüedi Ray, eds, *Chicago Architecture: Histories, Revisions, Alternatives* (Chicago, 2005)

Whitaker, Craig, *Architecture and the American Dream* (New York, 1996)

Willis, Carol, *Form Follows Finance: Skyscrapers and Skylines in New York and Chicago* (New York, 1995)

Wilson, Alexander, *The Culture of Nature: North American Landscape from Disney to the Exxon Valdez* (New York, 1992)

Wilson, Chris and Paul Groth, eds, *Everyday America: Cultural Landscape Studies after J. B. Jackson* (Berkeley, CA, 2003)

Wilson, Richard Guy, and Sidney Robinson, eds, *Modern Architecture in America* (Ames, IA, 1991)

Wines, James, *Green Architecture* (Cologne, 2000)

Wolf, Peter M., *Land in America: Its Value, Use and Control* (New York, 1981)

Wright, Gwendolyn, *Building the Dream: A Social History of Housing in America* (New York, 1981)

—, and Janet Parks, eds, *The History of History in American Schools of Architecture* (New York, 1990)

—, *Moralism and the Model Home: Domestic Architecture and Cultural Conflict in Chicago, 1873–1973* (Chicago, 1980)

Zukin, Sharon, *Landscapes of Power: From Detroit to Disneyland* (Berkeley, CA, 1991)

—, *The Culture of Cities* (Oxford and Cambridge, MA, 1995)

Zukowsky, John, ed., *Chicago and New York: Architectural Interactions* (Chicago, 1984)

Acknowledgements

I have lived with this book for four intense years, although several friends have recognized that it evolved throughout the course of my career. Vivian Constantinopoulos at Reaktion Books has been a remarkable editor. She conceived of the 'modern architectures in history' series, an inspired idea, and helped me conceptualize a book that engages the breadth, ambiguities and power of architecture in the USA. Everyone at Reaktion Books has been extremely helpful. A fellowship from the Guggenheim Foundation helped initiate the project. The Graham Foundation and Wolfsonian Foundation provided assistance for illustrations, as did the Beverly Willis Foundation, where Wanda Bubriski and Beverly Willis have been especially helpful.

The text has benefited from many friends and colleagues. Robert Beauregard, Robert Bruegmann, Kenneth Frampton, RoseLee Goldberg, Sandy Isenstadt, Richard Longstreth, Reinhold Martin, Felicity Scott and Kate Solomonson have read sections and offered valuable advice. I have also drawn much from conversations with Frances Anderton, Jean-Louis Cohen, Julie Eizenberg, Diane Ghirardo, Rosanne Haggerty, Laurie Hawkinson, Chiu Yin Wong Hempel, Alan Hess, Hilde Heynen, Thomas Hine, Mark Jarzombek, James Kloppenberg, Hank Koning, Jean-François Lejeune, Mary Miss, Robert Stern, Tony Vidler, and the late Jacqueline Tatom. This synthesis began with the Preston Thomas Lectures at Cornell. Yale, Harvard, Washington University, the University of Washington, the University of Texas, the University of California at Berkeley and the Radcliffe Institute for Advanced Study helped clarify my ideas.

Irene Cheng has been an indispensable help. She not only tracked down illustrations but sharpened my eye about visual continuities and uncanny surprises in various cultural media. Other students at Columbia's Graduate School of Architecture, Planning and Preservation have tested my speculations with perspicacity, especially Hyun Tae Jung and Inderbir Riar. Hannah Ilten helped in innumerable ways, not least of which her always cheery disposition.

Several libraries and photographic collections have been indispensable resources, especially Julie Tozer at Columbia University's Avery Library and C. Ford Peatross at the Library of Congress who shared his historical sensibility together with a magisterial archive. Special thanks to Erica Stoller and Christine Cordazzo at Esto, Erin Tikovitsch at the Chicago History Museum, Julio Sims and Anne Blecksmith at the Getty Research Center, William Whitaker at the University of Pennsylvania Architecture Library, Pat Ezzell at the Tennessee Valley Authority Archives, Patrick Lemelle at the Institute of Texas Cultures, Nancy Sparrow at the University of Texas Libraries, Erik Pepple at the Wexner Center and Crystal Zuelke at the Las Vegas News Bureau. Diana Agrest, Steve Badanes, Min Fung, Craig Hodgetts, Jake Gorst, Donlyn Lyndon, Richard Payne, Stanley Saitowitz and James Wines have been especially generous.

I learned a great deal from the experience of five wonderful years with the PBS series 'History Detectives'. In particular Chris Bryson, executive producer at Lion TV, illuminated new ways to use visual material and think about the nature of evidence for overlapping kinds of enquiries. The experience affirmed my belief that a wide spectrum of the public cares about the exciting processes of history.

My family tolerated my obsessions with this book while sharing myriad pleasures that enriched my life. David has given me wise insights about the role of history in cultural conflicts. Sophia's linguistic gifts are an inspiration, as is her palpable delight in all kinds of learning. My husband, Thomas Bender, has been remarkably patient and supportive. I have drawn from his appreciation for the richness of American history and his commitment to greater justice and beauty in today's cities. This book is dedicated to him.

Photo Acknowledgements

The author and publishers wish to express their thanks to the below sources of illustrative material and/or permission to reproduce it.

Photo Peter Aaron©Esto: p. 251 (foot); photo Berenice Abbott (courtesy of the Museum of the City of New York): p. 107; courtesy of Agrest/Gandelsonas Architects: p. 261; The American Institute of Architects Library and Archives, Washington, DC: p. 172; from *The Architect* (July 1918): p. 60; The Art Institute of Chicago (Bruce Goff Archive, Ryerson and Burnham Archives) – reproduction © the Art Institute of Chicago: p. 144; courtesy of Asymptote: p. 245; from Atterbury, *The Economic Production of Workingmen's Homes* (1930): p. 70 (top); courtesy of Avery Library, Columbia University: p. 117 (top); AXA Equitable Life Insurance Company: p. 20; © Steve Badanes: p. 221 (top); photo Donald Barthelme, from *Aluminum in Architecture* (Special Collections, University of Houston Libraries, Courtesy of the Estate of Donald Barthelme, Sr): p. 190; photo Jordi Bernardó: p. 177; photo Ruth M. Bernhard (courtesy of the Kiesler Archive): p. 110 (foot); photo Leslie W. Bland (UTSA Institute of Texan Cultures, courtesy of City Public Service Company Collection): p. 136; photo Michael Bodycomb, © Kimbell Museum of Art, Fort Worth, Texas: p. 232 (top); courtesy of Max Bond/Davis Brody Bond Associates: p. 228; photo Tom Bonner, courtesy of Holt Hinshaw: p. 246 (foot); photo Jack Boucher, Library of Congress, Washington, DC: p. 120; photo Ernie Braun, courtesy of the Eichler Network Archives: p. 168; photo courtesy of Judith Bromley: p. 34 (middle); courtesy of Will Bruder + Partners: p. 272 (foot); courtesy of the Estate of R. Buckminster Fuller: p. 102; courtesy Buffalo and Erie County Historical Society: p. 59; California State Library: p. 33; courtesy of Caudill Rowlett Scott: p. 138; photo Benny Chan/Fotoworks: p. 258; collection of Irene "University Library Archives (Joseph Urban Papers): p. 108; photo Will Connell (Department of Special Collections, Charles E. Young Research Library, UCLA): p. 106 (foot); from *The Craftsman* (1916): p. 62; courtesy Diller Scofidio + Renfro: p. 267; courtesy of Eisenman Architects: pp. 197, 265; Ford Powell Carson, Architects: p. 165; from *Fortune* magazine (July 1964): p. 227; courtesy of the Fountainbleau Hilton: p. 185; photo © Joshua Freiwald: p. 214; photo Clarence Fuermann (courtesy of the Metropolitan Museum of Art, New York): p. 58; courtesy *Good Housekeeping*: p. 174; photo Jonathan Green, 1976: p. 224 (foot); photo Art Grice, courtesy of Miller/Hull Partnership: p. 263; photo Tim Griffith, courtesy of Stanley Saitowitz Architects: p. 255; Gruen Associates: p. 184; frontispiece from Edward Everett Hale, *Workingmen's Homes* (1874): p. 30; photo Jim Hedrich, © Hedrich Blessing: p. 243; photo Ken Hedrich (courtesy of the Chicago History Museum): p. 93; photos Hedrich Blessing, courtesy of Chicago History Museum: p. 140; photo Ted Hendrickson, courtesy of Connecticut College: p. 130; from the Henry Ford Collection, Detroit: p. 56; Hewitt & Garrison Architectural Photography: p. 251 (top); Historical Society of Pennsylvania, Philadelphia (Medium Photo Collection): p. 19; photo © Hardy Holtzman Pfeiffer & Associates (courtesy of H3 and Holzman Moss): p. 223 (right); photo courtesy of Hirshhorn Museum and Sculpture Garden, Smithsonian Institution, Washington, DC: p. 198; photos courtesy of Hodgetts + Fung: pp. 225, 271; courtesy of Steven Holl Architects: p. 273; photo Robert Huntzinger from *Fortune* (October 1964): p. 150; photos © Timothy Hursley: p. 216 (top), 257, 274; from *Industrial Chicago* (1891), courtesy of the

Inc. – reproduced by permission of the University of Georgia: p. 65 (top); courtesy of Sandy & BabcockSB Architects: p. 194; photo Ben Schnall (Lescaze Archives, Special Collections Research Center, Syracuse University): p. 87; from *Scientific American*: pp. 42 (1884), 75 (1912); from *Second Homes* magazine (courtesy of Jake Gorst): p. 181; photo C. Segerbloom for the Bureau of Reclamation: p. 14; Sheldon Memorial Art Gallery, University of Nebraska – Lincoln (F. M. Hall Collection): p. 9; photo Julius Shulman, from *Deutsche Bauzeitung* (November 1966): p. 220; © SITE: p. 200; photo courtesy of Skidmore, Owings & Merrill: p. 224 (top); photo Craig Smith for the Phoenix Office of Arts and Culture: p. 241; courtesy W. Eugene Smith: p. 172; courtesy of SOM Archives and Hyun Tae Jung: p. 147; courtesy of Sony Pictures: p. 176 (top); State Library of Louisiana, Baton Rouge (Louisiana Collection): p. 116; photos Ezra Stoller© Esto: p. 139 (foot), 157, 160, 162, 163, 166 (top), 173, 187, 191, 209, 219, 232 (foot); Stone-Day Foundation, Hartford, Connecticut: p. 31; photo Roger Strauss©Esto: p. 125; photo Timothy Street-Porter©Esto: p. 221 (foot); courtesy of Studio Completiva, Denver, Colorado: p. 254; courtesy of Tennessee Valley Authority Archives: p. 119; *Time* Magazine, ©1936, 1949, 1952, 1963, 1964, 1979 – Time Inc. – reprinted by permission: pp. 12–13; photo Bill Timmerman (courtesy of Will Bruder + Partners): p. 272 (top); photo Judith Turner, courtesy of Smith-Miller + Hawkinson: p. 238; U.C. Santa Barbara University Museum Architecture and Design Collection: p. 96 (foot), 98; University of Arkansas Library, Fayetteville, Arkansas (Fay Jones Collection, Special Collections): p. 233; courtesy of the University of Chicago Press: p. 81; photo © Venturi Scott Brown & Associates: p. 218 (foot); *The Wainwright Building*, promotional brochure published by the Wainwright Real Estate Company, St Louis: p. 27 (top right); courtesy of William Massie Architects: p. 236; photo William Watkins (©Venturi Scott Brown & Associates): p. 210; from *Western Architect*, courtesy Art Institute of Chicago: p. 69 (foot); photos Gwendolyn Wright: p. 70 (foot), 74, 133 (foot); courtesy of Yale University Library (Saarinen Archive): p. 137 (top); © Mitsu Yasukawa/Corbis: p. 249; from Alfred Yeomans, *City Residential Land Development* (1916), courtesy of Avery Library, Columbia University): p. 72.

Index